The Survival Tales of John Hersey

Street scene in the Warsaw ghetto
From the television filming of *The Wall*
Courtesy of Time Life Productions Incorporated

The Survival Tales of John Hersey

by

Nancy L. Huse

The Whitston Publishing Company
Troy, New York
1983

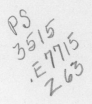
Copyright 1983
Nancy L. Huse

Library of Congress Catalog Card Number 82-50825

ISBN 0-87875-238-2

Printed in the United States of America

TABLE OF CONTENTS

ACKNOWLEDGEMENTS

We wish to thank the following for copyright permissions.

The Author's Guild, Inc., for a quotation from John Hersey. Reprinted by permission from *The Author's Guild Bulletin,* June-July 1965. Copyright 1965 The Author's Guild, Inc.

G. K. Hall and Co. for the excerpt from *John Hersey* by David Sanders. Copyright 1967 by Twayne Publishers, Inc., and reprinted with the permission of Twayne Publishers, a division of G. K. Hall and Co., Boston.

Harper and Row for the excerpt from *The Picaresque Saint: Representative Figures in Contemporary Fiction* by R. W. B. Lewis. Copyright 1956 by J. B. Lippincott Company, and reprinted by permission of Harper and Row Publishers, Inc.

Indiana University Press for the excerpt from *The Critical Path,* by Northrop Frye. Reprinted with permission.

Life for the excerpt from "The Marines on Guadalcannal" by John Hersey. *Life* (c) 1942 Time Inc. Reprinted with permission.

Modern Language Association of America for the excerpt from "The Naked, the Dead, and the Machine: A New Look at Norman Mailer's First Novel," by Randall H. Waldron. Reprinted by permission of the Modern Language Association of America from *PMLA,* 87 (1972).

The New Republic for the excerpts from reviews by Margaret Halsey, B. F. Skinner, Carl F. Hansen, Robert Gorham Davis and William Jay Smith, "What Shall We Do with the Gifted Child?" Reprinted by permission of *The New Republic,* (c) 1960 The New Republic, Inc.

FOREWORD

John Hersey occupies a somewhat lonely and anomalous position on the current literary scene, particularly in terms of his handling by literary scholars and critics. Though his novels and nonfiction documentaries have been frequent best-sellers, he is obviously too "serious" and philosophical a writer to be classed with the ever popular formulaic melodramatists like Irving Wallace, Arthur Hailey, Sidney Sheldon and Judith Krantz. On the other hand his strong interest in current topics of moral and political concern like racism, war, genocide, overpopulation and atomic holocaust have made him seem to many critics more a moral crusader than a literary artist. As a consequence, his work, though widely read, has never been subjected to the kind of sustained critical inquiry accorded to such twentieth century writers as Hemingway, Faulkner, or Bellow who have been treated as major artists by the critics. John Hersey has been widely reviewed, but almost never interpreted and evaluated until the present book.

Thus, Nancy Huse's book is an invaluable aid to our understanding of the scope and development of John Hersey as a writer. It is a comprehensive study which begins with Hersey's earliest published journalism and examines all his major works down to the present. Most significant of all in the present state of Hersey criticism, Huse gives us an artistic as well as thematic analysis of Hersey's development. Her discussion shows clearly that the common opinion of Hersey as an inartistic moralist is downright wrong. Instead, Hersey emerges from this treatment as a fine craftsman who has been highly sophisticated in his choice of literary techniques and structures.

Beyond its value as an analysis of John Hersey's literary career, this book also offers a number of ideas about two problems

of general literary interest. The first is that of the relationship between art and moral or political intentions. Huse suggests some of
the central characteristics of the kind of artistry that can be achieved
by a didactic writer. Many of her points about Hersey can also help
us to appreciate the accomplishments of other writers who have set
out with the purpose of illustrating or pleading their opinions in literary form. In addition, her analysis points to some of the central techniques available to writers for adorning a moral or pointing a tale.

Finally, this study also explores some of the key issues of
literary popularity. Hersey has continually sought to convey the
fullness of his concern about the issues of his time in as effective a
way as possible to the broadest spectrum of the literate public.
Huse deftly analyzes the literary techniques which Hersey has used
to reach a broad general public, and thus gives us insights into some
of the major artistic modes of the serious popular writer. These insights also help to explain the appeal and the achievement of other
writers like Leon Uris and James A. Michener who share with Hersey
both a concern for current social and political problems and an
ability to express this concern in a literary form accessible to a very
wide public. In sum, this book is a significant study in popular culture as well as the first sustained critical appreciation of John Hersey.

John G. Cawelti
University of Kentucky

INTRODUCTION

John Hersey is an impressive figure in contemporary American letters. Over four decades, his work has evoked relatively little critical comment despite his early Pulitizer prize for *A Bell for Adano* (1944), his acclaimed journalism in such works as the world-famous *Hiroshima* (1946), and a long list of novels which deal with contemporary events but actually represent a complex artistic response to post-World War II history. His 1950 novel about the Warsaw ghetto, *The Wall*, made into a play by Millard Lampbell, was, in 1981, the occasion for the first joint venture of Polish and American television; more importantly, it followed worldwide viewing of "The Holocaust," an earlier American series, as the catalyst for discussion and increased historical consciousness of an atrocity little understood despite its devastation of a people. With its focus on the resistance movement in Warsaw, *The Wall* should have an important effect in altering mass tendencies to blame the victims of the Nazis for their own deaths. The television production, however, is only one of many ways in which Hersey's life and work are dynamically intertwined with moral, political, social and aesthetic beliefs in an intellectual climate he has helped to foster and preserve. Hersey commands respect and deserves critical attention as a teacher at Yale; as a member of numerous groups to protect educational excellence and freedom of expression; as a writer convinced of the moral authority of the creative artist; as a friend and colleague of major figures of his age; as a journalist credited with influencing non-fictional narrative; and, finally, as a serious novelist whose works have reached a wide audience.

Only two full-length studies of Hersey have previously appeared. David Sanders' *John Hersey* (1967), written for *Twayne's United States Authors Series,* is important for its bibliography and for its thematic plot summaries. Sanders holds that Hersey has lacked critical attention for two reasons: his unclassifiable, varied forms and subjects, and his unstylish, forthright, narrations. Yet Hersey's insistence that human survival is important and possible is, Sanders suggests, a form of "radical innocence" as defined by Ihab Hassan in *Radical Innocence* (1961). [1] In this sense, Hersey's direct and mainly affirmative vision is his own manner of recoil from the horrors he viewed as a World War II correspondent. Sanders' point is interesting, for despite the simple directness of much of Hersey's work, the presence in it of a mind rebelling at the age's acceptance of nuclear weapons, the Holocaust, racism, and the annihilation of the individual in a technological society places Hersey as an intellectual contemporary of Bellow, Wright, Mailer and Agee.

An unpublished dissertation, *Against the Grain: The Achievement of John Hersey,* by Samuel B. Girgus (University of New Mexico, 1972) is the second full-length study of Hersey. Girgus, using an interdisciplinary American Studies approach, argues that Hersey's books offer philosophically complex interpretations of human life. Placing Hersey in the romantic-ironic tradition of Hawthorne as a fiction writer, Girgus theorizes that the author's political and cultural attitudes substantially agree with radical critics such as Herbert Marcuse, Ivan Illich and Charles A. Reich, with ideas about the individual and selfhood in common with those of Sartre, Camus, Tillich, Rollo May, R. D. Laing and others.[2]

Hersey's persistent use of the theme of survival through confrontation with the hostile forces of technological society is the vehicle for his special vision of individual freedom and responsibility. Concentrating on Hersey's anguished yet ultimately affirmative vision of man and using a philosophical-historical approach, Girgus demonstrates Hersey's contemporary distillation of intellectual experience; but this approach leaves virtually untouched several major questions about Hersey's work. Chief among these are traditional critical concerns such as the relationship of form to meaning, the artist's original contribution to our literature, and the effect of his personal aesthetic on his writing. Hersey insists that he works primarily in the field of fiction rather than in journalism, but he is world famous for *Hiroshima* and in spite of his denials, an important innovator in the significant twentieth century move toward nonfiction as a major genre. In addition to his nonfiction, however, Hersey has produced in *My Petition for More Space* (1974) a tightly controlled, carefully worded and original prose fiction, in *The Conspiracy* (1972) a suspenseful epistolary political novel, and in *Under the Eye of the Storm* (1967) an effective philosophical thriller. These and his other books deserve to be studied for their craftmanship and for what they reveal about Hersey's development as an artist.

Hersey has repeatedly been compared with writers of stature; Hawthorne, Conrad, Crane, Dos Passos, C. P. Snow; a case can be made comparing him with Steinbeck, Camus, Silone, and Mailer. Is the Yale teacher and earnest crusader merely patching together, consciously or unconsciously, bits of material taken from the great writers he is said to resemble? Or does he resemble them because of his weaving together in new ways various elements they too have employed, such as realistic reporting, a concern with both the individual and his existence in society, and direct commitment of the writer to a political or philosophical stand? Girgus has described Hersey's intellectual framework as one provided in raw form by his age but distilled by his personal experience and attitudes into a unique insistence upon the individual's ability to survive and even to transform a hostile society. If Hersey possesses a unique vision, can he have expressed it only in cliches and borrowed forms? His development as a writer, with the increasing irony in his still affirmative vision, is a matter of critical interest.

Hersey's philosophical view depends upon the individual's attaining authentic existence in the face of overwhelming odds. The characters in *The Wall* who survive as persons do so by accepting the ultimate horror of Nazi intentions as reality and throwing themselves into an attempt to reshape the reality by confronting it in brave, nearly hopeless battle. Their late but convinced rallying wins not a physical but a mental or spiritual battle. Boman in *The War Lover* (1959) comes to see his own guilt and responsibility; the engineer in *A Single Pebble* (1956) becomes aware of a dignity in human struggle he had not dreamed of; Sam in *My Petition for More Space* is a walking consciousness whose futile quest becomes an authentic existence in itself by reason of his total engagement in it. Each work takes on the aspect of Camus' Sisyphus myth, but Hersey has his own means of demonstrating the reasons for continuing and relishing the struggle. A glance at a list of Hersey's works evokes an image of salvation for the individual and for society as a whole which constitutes a kind of transforming vision in starkly modern terms.

The absurd labor of Sisyphus-man is the result of his passion for life in the face of death. Hersey's heroes display not the scorn and sorrow of the conscious sufferer, but that other side of the labor which, Camus, says "can also take place in joy." [3] Hersey's special chore has been the creation of fables which represent the human being engaged in an unceasing labor for survival with dignity. The very struggle becomes the essence of human life and its shadowed joy. Nowhere in Hersey's work is there a suggestion of an imposed external order or a divine destiny; yet humanity defines a kind of order and even a nobility by engagement with the challenge of staying alive in dignity, of carrying a burden which is both the result of personal choices and imposed from without by others. That Hersey has isolated the narrow moment when Sisyphus turns to take up his burden by choice, that he has omitted explicit portrayals of the design of the universe, that he has left untouched the realm of man's fall or choice of defiance of the gods in order to show human beings as straining but determined, never dreaming of refusing the task of life and rather absorbed in it by will, has caused the author to be faulted for simplification. His being unlike Dostoevsky (though like Crane, Dos Passos, Conrad and the others) has seemed to be a problem for critics.[4]

The age is impatient with such deviation from the tragic and the absurd visions of man. Social writers, Upton Sinclair and the Steinbeck of *The Grapes of Wrath,* are out of style; nevertheless, their names have a hallowed ring. Their achievements, curious and bumbling though they seem in comparison with more admired writing, once caught the public mind and gave a partial but startling view of life. In his depiction only of a "slice of the spirit," Hersey has recognizable and even deliberate limitations. But his wrestling with necessity, his concern with life rather than with death, is at very least an interesting variation of a dominant contemporary theme. R. W. B. Lewis, discussing what he calls the "picaresque saint" in modern literature, writes of heroes in Camus, Silone, and Faulkner and others: "The absurd, therefore, far from inviting the individual to quit his life, requires of him on his honor that he hang on to it; it becomes a rule, a principle of living." [5]

In examining Hersey's technical development and in specifying the nature of the survival theme that prevades his work, we must understand his concept of the role of the writer. It is this which separates Hersey from Camus and allies him with Sartre; it is this which makes Hersey, cool WASP writer that he is, the unlikely bed-fellow of the bad boy of contemporary American Letters, the unruly Norman Mailer. The question central to Hersey's carreer, as it has been to Mailer's, "what it is to live by and for writing," [6] pervades Hersey's rhetoric and that of his characters, often the most important ones.

Hersey's concept of the writer's role in society causes him to sound, at times, like an earnest do-gooder or revivalist preacher. In *White Lotus* (1965) for example, it is clear that Hersey has set out to tell us truth about the human condition, to make us recoil from slavery because his elaborate fiction demands—if we stay with it—that we imagine what it is to live as a slave. In *The War Lover,* too,—as in nearly all of Hersey's books since *The Marmot Drive* (1953)—it is apparent early in the book that Hersey has designs upon our ideas. He wants us to believe as he does; to do this he tells a story, as preachers always have. His didactic rhetoric is varied throughout his career, but it shows a growing sense of pain or disappointment without ever abandoning its principle tenet: that individuals, particularly those who have awareness, can and will continue to confront and re-shape social attitudes and political forms.

To look carefully, then, at Hersey, we must look at a message as well as at a style. Moreover, as we should ask anyone else who directed us to believe and act in a particular way, we must note what the exhorter does about his creed in his own life. It is interesting that many people, including academic critics, admire Hersey as a man even though they object to certain qualities (or lack of certain qualities) in his fiction. Hersey's prominent role in the civil rights movement, in education, and in politics grows from his conscience as a man; but this conscience shapes his books and determines their unstylish forms and tone. A look at Hersey's work as a man will give at very least an added dimension of sincerity to his work as a writer. For those who can see Hersey only as a mediocre writer, perhaps it will explain his important role as a respected cultural figure whose works mirror their times in a distinctive way; for those who admire Hersey's talent, it will help to explain the fund of experience from which he draws.

Since the general question of the artist's role in America is interesting in itself, knowledge about Hersey's public deeds, style of life and conviction of his truthtelling role is profitable for the way it shows his alignment with some of his most brilliant contemporaries and his small but vital contributions to the literary scene, which include both his writings and his actions. His early interest in writing "novels of contemporary history," his special gifts for description and for rhythmic or cryptic phrasing, his use of various types of reportorial forms and his relationship to the contemporary existential novel and to nonfictional narrative indicate both a sturdy individual talent and a kinship with the literary and intellectual milieu. His actions, in fact, have helped to create this milieu; he is therefore important even beyond questions of literary style and imagination.

Whatever credence Hersey's survival theme has besides his own insistence on it in life and in fiction comes from the way that his characters make their existential choices to rejoin, and yet remain free from, a rather threatening society. These choices are not made in a vacuum. The means of attaining true existence are offered through the communicative powers of those who feel set apart by their ability to present a vision of reality to other men. In *The Wall* (1950), for example, although Rachel Apt and Dolek Berson eventually emerge as leaders, it is Noach Levinson, historian, writer and cultural critic, who helps them to become immortal, who finally expresses the reasons for their will to survive. Hersey reiterates that there is a sacredness about representing one's concept of truth in written or spoken words through such culturally unifying figures as Su-ling in *A Single Pebble,* Kid Lynch in *The War Lover,* and White Lotus herself. The reaching out of one human being to another in order to share a vision, and thus to allow the other person to create his own imagined representation, has never ceased to inspire Hersey or his characters; in *The Child Buyer* (1960), this ability of Barry's is the essence of his genius and the great power which the computer will take from him.

The means by which Hersey has become famous, the reportorial earnestness, selectivity and skill he showed in *Hiroshima,* have remained the cornerstone of his creative gifts and the only explanation for his affirming human survival. The preoccupation Medlar has with the dolphins in *Under the Eye of the Storm* and the boorish presence of computer-loving Flick on board "The Harmony," are the outgrowths of Hersey's lifelong preoccupation with the wonders of communication. Human consciousness, beautifully able to share its vision of truth with others (and thus to help them toward the creation of their own) is the explanation Hersey gives for both our ability and our will to survive, his major theme and the determining factor of his style. *A Single Pebble, The Conspiracy,* and *My Petition for More Space* are directly concerned with this mystery; indirectly, other works are concerned with it as well. In *The Marmot Drive,* it is Hester's separation from others, in *Too Far to Walk,* it is John's abandonment of the tradition which account for their sufferings.

Hersey's preoccupation with the individual's transcending through communication and awareness the negative and threatening trends of history identifies him securely as a twentieth century figure. The coming of technology and the passing of Christianity have posed serious threats to the Western individual struggling to survive in a world gone meaningless. Cultural and literary critics typically pronounce that moderns fear loss of control over their individual fates. John Aldridge, for example, has substantially treated the problem of lost values and thus the passing of the tragic and dramatic from contemporary life in his study of American writers, *After the Lost Generation.* Hersey's use of existential thought in such works as *The War Lover* and *The Child Buyer* has been noted by Girgus and by early reviewers. It is not surprising that a writer who is awed by our capacity to survive and take responsibility for our existence would, early in his work, show he had absorbed the contemporary philosophy which attempted to define the human being in control, although alone.

In his own way, Hersey has both a debt to Camus and kinship with him. Camus, with his Sisyphus figure, and aware human characters, offers the beginnings of a modern mythology. Hersey's preoccupation with the Sisyphus image both elaborates the moment of assent and will power involved in fully living and attempts to explain the reasons why such a struggle is possible and even desirable.

In his use of the Sisyphus myth and other existential themes, Hersey bears a resemblance in our age to storytellers such as Hans Christian Andersen, who freely used old folk tales, modified forms of them, and new forms including the satirical fantasy. The comparison of Hersey to Andersen, although incongruous in some ways because of their different times in history and manner of communicating, nevertheless is valid. Both are versatile storytellers who freely use old material, sometimes in new forms; both bring to their stories strongly felt emotions and observations about contemporaries. Both sometimes lose an audience because of moralizing too openly. Andersen is known for a common popular form of his day, storytelling, but he always aspired to write serious drama. Hersey has used the skills of a modern reporter in his most satisfying works, and like Andersen will not be best remembered in his preferred field as a serious, original novelist (*The Marmot Drive* has been called his greatest failure) but rather as a talented chronicler or inspired reporter of his times. As with Andersen, there is a strain of the didactic in Hersey's stories which cannot be removed or ignored in defining his essential meaning as a writer.

In the obvious urgency of Hersey's voice in such works as *White Lotus, The Child Buyer* and *The War Lover* and even in its controlled urgency in the later *Under the Eye of the Storm, The Conspiracy,* and *My Petition for More Space,* there is less of Camus' artistic concern with communicating real experience than of Sartre's

Promethean desire to create a world that is lacking.[7] Although Hersey's collection of essays about writing, *The Writer's Craft*, includes famous critical essays by Lubbock, Forster and Bowen, his introduction uses the *O. E. D.* definition of "craft" to present the act of imaginative writing as one not only of skill but of power, "a life to which one must wholeheartedly give himself over." (p. 3) Beyond what Hersey calls "the naive stage of self-expression," writing demands dedication; it must "be seen and felt, or at least tasted as the central activity of a way of life." (p. 5) The story-teller's basic and constant motive is "the urge to hand along to another person a story, a vision, a mood, or, as Tolstoy insists, a set of powerful feelings." (p. 5)

The tone Hersey uses here echoes an earlier essay written at my request for the first issue of the literary magazine at John Hersey High School, Arlington Heights, Illinois in 1969. After insisting that the printed word will endure because it comprises a double act of creation, with the reader transforming the writer's vision into his own personal one, Hersey takes on the passionate tone and rhetoric of one who has authority, conviction and the desire to convert others to his viewpoint which is characteristic of most of his work:

> But in writing and reading, we are all makers, creators, artists, passers on of the shimmering, awesome, short, pain-struck, joy-strewn mystery that we call life. The written and printed and seen word cannot die, nor can we in seeing it, because it contains and hands on the record, the perception, the highest possibilities, the trembling essence of life itself.

The phrase which expresses Hersey's view in theory and in practice is the one that proclaims writing to contain and hand on the "highest possibilities." His earliest discussion of writing, "The Novel of Contemporary History," in *The Atlantic*, November, 1949, sets as the aim of authors and standard for critics of the genre an implicitly social value.

> Above all, this kind of novel should make anyone who reads it better able to meet life in his generation—whatever that generation may be. This is the highest aim of any piece of fiction . . . [8]

His words, Hersey added, applied to the novel of contemporary history in only one respect. The chaos and complexity of modern times have confused and harrassed present generations more than most other peoples had ever been by their own times. Fiction, unafraid of complexity, could "illuminate the human beings who are caught up in the events," could give its readers an opportunity to live history, not merely to witness it through journalistic attempts. A search for understanding and a desire for communication, he stated are the chief aims, along with anger at social conditions and a will for world citizenship, which a writer of "novels of contemporary history" can validly pursue.

"Understanding" and "communication" are words which describe Hersey's attempt in fiction to pass on "the highest possibilities" and to make "anyone who reads it better able to meet life in his generation." Although the early articles as well as the recent collection about writing contain references to style or form, these things are secondary to his ultimately didactic concept of writing. Hersey says that he agrees in substance today with the tone and content of the *Atlantic* essay.[9] His later essay affirms this.

Hersey is less concerned with *technique* as part of the writer's craft than with the peculiar *power* of the craft, the resonance of the writer's voice speaking to his audience within his culture's limitations and yet echoing the writer's idiosyncratic viewpoint. Hersey's essay builds to a climax where he pronounces as central to the writer's vocation its power to help or to improve the world. He uses E. M. Forster's distinction between preacher and prophet, dismissing novelists who are simply preachers and endorsing those who speak with the resonant, timeless voices we associate with prophets. (10) Referring to Faulkner's remark that he would like to think his behavior better for having read *Don Quixote*, Hersey states:

> I do not think Faulkner was speaking of a socially useful morality he learned from Cervantes, or which *Don Quixote* roused in him. I believe that after reading Cervantes he kept hearing the sonorous, echoing tones of a seer, and that this distant thunder set him thinking, as he was prone to do anyway, of his relationship as an artist to the issue of an honorable survival for mankind. (10)

Here the author of *Hiroshima* and *The Wall* demonstrates the continuity of his own vision of the writer's work. Having the artist concerned with "the issue of the honorable survival for mankind" touches again upon his insistence in "The Novel of Contemporary History," that fiction is remarkably able to clarify and to illuminate the disturbing and confusing nuclear age. In the introduction to the anthology he cites Solzhenitsyn's belief that art can " 'help the modern world.' " (10) Art, Hersey maintains, makes people want to live.

> Art praises and nourishes life, art hates death. This is what we mean when we say we recognize power in a work of art: The life forces in us are encouraged. We want to work, we feel a surge of sex, we can weep again, we are suddenly famished, our sufferings too are more acute, yet we seem to know better how to give and take. (10)

In emphasizing the role of art (the literary art) as a catalyst toward a richer existence, Hersey crosses the path of Sartre briefly but intensively. Sartre's conviction that the writer has a moral mission to illuminate and to influence his own historical period, with history rather more important than literature, seems closely allied with Hersey's explanation, in the *Atlantic* essay, of the writer's obligation to and effect upon his age in "the novel of contemporary history." Showing the "constants of human character" within the ferment of contemporary events, Hersey's writer differs from Sartre's situational vision of man very little; the "constants" of Hersey's own characters have emerged as human needs for individual responsibility, awareness, and assent. Hersey's human being is as alone as Sartre's until he enters into valid relationships. These become more and more difficult as Hersey deepens his criticism of social and political systems; a recent book, *My Petition for More Space,* is a futuristic novel which demonstrates the stifling of human relationships in a totalitarian society at the same time that it breathes with the all-but hopeless struggle of the individual (the writer) to remain free and to envision freedom for others. Hersey's work has been to portray possibilities in a given world rather than to preach revolution; nevertheless, like a back-door Sartre he has repeatedly implied that the contemporary world is one an awakened individual cannot accept without pain, without "the absurd."

Hersey sees the writer's role as questioning and visionary in any society; he does not share, and probably never has, Sartre's conviction in *What Is Literature?* that the writer is capable, that people are capable, of achieving a classless and peaceful society through a commitment to socialism. He sees the writer as independent of idology, Plato's poet with a vision of possibilities which he leaves to others to put into action. Not literature-as-action in the Sartrean sense, but literature-as-suggestion-for-action is Hersey's sense of commitment.

> That art can have devastating effects in the real world is all too vividly borne out in the totalitarian states, which do not care for it. Some revisionist critics have been arguing lately that all art is reactionary, that all art is conceived for the purpose of keeping things the way they are. This is false doctrine. True art is neither revolutionary nor reactionary. This does not mean it is neutral. No. It is rebellious in any setting. It will not accept lies, which are the essence of violence of whatever kind or color. Precisely because of art's foundation in temperament, it rejects systems altogether. This is why art says preacher no, prophet yes. Art enrages the ideologue because it attacks the lie in his ideology; he is too obsessed to notice that it also attacks the lie in his enemy's ideology. (10)

This sense of the idiosyncratic voice of the writer, the sensitive and aware individual who can convey the truth of his gifted vision, whose temperament is"played upon by intellect in quest of the whole truth" (11) helps to explain some aspects of Hersey's own career. A Platonist in an age of Aristotelian criticism, a man obsessed with his truth-telling role and yet aloof from the Marxist interpretation of history, concerned deeply with topical subjects because they are the burden, and the Sisyphus-task of man, Hersey has been uniquely of and outside of his times. The writer, he has said, "must want to pierce reality with his personal vision and tell someone else what he has seen."[10] Alone and yet in touch, Hersey's life is the raw material for the characters of his books. The paradox of singularity-in-community, Hersey's philosophy and major theme, may account for the remoteness and alleged oversimplification of some of his work. It also accounts for the many strengths of his art.

In an interesting way, Hersey's life and reputation as the reporter who wrote *Hiroshima* and the consoling storyteller who won a Pulitzer prize for *A Bell for Adano* create a ready market for his books because of the positive reaction people give to his name. Coupling this fact with the complexity of Hersey's intellectual vision, his unique distillation of existential ideas and the common ground between Hersey and the more radical intellectual historians such as Marcuse and Illich, gives ample evidence that—entirely aside from the question of the literary value or originality of his books—this author shares with other popular and literary writers the responsibility and the distinction of disseminating important cultural ideas and attitudes. With his distinctive name and reputation for being "an unusually decent fellow" (one professor's description even as he dismissed impatiently the "thin" writing in the novels), this famous author attracts a somewhat different type of audience than does a Sartre or a Mailer. As the bright and apparently honest reporter of World War II and its aftermath, as the known advocate of racial equality and of effective education, as an observer of the youth cult of the sixties and a compassionate commentator mediating between generations in *Letter to the Alumni* (1970) he communicates as a loyal and dignified, frank and warm, old friend. Yet—in the way that popular writers have—Hersey is spreading a version of the age's representative intellectual tenets. Unlike popular writers who merely reaffirm comfortable mores, however, Hersey challenges the American reader's view of the world.

CHAPTER I

TOWARD A PRIVATE VISION

In the final paragraph of *The Rhetoric of Fiction,* Wayne C. Booth provides a concise description of the relationship among author, reader, and subject matter which has compelled John Hersey's attention in his few essays on literary theory and, more significantly, in the form and content of his fiction.

> The author makes his readers. If he makes them badly—that is, if he simply waits, in all purity, for the occasional reader whose perceptions and norms happen to match his own, then his conceptions must be loftly indeed if we are to forgive him for his bad craftsmanship. But if he makes them well—that is, makes them see what they have never seen before, moves them into a new order of perception and experience altogether—he finds his rewards in the peers he has created.[1]

The writer, Booth explains, need not discover new truths, need not even explain his norms, but must transform a private vision into a public one. Hersey had to go from conveying the generalized national vision of his early days as a foreign correspondent for *Time-Life* to possessing and displaying a private, independent one; from having flocks of assumed readers and comrades, he had to pass to letting his verbal creations convince and appeal on their own merits. For special reasons, however, his work would never exhibit a complete transition from one area to the other.

Because Hersey's first published writings appeared in news magazines with a nationwide circulation, his wartime reports conformed of necessity to the style and attitude of the Luce syndicate which controlled them. An audience of Americans interested in winning the war and in knowing facts about the conflict tailored to the notion of a just cause was an assumption Hersey was willing to make at the beginning of his career. His growth as a writer during his years of journalism (1937 - 1950) from a cub reporter swayed by external assumptions about the nature of his wartime experiences and the needs of his ready-made audience, to a capable artist organizing experience and leading readers to accept his perception of the Warsaw ghetto, is an interesting study in personal as well as literary maturity. The war years were important for Hersey's career because he grew in compassion and acquired varied experiences he could translate to fiction, but they were even more significant for his art because they inspired him with the vision of the writer's role in society which has been, essentially, his own "private vision" in Booth's sense of the term.

Hersey's earliest reporting under a by-line, 1940 - 42, and his first book, *Men on Bataan,* give potent examples of his problem— no doubt unrecognized by himself or anyone else as a problem at this time—of playing to a house which needed, demanded and got an uncomplicated agreement with its basic conceptions and attitudes. His first important article was a breezy assurance that "Joe Grew, Ambassador to Japan" (*Life,* July 15, 1940, pp. 76 - 83) had an "appeasing" nature made up of attributes for which the Japanese are "temperamental suckers." [2] To people "repressed poetically" and "stunted physically," (78) Hersey wrote, the hearty and sports-loving ambassador had a special appeal. Even so, Grew's policy of "dynamic appeasement" would not, according to Hersey, hinder Roosevelt from thwarting Japanese attempts to bully the United States.

The remarks about the Japanese Hersey made in this early article seem startling when balanced against *Hiroshima,* the peak of Hersey's reporting and the objective correlative, in a sense, of an attitude, a rhetoric and a world view which still mark Hersey's writing. Three other articles in 1942 are better examples of his even then considerable power to involve an audience through the use of selected concrete detail, suspense, and pleasing form; they also contain traces, expressed as generalizations and cliches, of Hersey's personal empathy, the quality that has informed his life and his fiction.

"Nine Men on a Four-Man Raft" (*Life,* Nov. 2, 1942, pp. 54 - 57) is a story Hersey presented using a single narrator to control the results of interviews with the seven survivors of a plane crash in the Pacific. It is interesting that, like *The War Lover,* the article has the co-pilot as narrator of the suspenseful and nearly fatal event. The camaraderie Hersey noted among pilots and other airmen is an interesting sentimental detail in view of the same author's later story of survival by Boman's tightly knit and emotionally complex crew. The article is significant mainly for Hersey's arranging of one calamity after another—struggles with a delirious man, failure of rations, attacks by sharks, loss of flares, and sighting of planes which continued on without notice of the men—laced with physical description and accounts of the men's loyalty and mutual help. The other stories from this period, "The Marines on Guadalcanal" (*Life,* Nov. 9, 1942, pp. 36 - 39) and the source for *Into the Valley,* "The Battle of the River" (*Life,* Nov. 23, 1942, pp. 99 - 116) show Hersey becoming personally involved in the writing. The November ninth article is filled with appeals to the reader's emotions through simplistic and sentimental touches such as his description of the marine as a fighter; ". . . a cross between Geronimo the Indian Chief, Buck Rogers, Sgt. York, and a clumsy, heartsick boy," (36) and through direct pontificating: "The marines on Guadalcanal have passed their test with high marks." If these men were typical of the fighting men still in training camps, Americans could "look forward with confidence to the next great blows to come." Hersey became a participant rather than a witness of the "great blows;" the November twenty-third article carries a picture of the author wearing a green head-net he found on a dead Japanese soldier, and also of a flag on which the soldier had written some poetic and militaristic sayings. There is a touch of empathy with the dead enemy, a contrast to the November ninth characterization of the Japanese as "our animal adversary." Hersey's tone after helping to move wounded marines during an ambush is humbler than in the preceding article; he calls himself an"unprofessional onlooker" with "new faith" in U. S. chances of winning the war in the visible future. (116)

If Hersey was an "unprofessional onlooker" of the war, he had already showed professional ambition and energy with his first book, *Men on Bataan* (1942), a work he researched from the files of

Time Life. The book had a sliding form reminiscent of Dos Passos. One chapter would focus on MacArthur; the last sentence would supply the heading of the next chapter on MacArthur's men, and then back to the general. The effect suggests a newsreel camera in motion. Chapter five, for example, describes the courage MacArthur's mother passed to him, then states that the men noticed it and "were a little infected, and almost immune to fear." (32) The following chapter describes the atmosphere of rumor and excitement in Manila before the Japanese invasion. It also provides an example of the type of quick advice Hersey was prone to insert in his writing— an example true to *Time*-style, but significant for the way it relates to Hersey's favorite theme, survival through communication: "If, when you experience your first air raid, you happen to be in a town where there are no air raid shelters, walk, don't run, to the nearest human mind." (48) Such a sentence actually is a good indication of what Hersey was trying to accomplish in this book, and the simple but direct way he accomplished it. David Sanders has commented, "The writer, plainly caught up in the war effort, was doing a book that he felt had to be published for the sake of morale and truth in this year of American defeat." [3] In addition to his own impulses to explain the war even at this early date, Hersey indicates in *Men on Bataan* a high consciousness that he may be directly preparing some of his readers to take part in battle in the near furture. As the "nearest human mind" to the subject and the audience of the book, Hersey tries to bring both together.

In describing the common men, Hersey gives a typical rally-round exhortation that effectively summarizes most of his future books: "They have reacted as you will when your crisis comes, splendidly and worthily, with no more mistakes than necessary." (7) With a curiously prophetic touch that Hersey would demonstrate much more fully in later work, he states that he rejects the notion of MacArthur or anyone else as an omnipotent hero whose mythical abilities would remove responsibility from ordinary individuals.

Although the vignettes about the fighting men do seem more interesting and effective than the biographical commentary on MacArthur or the long quotations from the general's speeches and writings, Hersey does not really succeed in "understating" Douglas

MacArthur. He carefully defends MacArthur's decision to declare Manila an open city (1), prints criticism of MacArthur to balance overpraise, but effectively smashes his own and the reader's neutrality by saying that it was made by "two newspaper columnists whose stock in trade is irreverent gossip," (230) and builds the book to a dramatic ending with MacArthur's escape from Bataan. In fairness to Hersey, it must be said that " 'I came through and I shall return' " (311) is dramatic enough in itself to make the brief chapter about the surrender of Bataan seem like falling action. The reporter had a natural affinity for his subject.

In a sense, the press in *Men on Bataan* is a third character interpreting for and communicating with a fourth character, the audience. To overlook the emphasis Hersey places even in his first book on the act of writing and the role one person's vision can play in other lives, is to overlook the true structuring element of the war journalism he produced, as well as the dominant theme of his career.

MacArthur is depicted as a "lover of words" who was also the master of symbolic gestures. In his dealings with the government, Hersey describes him as furious with Roosevelt in 1943 for pushing legislation through the House which would have declared Army personnel on half-pay for the duration. He was furious with the idea itself, but—Hersey stresses—also with the underhanded way Roosevelt chose to act. He threatened resignation until the President granted an appointment to discuss the matter, and then spurred a public relations compaign which resulted in a defeat of the bill by the Senate. This pattern of the individual effecting change through persuasion and example is one of Hersey's most frequent portrayals in journalism and fiction. His tone here is one of complete concurrence with the General's reaction to "underhandedness" and with his belief that the Army must be kept in high morale and readiness.

MacArthur's relationship with the press is described at length. He allowed the reporters and editors full freedom and responsibility to do their own editing after he expained their important role in shaping history. One of his examples was Sherman's march through Georgia, the result of news printed in the South and reprinted in the North about Confederate strategy. As conscious observers and self-censors, the press would be "the people's means of information and mouthpiece," and also, in effect, powerful agents in the war. Hersey also notes that, even after his libel suit against Drew Pearson and Robert S. Allen was settled out of court without payment, the General was not vindictive and never, "by flicker of eye or lash of tongue," showed bitterness toward the press.

The common men also interact with the reporters—" 'Write my mother I'm a hero,' " (28) they say. Visible proof of this dialogue with the correspondents is Hersey's use of several letters the men sent home and of interviews and other descriptive material from correspondents. The eve of the invasion of Manila is related mainly from the reporters' viewpoints, and one chapter defends the Associated Press correspondent whose first reports describing a feeble and ill-equipped Japanese army resulted in a press conference by Secretary Stimson to explain the American's defeat. The reporter, Hersey insists, had sent all that he could discover, "a compendium of the reactions of men, who had not done much of it, to the act of killing." (97)

The author's sense of responsibility in his task to communicate pervades the book in spite of the smooth, quick tone and full alliance with the common desire to build morale and to "win" the war. His frequently used formula, "I think you ought to meet . . ." is matter-of-fact rather than patronizing, an obvious move toward personalization. The crusading, committed tone would be more apparent in his next book, but even in this one Hersey allows himself to give an eyewitness account—the only one, since he never worked on Bataan—which stands out for its sensory effectiveness and undisguised search for human motive and toleration. On an assignment in 1939, Hersey had met General Masuhara Homma, the Japanese general who had been rumored a suicide during the Bataan invasion. His account of the general is both humorous and slightly grotesque, and Hersey tends to be defensive of him: ". . . if he did kill himself, it is safe to say that he did it for the Emperor." (85) Such tendencies to explain motives and bring mutual understanding of all comprise both the form and the theme of the book.

Hersey's second book, *Into the Valley,* based on the same experience as the November twenty-third *Life* article, is a slim but memorable volume.   Besides earning the first hints of a literary reputation, with at least one reviewer noting the power of sense and emotion that resembled Crane's in *The Red Badge of Courage,* [4] Hersey had begun to deal with the experiences of the war and his role as a correspondent in a serious, personal way no longer derivative of the patriotic and editorial fund of generalizations much of his beginning work depended on.   In the account of an unsuccessful skirmish by a small group of Marines, Hersey found a theme and a form to express the growing perceptions of his life, including his own responsibility toward his audience.

Into the Valley is more than a personalized report or an impressionistic essay.   It is a piece of journalism in the form of a personal narration, a drama whose chief character creates and controls both the material and its telling.   The now familiar technique of Mailer in starring himself in historical accounts was used subtly by Hersey as he attempted to give meaning and beauty to the events of the war.   The humble account of a correspondent who became brave in spite of himself through volunteering for something he did not understand, and through responding to the needs of the moment by an existential surrender to it, is held together by Hersey's questioning and sympathetic presence.   The theme of communication and its relationship to survival emerges during the account, with the writer-turned-marine performing his special task, the search for coherence and purpose that make survival worthwhile.   As he enters the jungle, he frames questions about the war aims of the marines, and makes a contract with the reader to resolve the quandary: "Not only down the first slippery steep, but far along the trail into the jungle I wondered about this, until I asked and got a strange answer, as you will see." [5]

The writer's role as supplier of truth and sharer of experience was stated even earlier in the essay: "This book is an attempt to recapture the feelings of Rigaud, his men, and myself, when we went into that jungle valley.   If people in the homes could feel those feelings for an hour, or even just know about them, I think we would be an inch or two closer to winning the war and trying

like hell to make the peace permanent." (4) The reader is someone
in need of vision, not of reassurance or praise or entertainment. To
supply the vision, Hersey relies more fully on his storytelling than
on his sermons.

Paralleling the formal structure of telling facts and the importance the correspondent assigns to his role is the thematic structure
of the men's telling one another the things that make a difference
to the immediate mission as well as to the entire war and their lives
outside of it. The essay contains a dual set of communications;
the outer group concerns Hersey's mission to report on the war
and to effect change through this, while the inner set is made up of
the marines' communications to one another, and especially of
Captain Rigaud's climactic command at the moment of retreat.
Because the correspondent-narrator has voluntarily joined the
mission, there is an interesting fusion of the narrative form with the
thematic content.

For a time Hersey's life depends upon Rigaud and his men,
yet when he leaves, Rigaud implies that the writer's freedom to leave
can, in a sense, ultimately free him and his men. In their final conversation, the writer offers to do favors for the men when he returns
to the States. Rigaud's request is similar to those of his men who
have asked Hersey to "eat me a piece of blueberry pie" or "give my
mother a telephone call," (137) but it is expanded to the point that
the writer will be so nearly identified with Rigaud that he will be
another self. He will dress as Rigaud specifies, go to a bar, and then
will order two Tom Collinses. "I don't care how you drink yours,
gulp it for all I care; but Captain Rigaud's drink, sip it, take a half
an hour if you got to." (138)

The important role of communication in the essay is indicated
first when Hersey mentions that the only intense scene he saw
during the preparation for the mission was that of a boy "sitting
beside the road against a tree trunk reading what must have been
ten large pages of closely packed writing. The paper was crumpled
and soiled: obviously he had read the letter right into his memory.
After he finished, this time, he tore the halves into quarters, and
kept tearing until there was a pathetic little confetti of farewell

beside that Guadal road." (14) This incident of pain and awareness contrasts sharply with the deceiving atmosphere of casual waiting with the marines looking like "Americans waiting for a ball game to start, or merely getting rid of Saturday afternoon." (13) The dramatic meaning of the events is conveyed only through the boy's response to his letter and through the obvious intensity of the ten-page letter. Human beings achieve whatever control or dignity they have in their lives by virtue of their impressing, persuading one another of meaning.

At the climax of the narrative, when the men have found a dead marine from their own front ranks, a runner appears on the jungle trail. Although this appearance is a historical fact and not one Hersey created to supply meaning, he uses the occasion to comment directly on the importance of the runner and of communication itself. "These runners are an anachronism. They make up human lines of communication; they do the jobs that copper wire and short waves ought to do . . . . Their fellows take them for granted, but there are no men who are braver or stronger." (66 - 67)

Rigaud is not satisfied when the runner cannot say why the men have unexpectedly come upon two other marine companies, one forward and one to the right. He and his men guess correctly what the plan is, but send off for confirmation of their ideas. Hersey comments at some length about the unpleasantness of the men's isolation, of having to act without knowing why. Then he relates the use made of the waiting period before the runner returns.

The men have a strange, whispered conversation with Hersey. They ask him questions about the war outside and about their own mission on Guadalcanal, the reason for strategy—"Why the hell isn't Dugout Doug doing anything?" (71)—and about the Allies, the new weapons, and the war effort at home. As their questions become pounded into formulas, Hersey realizes that they do not want answers so much as the opportunity to toss out questions, as though they were "merely waving their arms in angry gestures of protest;" (71) they were "perhaps about to give their lives for their country, and yet exercising, until it nearly collapsed from being exercised, the right of free speech." (73) And so Hersey the writer asks the question he has framed for them out of their own doubts: " 'what are

you fighting for?' " The men cannot or will not answer in concep-
tualized terms. One whispers, "Jesus, what I'd give for a piece of
blueberry pie" (74) and the others follow with " 'mince,' " " 'ap-
ple.' " Hersey explains at length that " 'pie' " is a symbol of home,
of things worth fighting for. Home means generosity, good pay, comforts, democracy, pie.

Girgus has commented that Hersey's self-conscious and stilted
explanation is a composite of popular war aims and attitudes the
marines "may have forgotten, may have been embarrassed to repeat
or may never have believed. . . . "[6] Had Hersey stopped there, Girgus
speculates, his place in American literature would differ from the
one he now deserves. Hersey's search for a meaning behind the war
would provide material for several better books.[7] But it also, with its
tone of kindly explanation—kindly toward the marines who expressed
their war aims in this simple, partially humorous way, kindly toward
the reader—implies more than a search for meaning on Hersey's
part. It carries the note of authority and mission that has characterized Hersey; although confused himself, the writer can and must
explore meanings through his tales and give some clarity to events.[8]
This is just one of many such direct commentaries which call attention to Hersey's concept of his role. This one is interesting for its
context, the aftermath to moments of intense but imperfect communication in the jungle, where the men were waiting for an answer
to a smaller question about their role in the compaign.

The idea behind Hersey's didacticism, that an individual or
a small group can decide outcomes by making their courage and
ideas known, has its strongest incarnation in this work as the group
encounters deadly machine gun fire on their way to the river. A
message to withdraw passes through the ranks. The movement
begins slowly, then turns to a wild scramble for cover. Hersey describes himself "eager to be away from that spot," (89) yet distressed
to see the myth of the brave, even invincible marines destroyed
before his eyes. "I had a helpless desire to stop the flight. It seemed
wrong." (89) His problem was that he was caught in a general
feeling which the men were communicating to one another, that
they could no longer act with courage, "which is largly the desire
to show other men that you have it." A person alone in a large
group which has given up finds it almost impossible not to quit.

Explaining this in the midst of his narrative, Hersey focuses on the idea which, by constant refining and by amplification as well, he would make uniquely his own in writing theory and in subject matter: "The only way to avoid it [the desire to give up] is to be put to shame by a small group of men to whom this acting is life itself, and who refuse to quit; or by a naturally courageous man doing a brave deed." (89 - 90)

Later, Hersey would develop this insight into the chief characters of *The Wall*, and he would re-examine it with much more complexity in works such as *The Conspiracy* and *My Petition for More Space*. Here it explains why the marines could retain their reputation for toughness in battle; Rigaud coolly orders the men to counterattack and then to retreat in an orderly fashion. He notifies his field officer so that the men will not be acting in isolation, apart from the system they had felt free to criticize earlier.

The reporter helps to carry out wounded during the retreat. One man tells of a sergeant, Bauer, who had been shot holding his post at a machine gun. The men who go back for him find their way out by following a telephone wire. Hersey, earlier in the account, had nominated the wire stringers for medals along with the medical corpsmen. The theme of interdependence and communication to effect survival is illustrated in a few additional anecdotes, notably the case of one of Bauer's stretcher bearers. Two of them were named Cox, but no one knew that. One went to sleep during a break for rest, after telling some of the men to wake him when they started again. Their whispered calls were answered by the other Cox, and the man left behind had to find his way out alone, waiting until morning to find the saving telephone wires.

Not only the numerous references to communication by direct comments and selection of incidents to illustrate it give *Into the Valley* its strength and meaning. The form itself, with its devices to make the reader "feel these feelings for an hour," contributes to the meaning. The first person narrator's tone is one of empathy for the men, and it even takes on empthy for the Japanese when Hersey senses the presence of a sniper just above him in the jungle. The reader is drawn into the narrative as an informed observer, for Hersey shares his knowledge at the outset that Rigaud's mission was doomed before it began. He sacrifices suspense, or part of it, to draw out and deepen the effects of identification and sympathy. Frankness, such as his allusion to the Geneva Convention "which the United States humanely (and out of fear of reprisal) still observes," (57) numerous appeals to the reader such as the analogy between firing mortars and trying to judge a fly on the outfield, (83) as well as references to his own fears and motives—all suggestive of Mailer's personalized histories—work to give Hersey's readers the idea that, as nearly as possible, his simple language is giving them an opportunity to relive his experience.

Into the Valley, which reviewers were virtually unanimous in praising, shows for the first time Hersey's rich gifts as a writer. The tone, the skillful use of flashbacks and character sketches, and the evocation of jungle sounds and scenery to convey mood are accomplishments which indicate considerable power. Hersey's concept of the writer's role, already suggested in this early work, helps to explain why he has chosen to write in a variety of modes to reach his audience.

Hersey's assignment in the summer of 1943 took him to Europe, where he observed an Army major, a "masterpiece of fact" whose work with AMGOT (American Military Government Occupied Territories) in Sicily seemed to the reporter touched with humor and sadness. Six weeks after filing a story with *Life* about the major's work ("AMGOT at Work," August 23, 1943), Hersey had completed the novel which would win the Pulitzer Prize of 1944, identify him to a large audience as a moving, humorous storyteller, and remain one of his most famous works. The book, later adapted into a critically well-received play by Paul Osborn and into a popular war movie, met most of the requirements of the ordinary best seller. It was simple to read, sentimental, held a certain amount of romantic interest, and seemed to reviewers and other discerning readers at the time a pleasant, even a compelling story. Edward W. Rosenheim, for example, remembers reading the book with much pleasure at the time of his discharge from the Army. Although *A Bell for Adano* has usually been read as a happy but touching story of a well-intentioned and kind-hearted officer, and as a typical best seller, very recently it has received attention for both its relationship to Hersey's total achievement and for its early use of an important post-war theme in America.

Girgus' discussion of the novel is the first serious critical commentary the book has received. He argues that the work is misread when it is treated by such reviewers as Diana Trilling as a mere reflection of popular assumptions and folk idealism. [9] Hersey's novel expressed not only a "Platonic ideal of Americanism" (Trilling's phrase) but also outlined the forces that were challenging this ideal and absorbing it into a new kind of political and economic system. Girgus sees Major Joppolo essentially defeated by the emerging machine.[10]

Writing in PMLA, a critic of *The Naked and The Dead* places Hersey's book first in a long line of American World War II novels which focus on technology and protest it. "Underlying the lighthearted story of John Hersey's *A Bell for Adano* (1944), the tension between mechanism and humanism is symbolized by the conflict between General Marvin's armored cars, tanks, and guns and the painted wooden carts of the Italian Villagers."[11] Hersey, who has rarely commented publicly about any of his books, seems to feel strongly about his intent and its effect in this novel. Discussing in a letter to Girgus the possible reasons for his poor reception from critics, Hersey mentions that he has "always written against the grain, both of literary fashion and of establishment values (e.g., although *A Bell for Adano* appeared to be a rather sentimental novel about a 'good guy,' the significant thing about it at the time— 1943, while the war was far from won—was that it pictured an American hero, or at least a high American officer, as a dangerous shit—and did this several years before Mailer wrote about Croft and Cumming. . . ."[12]

Despite its surface characteristics and statements critics such as Warren French make that the novel is useful now only as evidence of what war-time Americans could be prevailed upon to accept as serious literature, [13] a close examination of *A Bell for Adano* shows it to have a basic structure that differs from the ordinary pattern of the crowd-pleasing best seller. In an important study of the commercial novel, Albert Van Nostrand comments that popular fiction comforts the reader about himself and his possibilities, about humanity's natural goodness, the individual's worth and its proof through material success.[14] Very few competent writers believe that good will win. Popular writers choose to entertain without offending, satisfying the powerful common longing for goodness to vanquish evil. *A Bell for Adano*'s narrow escape from such a pattern lies in Hersey's partially realized ironic treatment of the hero.

Although Joppolo represents "the best of the possibilities,"[15] and stands for the merit of the individual, he is depicted as unable to achieve his desired goals in Adano. He brings a measure of organization to the town, but does not succeed in sharing his own poorly articulated ideals with the townsmen. The climax of his work, the mounting of the bell, takes place in his absence, and although it represents his personal interest in the people of Adano, they never learn its origin and its place in the larger historical framework. Interpersonal communication is affirmed within the text to a degree, yet Joppolo is ineffective in dealing with Purvis and Marvin, who have the real power. Hersey's rhetoric in presenting the character suggests that, although he believes "the quality of the men who did the administering" (vi) to be the important factor in the American military government, the system itself both prepares the men poorly and then abandons them—a system composed of other human beings insensitive to personal feelings or unable to take a stand. The hero, at times, becomes the butt of the narrator's bemused condescendence because he is not conscious of his own shortcomings.

The narrative implies that Joppolo remains unaware of his true alienation from the governing system he represents; because of this he is too weak to accomplish more than isolated good will. He is only half alive, a shell, as Hersey presents him. There is no one in the novel who can be his equal in compassion because he does not understand his own idealism and cannot convey it to others. His lack of awareness or of valid human relationships, his inability to share his vision and help the people of Adano to create their own version of it, mark him in Hersey's canon as an undeveloped character type, rather than a truly ironic hero.

The playful tone of the entire book, especially as it treats Joppolo, accounts for the relative submerging of this book's serious side. Although Hersey treats with some complexity an important popular assumption (that the common man in his limitations is capable of good), most people overlook the serious theme. The almost frivolous tone of the book and its form as a fable in which the main character shows a lack of ordinary common sense, and whom the reader feels sorry for rather than respects for his growth, account for this. A close look at the form can, without discounting the seriousness of the theme, explain why it seems more a sign of Hersey's potential than an indication of his true accomplishment.

In a foreword to the book, Hersey sets the narrative tone by pontificating in a playful manner. "Major Victor Joppolo, U. S. A., was a good man. You will see that. It is the whole reason why I want you to know his story." (v) The sense of didactic purpose is lightened by his implication that "the authorities" are in general idiots and that Joppolo with all his goodness was "weak in certain ways." The author conveys that the system itself was a muddle, and that the works of a good man in such circumstances represented the "best of the possibilities" for it. Up to this point, the middle of the foreword, Hersey could have placed equal emphasis on the failure of the system and the crippling of even its good men by its deficiencies. He does not do this, however, in the rest of the passage. He spends four paragraphs eulogizing "our Joppolos," "our future in the world," the sons of immigrants who can understand the ways of Europe as well as of America. The sweeping prose of the last paragraph cancels out the small doubt the reader could have by this time about Joppolo.

> Neither the eloquence of Churchill nor the humaneness of Roosevelt, no Charter, no four freedoms of fourteen points, no dreamer's diagram so symmetrical and so faultless on paper, no plan, no hope, no treaty—none of these things could ever guarantee anything. Only men can guarantee, only the behavior of men under pressure, only our Joppolos. (vii)

Aside from the grandiose crusading tone of this statement, Hersey creates a problem immediately for most readers. He has hinted that Joppolo may not be infallible, but he has posited that

that he is the ultimate resource of the nation. Throughout the book, he fails to waken Joppolo to his lack of power and his unconscious motives, yet he offers him as the only hope we have. The great-hearted but unthinking Joppolo, crucially different in perspective from later Hersey characters, simply is not equipped to do what the foreword promises. It is significant that Girgus' strongly ironic reading makes no mention of the foreword.

The main barrier to an ironic reading is that Hersey is not fully aware that his hero has been taken in. He thinks in terms of "good men" and "bad men" and not of the evils of technology per se. Writing the story of the good man, he incidentally writes a con-demnation of a system. The focus on the "good man" who is more a helpless innocent than a leader makes the story cute, engaging, warm, and reassuring, but not strong criticism of the system which failed Joppolo and which he failed. It provides a one-time pleasur-able experience for most readers, and it does not portray Joppolo as a traitor to himself or the villagers.

Besides touching the soil when he arrives in Italy, his parents' homeland, Major Joppolo shows the seriousness and sentimentality of his personality in the first few pages of the novel by his dialogue with the cynical Sergeant later relegated to the background. Hersey evokes empathy with the Major as he responds "Cut the kidding" to Borth's "I don't trust you men who are so sentimental and have too damn much conscience." (5) Hersey's comment is typical of the superior and somewhat oracular or patronizing tone he takes in discussing the hero: "There was an echo in the way he said it, as if he were a boy having been called wop by others in school. In spite of the gold maple leaf of the rank on the collar, there was an echo." (5) The major is childlike in other respects; he has the habit of expressing feelings directly, of assuming that people are basically good, and of proclaiming his own honesty: "Usher, I love the truth," he tells the first Italian he meets. (10) His simplicity in some ways equals that of the people he governs; Zito, the usher, fools him into believing a picture in his office depicts Columbus discovering Amer-ica.

Hersey uses the boyish, simple, yet personalistic Major in

connection with a plot device that works quite effectively within the limits of the sentimental story: the bell that is needed for Adano. The Major spends his first day in Adano with the townsmen Craxi, Cacopardo, Giuseppe, Zito and a priest, who convince him of the need for a bell. The old bell had been the unifying voice of the town, and it united not only the people of the village in their labors, pleasures and sorrows, but it brought a unity of past and present with its long, rich history. Joppolo's search for a bell to replace the one taken to make Fascist guns is, of course, the symbol of his attempt to replace the Fascist system with his version of American democracy.

It is somewhat ironic—although there is no indication that Hersey intends the irony—that Joppolo flatters a Navy officer to get the bell. His flattery is thoroughly pragmatic and not commented upon except by the fact of success. The character who is capable of saying to a returned Italian soldier, "I don't know, Nicolo. I think the cause is there, all right. We've got to get rid of the bad men, and the Germans have some, and I'm afraid you did—and of course we have some, too. I just don't know whether our soldiers think much about causes. That's the one thing that worries me about this war," (299) never examines the validity of his own beliefs and motivations. Even as Hersey depicts him, Joppolo seems a bit thickheaded. But there are many occasions where the narrator seems equally unaware.

The theory that the Major's kindly administration was really calamity and not salvation for the Italians because it brought technocracy is not consistently supported by the narrative tone. Had there been a working out or development of Joppolo, had there been some recognition of his shortsightedness or weakness within the story, the book would more clearly be a condemnation of manipulative society. As it stands, *A Bell for Adano* is a sentimental story of a "good guy"—as Hersey puts it in his letter to Girgus— with a few "bad men" such as General Marvin having the upper hand. The foreword, the narrative, and the character portrayals do, however, comprise an expression of Hersey's essentially didactic attitude toward writing.

A few years later, writing for the *United Nations World* (May, 1947) Hersey would ask:

> Is a man of any use against an avalanche? . . . Higher up on the mountain, right now, there are sounds of boulders sliding: what should one man do alone?[16]

He replies that each person can do a few specific things so that he

> will have a sense that he is participating; that he lives in the community of those who want peace, no matter how divided, helpless, and even hopeless that community sometimes seems; and that he is not alone, and really without hope, outside the community; that he is trying to be a citizen of the world. (20)

Here he urges people to join a group devoted to the study of world organizations, to read, to question, and to work for concrete goals while in the process of working for theoretical ones. Much as Joppolo worked from basic humanistic values without being either complacent about the system or alienated from it, Hersey advocated responsibility for one's own actions and belief in our power to accomplish much in a world or system that is far from ideal. The emphasis Hersey places in the 1947 article and in all later writings upon the importance of education and co-operation even with an imperfect community indicates that he would eventually examine that side of Joppolo, the weakness and the vagueness, that was overlooked in his six-week composition of a sentimental and entertaining best seller.

One way Hersey would find to develop his theme of the informed individual's Sisyphus-task in a possibly hopeless world would be his scholar-narrator, Noach Levinson. From the too-simple Major to the varied characters of *The Wall* would be both a literary and a psychological journey. But even his experiences at Hiroshima and Warsaw would not make him cynical of the possibilities of humanism. They would cause him to write from an increasingly individualized position while at the same time determine him to bring his vision to as many people as he could. These two factors would help decide his forms, his themes, and his reputation.

During an assignment to Moscow in 1944 Hersey had an experience which apparently has affected his work. His interviews with Russian writers reflect an interest in the social role of the writer close to the description Frye gives of the humanist, whom he sees as departing from conservative ritual and belief, the "myth of concern," to take up a questioning, liberal stance, the "myth of freedom," much as Cressida left the defending camp for the beseiging one. [17]

In Hersey's time, "the myth of concern" would place loyalties in the American liberal system; the "myth of freedom" would call for the radical left and, finally, for alienation such as that described by Aldridge or Hassan. Hersey had expressed a view which is perhaps more difficult to describe or to maintain than conformity to either dominant myth; he is the Cressida not ready to move from one camp to another, less concerned with forming a new allegiance to a rising force than with wringing the last usefulness out of the old as long as it still functions in the lives of most people. It is not out of order to speculate that what he recorded about the Russian writer's position in his society may have been a shaping factor in his own stubborn vision.

Hersey used a Gorki phrase to name his first article from Russia, "Engineers of the Soul," (*Time*, October 9, 1944), and stated, "Not a word is written in Russia which is not a weapon." [18] Because writers in Russia at this time have philosophical unity with their audience and exercise great influence and responsibility toward them—because, in effect, they write within a "myth of concern"—they can be judged solely by their aims: " 'to tell the truth about the war,' " to depict " 'the heart and soul of the Soviet man.' " (100) Their styles are "muscular, bitter, mystical and adjectival" (100) and exhibit terrible hatred toward the Germans. One writer, Sholokhov, says his censor is truth itself, and that he has uttered no cliches about patriotism. Vishnevsky, a playwirght, outlines a program for Russian writers which speaks implicitly of the closed myth of concern in which they would write after the war; in fact, it reads almost like a litany to the closed myth:

to gather the whole truth about the war

to glorify heroic tradition
to occupy themselves with human honor, conscience, soul
to call on Russians for a new effort of creativeness for peace
to explore England and America. (102)

" 'We shall talk,' " Vishnevsky said, " 'plainly, clearly and with polemical incisiveness and we shall expect our British and American colleagues to speak to us in the same language and in the same spirit.' " (102) Hersey's reaction to some of this shows in his tone in another article, "Dialogue on Gorki Street," (*Fortune* xxxi, Jan., 1945). "We must have no secrets from each other," he reports himself as saying to the "amalgam" Russian he is interviewing. (149) The "Russian" replies in terms of a closed society—that it is necessary to hide some things until the world is reconstructed on principles of thought, before secrets fall into the hands of the wrong people. " 'We must go very fast to a rational world—every father in the world must realize that somehow he is the father of every child.' " (151)

The concern with conscience was something Hersey was beginning to display as a writer, and after this visit it deepened. But he wrote, as his question above indicates, somewhere between the closed myth of concern and the open myth of freedom to construct a new society. He would be a strange new voice, and an isolated one, in his country, lacking the full support of either dominant myth, like an artisan carving details on a building in need of renovation or even demolition, but still in use. His work would express "what to do until the revolution (sic) comes," with far more concern about present reality than revolutionary possibility.

In other articles during 1945 and 1946, Hersey sounds a more independent voice than he had previously. For example, a report on kamikaze pilots (*Life,* July 30, 1945) condemns their training, where human life is cheap, where leaders "have systematized suicide; they have rationalized a morbid, sickly act." (75) A few months later, in "Letter from Shanghai" (*New Yorker,* Feb. 9, 1946) Hersey shows again that he is concerned less with the idea of American victories and policies than with human life and its quality. The journalistic practice of selection he would use in *Hiroshima* gives this essay an implicitly critical tone without a rhetorical attack on American policies. A mass of detail, including the sounds of "O Susanna!" on a Chinese fiddle, the conversion of a customs jetty into an American prophylactic station, the American conductor of the Shanghai Municipal Symphony, the angry victims of jeep accidents, is permitted to stand as evidence for the reader. He refrains from comment, even when he reports the enlisted men's "rickshaw derby" in which girls were "jockeys" and coolies were "Horses" with a floral horseshoe and $7.00 as prizes. One point of criticism he does make openly is stated in words which have interesting connotations; "American openhandedness has dislocated the economic life of the city." Not "generosity" or "wealth" but not "capitalism" or "greed" either; not "reformed" and not "destroyed." The words "open-handedness" and "dislocated" give an interesting reflection of the writer at this time.

During the China assignment, Hersey met General Marshall, who impressed him significantly with his ability to remember and select details and work for agreement among the divergent groups in Chungking. His difficult task of working with Chiang as well as with other parties found some inspiration in a passage from Franklin's autobiography. Hersey was moved to quote the passage; judging from his recent writings it may be useful in determining his own outlook as well as that of Marshall, who is the figure Hersey praised most of all of those he interviewed in depth during the journalism years.

> When you assemble a number of men to have the advantage of their joint wisdom, you inevitably assemble with those men all their prejudices, their passions, their errors of opinion, their local interests, and their selfish views. From such an assembly can perfection be expected? It therefore astonishes me to find this system approaching so near to perfection as it does. [19]

Hersey's habit of closing in for an observation of an individual and his theme that "good" or "bad" men make palpable difference no matter what the organizational structure, appears in a report he made of a trip from Shanghai to northern China. The two-part article is a detailed account of a voyage nearly ruined by the American Skipper, "an extremely bitter man. The only two things he seemed ever to have enjoyed were nailing shingles on roofs, which he had once done professionally, and the time he had temporarily deafened his wife during a squirrel shoot by firing too close to her right ear." [20] The officers agreed with Hersey's appraisal, and the Chinese soldiers—who were living on one scant meal a day in contrast to the captain's excellent meals—observed, " 'The American water soldiers on this ship are interesting. . . . In every country you have men who get angry easily and others who are quiet.' " (60) An interesting contrast to the boorish skipper, whose excuse for his unfair treatment of the Chinese is " 'The Americans won the war, didn't they?' " [21] appears in the Chinese major who politely tries not to lose face with his men because of the captain's abuse. The man had made an American friend early in his career, and when he becomes seasick on the nervewracking journey Hersey lets the irony and the wonder stand for itself: "All the rest of the voyage he lay there, fully clothed, sick, and with a letter in his pocket from an American Major promising to pay all his expenses whenever he decided to visit the U. S."

Hersey recorded many such contrasts in men. Perhaps because he knows a great deal more about many places and events than most writers can hope to find out—more, that is, of externals than most people can observe—he has continued to use concrete observation rather than psychological probings in most of his work; perhaps, too, he has tried to convey his humanistic vision in the same way he has learned it: by observing and noting detail, by piling up contrasts and similarities, by relating known experience to the philosophy he has consistently maintained, the primacy of the individual despite whatever doom we can prepare for one another. Choosing to write in such a mode has had its literary price for Hersey, but it has also been the shaping force of *Hiroshima* and other interesting and reasonably significant works.

Like *A Bell for Adano*, *Hiroshima* has been called an event rather than a book. [22] More than any of his other works, it has shaped Hersey's common reputation as a good-hearted but biased reporter, a writer who sees people in terms of events. [23] It has also caused him to have a widely recognized name as a skilled and sensitive reporter, whose account of the atomic bomb's effect is still read and discussed. It is the first of Hersey's books to appear on

college reading lists in history, social studies and journalism, and it
is also used in high school classes. As an early example of the nonfiction novel, it now receives attention in college literature classes as
well.

A critical work on postwar American writing, *The Mythopoeic Reality* (University of Illinois, 1976), analyzes *Hiroshima*
as an example of a new genre which reveals the "inner turbulence of
facts." [24] According to Mas'ud Zavarzadeh, Hersey's method
"followed the contours" of the horror without attempting to interpret it; the author-scribe recognized that the facts of the bombing
and its effects were beyond systematizing by means of mythic views
such as Christianity or humanism. Acting as the " 'midwife' of
experiential reality," Hersey offered the reader an awakening to the
untamed nature of facts in the twentieth century. He is one of a
number of artists who force the reader to confront "fictuality,"
the unimaginable and ungovernable nature of reality in the postwar
era. Unlike writers generally praised and analyzed by academic
critics—Bellow, Roth, Oates—authors like Hersey, Capote, Agee and
Oscar Lewis have provided truth in our century when what Zavarzadeh calls "the totalizing novel" and its imposed world order no longer is honest.

Zavarzadeh, in my opinion, has accurately placed Hersey
within a tradition of journalistic creativity. His thesis that this
new genre, the nonfiction novel, supercedes the traditional novel
as the dominant form of our age assumes that conventional fiction
writers impose unverifiable organizing principles on their narratives;
without using the phrase "death of the novel" the analysis assumes
it as a given. In the thirty-six years since Hersey wrote *Hiroshima*
few of his critics have worked from this assumption. While I think
Zavarzadeh offers a compelling case for recognition of the value of
the nonfiction novel and its place in a tradition that includes *Walden,
Life on the Mississippi* and perhaps *Moby Dick*, I believe that fiction
is still a viable and revolutionry genre today in the hands of such
writers as Christina Stead, Tillie Olsen and V. S. Naipaul who reject
dominant myths. Hersey, of course, has chosen fiction as his way
of responding to what he has seen. Recognition of his accomplishment in *Hiroshima* should take into account Hersey's arrangement

of facts within the work in the context of his emerging critical view of American life. Zavarzedeh's isolation of one Hersey work permits him, I think, to supply an interpretation of Hersey as a "sympathetic registrar" of the facts gained through interviews and other research. Hersey's reporting skills are certainly at their peak in *Hiroshima*, but the notion that his own consciousness is overwhelmed by fact in the writing is not entirely borne out by a close reading of the text. The writer's eleven subsequent novels, at any rate, indicate his stubborn endorsement of the power of fiction and provide a fuller understanding of what one American writer has done in an attempt to respond adequately to the chaos he documented in 1945. The response of early critics to *Hiroshima* is instructive, for they attest to the limitations of traditional fiction without imagining that a new genre would emerge in response to mass annihilation.

The work has had a wide and unique circulation, beginning with its publication in full in *The New Yorker* on August 31, 1946. For the first time, one report made up the entire magazine, with a black-bordered cover to express the editorial feeling about Hersey's essay. Other well-known facts about *Hiroshima* are that the Book-of-the-Month-Club distributed copies free to its membership because its directors found it "hard to conceive of anything being written that could be of more importance at this moment to the human race," that Albert Einstein and Bernard Baruch purchased a total of fifteen hundred copies, and that it was read aloud on four hours of prime-time radio. [25] All of this provides a basis for saying that Hersey's account helped to shape the thoughts of millions about the disaster. The book was printed in nearly every country by 1946, with the ironic exception of Japan. Hersey donated proceeds to the Red Cross.

Twenty-five years after its publication, my ninth-grade class at John Hersey High School noticed and argued about the major assumption of the work: that the atom bomb was an inhumane and unfathomable weapon whose users were guilty by implication. The students who felt the use of the bomb was justified in the circumstances expressed anger that Hersey gave a "one-sided" report, but most of them thought the book an effective warning about atomic power. The reaction of young students so many years after the use of the bomb and Hersey's report on it, during a time when young people were rather sensitive to public issues, is an important factor in the continuing impact of the work. Neither the fluid prose nor the philosophical assumptions of *Hiroshima* seem dated today. The book does seem to anticipate the anti-war views of liberals of the early sixties and the continuing opposition to the use of nuclear weapons. Its early effect of rallying a large number of people to emotional and intellectual rejection of atomic weapons must be seen as an important cultural event. Although the essay was partly shaped by Hersey's editors, his name is the one permanently associated with the work and its vivid picture of Japanese citizens caught in inexplicable chaos.

For a long time, critics who have found Hersey's didactic novels overbearing have either conceded that *Hiroshima* is a historically important and even a well-written piece of journalism, or else have ignored the work as irrelevant to Hersey's position in literature. Sanders' book mentions that no one has ever said that *Hiroshima* was an inferior work or even found adequate words for praising it. Kingsly Widmer, however, has written a harsh indictment of the work, Alfred Kazin has defined some of the problems of the form, and Girgus has examined *Hiroshima* extensively in a cultural context. Their comments are useful in this analysis of Hersey's rhetorical form and moral statement.

The chief objection Widmer raises to the documentary novel, and to *Hiroshima* as its prototype, is that it is actually an impossible attempt to "reduce vast horror to recognizable scale"—impossible in the sense that its literary devices meant for affective appeal cannot carry the factual authority the form claims. [26] Literature by its very nature calls for the personal integration of material, such as that given in a memoir, while history demands factual organization. The documentary novel gives neither of these, Widmer maintains, and in his opinion gives nothing else of value. The treatment of character, especially, is harmful; persons are never viewed apart from the event, but serve as material for the author to manipulate from a supposedly sympathetic stance which really implies a patronizing contempt. Description is not enough for awareness; the work lacks the quality of "survival-guilt" found in Japanese and European literature on the war which forces a response of horror and shame at the human condition.

Widmer insists that the imagination has added little to the affective power of literature on the bomb. The immediate and long-range public reaction to *Hiroshima,* however, indicates that Hersey's non-fiction novel did present in stark, effective form the sense of chaos, brutality and marvelous human resilience he observed in the survivors' accounts. Kazin's remarks on the "non-fiction novel," which give a more balanced description of the form before dismissing it as lasting art, explain that the imagination really cannot find a more adequate way to deal with mass horror. Tragedy is assimilated as individual fate but "death in round numbers is the death of strangers." [27]

From such criticism, which seems dated in comparison with that offered by Zavarzadeh, one gets the impression that Hersey stepped into the breach with his nonfiction novel. Had he written a straight historical account he would have told of "death in round numbers" and brought nothing of invention to make the work as distinctly memorable as it is. Kazin argues that the invention of one mind can stand as a fable, while publicly recorded facts have an unmemorable form; he assumes that writers must be judged within a hierarchy in which fiction must be valued more than non-fiction. By using hybrid techniques, combining research with conscious structuring of language for effect, Hersey has dramatized and made more vivid, although not really less true, the effects of the bomb.

Although Kazin, unlike Widmer, attributes affective power to the form, he rejects it because it seems unworthy of public acclaim. Why, he asks, should writers seize greedily on essentially meaningless events and try to make art out of them? Kazin's objections on grounds of exploitation are specifically for Capote and Mailer; moreover, they assume that the artist must share the intellectual and political grounds of the critic in order to produce a worthwhile work—that is, must affirm meaninglessness. Even Hersey's severest critics do not accuse him of self-aggrandizement at the time he wrote *Hiroshima,* and the continuing debate over the literary reputation of

Ezra Pound indicates that the artist need not share the dominant literary or political view. Hersey's belief that individual actions have meaning in and for themselves as long as human beings can endure, a theme that other artists such as Malamud, Bellow and Mailer find their own ways to explore, is more startling or hard to accept in his works than in theirs because he deals as a reporter or chronicler of this human activity rather than as an agonized symbol-maker. The artist's changing relationship to facts in this century is exemplified in *Hiroshima;* Hersey's nonfiction has a compelling beauty and sadness in recounting the incredible.

Kazin, who sees the documentary novel as a form that adds to—affects—the crisis it depicts is an effective counter to Widmer's argument that the form is a total failure. Since Hersey's didactic conception of his art and dogged use of it in every book, as well as his actions for the sake of various causes, can to a large degree spare him the label of opportunist that Kazin gives to similar writers, much of the rest of Widmer's argument also seems questionable. Does Hersey's editorial stance in *Hiroshima* really imply contempt for the survivors? It is probably safe to say that few people ever have or ever will read it that way. Widmer's final statement that literature must—in effect—prove that man is not a worthy creature, is out of the same reservoir of assumptions that Kazin's insistence on meaninglessness comes, and is typical of the major part of Hersey criticism before Girgus. As a singular voice he is guilty by association both with opportunistic non-fiction writers and popular noelists who assure the public that all is well. Fortunately, *Hiroshima*'s artistry has been better appreciated of late, though Hersey's name is notable for its absence in widely-circulated criticism.

With his emphasis on Hersey's exploration of the individual's role in the technocracy, Girgus argues that *Hiroshima* itself is a technological form in which the modern writer attempts once again to gain control over his material by combining art, life and personality in a way that responds to the challenge of new communications media. The danger that the individual writer, such as Mailer, may actually further the spread of dehumanization by employing mechanical means or topical situations to enrich or aggrandize himself, is one that Girgus resolves by stating that the organization of the material and detail provokes a moral response from the reader. Hersey does not need to talk in moral terms directly in *Hiroshima* because the facts and details speak for themselves. Girgus thus implies that Hersey had a sense of moral community with his audience. He did not need to convince them of new values, but to speak as a peer exceptional for his firsthand experience. [28]

For this reason, Hersey's work has seemed pedestrian to traditional critics. Frye has described the problem of the contemporary poet's isolation from society to the point that he violates the common notion of art if he attempts to adopt the kind of leadership role that Hersey seems to take, one of working within a community of established values with a Socratic belief that revelation must necessarily bring awareness. "In the twentieth century an important and significant writer may be reactionary or superstitious; the one thing apparently that he cannot be is a spokesman of ordinary social values."[29] Hersey, like a photographer taking pictures of a ruined building whose owners have unwittingly employed arsonists on their staff, brings the evidence of human destruction and fortitude to those he assumes will act upon the evidence in a way to curtail destruction and be consoled by fortitude. The photographer would not set out to condemn the employers of the arsonists, because they are his employers too, and have made a mistake which, by sending them out to gather evidence, they show themselves willing to correct. Hersey, with his concept of the writer as a gifted individual with a primary responsibility to help readers see and experience events for their own good, because such an experience is what they want and need, is in a different relationship to his audience than most contemporary artists.

Even though *Hiroshima*, like the three earlier books, proceeds on the knowledge of a community of human values with his audience, the book draws its superiority to them from its rightness for the occasion. Unlike Booth's artist, Hersey has been spared the need to express values much different from those of most of his readers—that is, of most literate people. The nature of his subject matter and his reasons for writing about it preclude this difficulty and make his writing exceptional; that also bring the dangers of being prosaic, ordinary, pedestrian, and unenlightening, as is clear from some aspects of all three preceding books. With the report on the bombing, Hersey becomes one of the few writers of his time to work with the purpose of providing drastic, dreadful information in such a way that individuals might develop the humanistic instincts they retain in a corrupt system.

Hersey clearly sets out to involve the reader's sympathies and to point out the likenesses of the Japanese victims to his *New Yorker* audience. Just as he later would define the task of "the novel of contemporary history" as not to illuminate events but to illuminate the human beings caught up in them, he sets that goal for *Hiroshima* also. Rather than reviewing the damage he saw on his visit, rather than giving a chronological account of the city's destruction from historical records of the extent of the damage, he chooses, as in the previous books, to focus on a few individuals who happened to be good interview subjects. Unlike the distinctions of nerve, courage or compassion he attributed to chosen individuals in the other war books, the qualities of his six subjects deliberately level them to randomly chosen, ordinary people from different occupations with nothing more in common with each other than they have with the readers, except for nationality. The statistical information that one hundred thousand people had died from the blast is given here for contrast, to build up the enormity of the catastrophe, and to put the reader's own sense of helplessness against such odds in abeyance before the account of the six other selves who really acted quite forcefully to save their lives despite the insignificant effect their actions could have. Later in the book, Hersey gives a more accurate factual account about the number of deaths when he explains that the figure is based on the thousands of corpses dug up after the American occupation forces recorded an official 78,150 as the number of dead. [30] This is one of many instances of authorial control of audience reaction. To enlist sympathy and ultimately to evoke astonishment leading to outrage is the aim of the work, not to create a historical record or an imaginative art form. Literature and history are brought to bear on reality as the writer judges them useful for his purpose. The form is much more controlled than it had been in *Into the Valley,* and it works toward a clearer end than does *A Bell for Adano,* for here the author is certain both of what he sees, and what he wants the reader to see.

What the reader sees are Japanese people so like himself or

herself in the details Hersey selects for viewing, and so sympathetic-
ally drawn in their few differences—such as the formal politeness
with which buried victims scream for help—that, coming from the
pen of the same war correspondent who wrote for *Life* about "weird
little Japs" in the early forties, conveys a change of outlook which
convinces the reader of the mistake made in bombing the city. The
first sketch of a survivor, the Reverend Mr. Tanimoto, draws the
reader still further into identifying with the subjects. Tanimoto
has a special worry because he has had an American education and
still had American friends.

Hersey is attentive to his now-involved reader's need to visual-
ize the event; for example, he sets up a distinct, concrete vision
of the scene before the bomb:

> Like most homes in this part of Japan, the house consisted of
> a wooden frame and wooden walls supporting a heavy tile roof. Its
> front hall, packed with rolls of bedding and clothing, looked like a cool
> cave full of fat cushions. . . . There was no sound of planes. The morning
> was still; the place was cool and pleasant. (8)

The structure of the book very effectively reinforces the
sympathetic involvement. Hersey returns five more times to the pre-
explosion hours as he describes each of the people he had briefly
mentioned at the beginning. The reader receives simple evidence
of common bonds with the victims (such as Mrs. Nakimura's weary
night with her three children, and Dr. Fujii's relaxed reading of the
newspaper in his underwear) and is taken again through the inexplicable destruction of the clearly depicted personal world of each
victim. From a self-sustaining citizen with individual problems,
responsibilities, and joys comparable to those of the literate and
probably middle class audience, each turns into a confused auto-
maton in a swarming mass of survivors and doomed. One of Hersey's
few explicit interventions occurs at this point, and it comes as a
trusting remark to an audience in accord with him. Describing
Miss Sasaki's ordeal he says, "There, in the tin factory, in the first
moment of the atomic age, a human being was crushed by books."
(23) Miss Sasaki, saved until last, is probably the poorest person
among the survivors; Mrs. Nakamura is poor, also, but her relatives
and friends survive and are supportive. The clerk is left alone and

crippled, least able to cope with her life after the bombing. More than any other figure, Miss Sasaki was "crushed" and both Hersey's comment and his detailed account of her bleak life serve to bring an effective end to the section.

The second section, the account of the six persons after the bomb struck until the following day, is called "The Fire" and depicts the pain and chaos by showing the people scurrying like ants under a human heel. Each person, even under these circumstances, finds a way to endure without controlling events, and to carry on without knowing the cause of the damage, the extent of it, or the hope of overcoming it. In a dazed blindness, each does what he or she can to stay alive and sane. The mother saves her children and tries to save her sewing machine, her means of livelihood. The clergymen try to help the wounded; Miss Sasaki waits in great physical and emotional pain; the idealistic young doctor works until he is numb, and obsessed with worry and consideration for his mother, and the older doctor is wounded, stunned and capable of worrying about being seen in ragged, bloody underwear. None of the actions are made to seem better than the others, yet each is predictable from the earlier vignettes. The reader is not surprised at outstanding courage, nor made disgusted about the lack of it. The extreme physical and emotional suffering of thousands of people surround the survivors, and their actions by contrast seem miraculously sane, practical and heartening without being held up as heroic in any way. The six people are a part of the most horrendous chaos, yet even in their utter confusion and agony they function as individuals the reader can identify with.

Significantly, the survivors begin to find strength and a reason for continuing to live in their interactions with others, yet the interaction is the most painful part of the account for both readers and characters. In two places, Hersey uses extremely graphic sensory details of the suffering. Both times, it is a clergyman who is faced with the horror when he exerts himself to his limits to help the suffering. In Part III, "Details Are Being Investigated," which shows the people beginning to put the pieces together with very little help from authorities, Mr. Tanimoto uses the boat he had found to rescue several of the most helpless people from the danger of fire. On a special trip to help people who had called to him, he has the horror of grasping a woman by the hand, pulling off her skin "in huge, glovelike pieces." (60) Father Kleinsorge, a German priest, has a similarly horrid vision of wounded soldiers to whom he brings water: "their faces were wholly burned, their eyesockets were hollow, the fluid from their melted eyes had run down their cheeks." (68) No other details in the book are as grotesque as these. Rather than simply presenting a list of ultimate horrors, Hersey uses a dramatic technique which engages the reader more effectively because the two compassionate clergymen are struggling to relieve their own and others' misery and are confronted with the worst signs of it. To the already vulnerable reader, these anecdotes act as capsules containing the essential truth of the essay, that well-meaning kindness is all but useless to repair such damage, but it is better than apathy. Tanimoto's response to his moment of extreme shock is one of rage at the lack of help supplied by the government and the doctors, and he continues in spite of it to supply help to those he can. Kleinsorge gives the grotesques a drink of water by improvising a straw from a piece of grass, and also gives them the illusion of hope: " 'There's a doctor at the entrance to the park. He's busy now, but he'll come soon and fix your eyes, I hope.' " (69)

The title of this section of the essay is another way that Hersey creates empathy for the survivors and anger at the military and political systems. " 'Details are being investigated' " is the way the Japanese radio coldly comments on the destruction of Hiroshima. Hersey notes that few people probably heard the short-wave rebroadcast of Truman's "extraordinary" announcement identifying the bomb. His intention to condemn the use of the weapon—already clear and appropriate through his account—is voiced with irony as he relates that the people were too busy or weary or hurt to know their use as objects of a great scientific experiment "which (as the voices on the short wave shouted) no country except the United States, with its industrial know-how, its willingness to throw two billion gold dollars into an important wartime gamble, could possibly have developed." (66)

The people's acquiescent role toward the Emperor and the other authorities is contrasted with the efforts they made to re-order their lives in section IV, "Panic Grass and Feverfew." They are left with unexpected side effects, with loss of energy and mysterious wounds that do not heal. They are the victims of technology out of control, but are also somewhat indestructible, tenacious victims. Each grasps at ways to continue living and each seems rather brave and, paradoxically, rather fortunate. Even Mrs. Nakimura in her poverty considers the suggestions Father Kleinsorge offers, of working as a domestic for some of the Allied soldiers, or borrowing money from her poor relatives to repair her sewing machine. (111) Miss Sasaki finds some assuagement in her conversion to Catholicism, but—like the mediocre alternatives open to Mrs. Nakimura—this is obviously no compensation for her troubles. (113) Hersey makes this point openly by a summary of the six people's situation at the end of the essay.

The reader can identify with the Japanese victims closely; Hersey says their common feeling was "a curious kind of elated community spirit, something like that of the Londoners after their blitz—a pride in the way they and their fellow survivors had stood up to a dreadful ordeal." (114) The question of the ethics involved in the use of the bomb is presented directly from the viewpoint of the Hiroshima survivors. Their attitudes range from the passive and fatalistic to deep hatred for Americans, but the problem of ethics itself is left to the German Jesuits who were present during the calamity and its aftermath. " 'The crux of the matter,' they concluded, 'is whether total war in its present form is justifiable, even when it serves a just purpose. Does it not have material and spiritual evil as its consequences which far exceed whatever good might result? When will our moralists give us a clear answer to this question?' " (118)

Hersey uses a fifth type of reaction as a poignant finish to the essay, and his own opinion appears in the way he introduces the paragraph dealing with their memories: "It would be impossible to say what horrors were embedded in the minds of the children who lived through the day of the bombing in Hiroshima." (118) A child, Toshio Nakamura, is quoted using the same kind of factual form Hersey had used, with a striking effect: " . . . Next day I went to Taiko Bridge and met my girl friends Kikuki and Murakami. They were looking for their mothers. But Kikuki's mother was wounded and Murakami's mother, alas, was dead.' " (188)

Booth has stated the Aristotelian criterion for good writing this way: all that is in the work must relate to the work, its object, purpose and form. [31] *Hiroshima* stands as such a work. In it the author himself carried out a Sisyphus-task, and he has been credited with being a cultural hero of sorts with good reason. The vision and mystery Hersey sought in his observation of the war finds an unforgettable expression in his most famous work. From being a reporter serving a ready-made set of values, he had moved to the position of an author expressing reality in a new form. In a modest way Hersey achieved what Booth suggests as an option for the modern artist:

> One possible reaction to a fragmented society may be to retreat to a private world of values, but another might well be to build works of art that themselves help to mold a new consensus. (393)

Hersey had plumbed to universal values, not created new ones; but he made his audience see what they had never seen so clearly before, moved them into a new ordering of experience and perception, and found his reward in the peers he created.

Tom Conti and Eli Wallach
In a scene from the television production of *The Wall*
Courtesy of Time Life Productions Incorporated

CHAPTER II

THE WALL: "AN ACT OF HUMAN SOLIDARITY"

Hersey's writing career, at the time of *Hiroshima*'s publication in August, 1946, was heavily balanced on the side of journalism. He had produced only one novel, *A Bell for Adano*, the winner of a war time Pulitizer Prize but not of serious literary attention. In the years since *Hiroshima*, Hersey has chosen to publish eleven novels, one work of journalism (*The Algiers Motel Incident* in 1968) and a few critical works. For Hersey at least, fiction has beckoned as a more durable, entertaining and effective medium than journalism. Although *Hiroshima* has been and continues to be the most respected of Hersey's individual works—the meeting, perhaps of the right minds at the right time—his chosen and desired vocation as an American artist has produced an intriguing and varied collection of fictions about human life.

Of his novels, *The Wall* (1950) stands as Hersey's most remarkable and worthwhile achievement; it may be the best novel because it allows free range for Hersey's impressive gifts for journalism and storytelling alike. It is outstanding for its massive strength and sympathy, its narrator Levinson, and its focus on Hersey's special perspective, communication-as-life. In assessing the book, neither Girgus nor Sanders rules out the author's obvious and enormous sympathy for the Warsaw Jews; like any favorable criticism of Hersey, their work deals with this artist in terms of his didactic purposes. Hersey does best under critical standards such as those he proposed for post-war Russian writers. As a memorial to six million victims of Nazi monomania, *The Wall* is hard to fault on humanitarian grounds.

Even acknowledging the journalistic and moral merits of *The Wall*, a critic of Hersey must recognize that it is a contribution to post-war fiction as well. Vastly different from *A Bell for Adano*, yet alive with the compassion, humor and cleverness of that book, *The Wall* includes careful plotting, effective characterization, and thematic patterns that have consistently engaged Hersey. It is a much better novel than *A Bell for Adano*, not only because Hersey spent nearly three years researching and writing it, but also because he had developed his powers as a writer of fiction during the years that elapsed between *Hiroshima* (1946) and *The Wall* (1950). A group of stories published during those years in *The New Yorker, The Atlantic Monthly* and '*47, Magazine of the Year* have not received critical attention, yet they show the author's growth in form and idea rather well. They reveal a Hersey truly convinced of the writer's moral responsibility toward the society which inspires his work, and a curiosity about the creative process he himself wished to take part in. The content and themes of these stories seem a direct preparation for what may be Hersey's best character, Noach Levinson, and for the numerous writers and communicators who people his novels.

The first of the stories, "The Death of Buchan Walsh" (*The Atlantic Monthly*, April, 1946, pp. 80 - 86), tells of a young man who is both appealing and exasperating to the narrator. This narrator is a writer who tries to make Buchan Walsh, a close friend, the hero of a story in which the uncommitted, purposeless young man would display unexpected strength and courage, beyond that of his "super-conscienced" socially concerned wife, in a moment of physical crisis. The climax, to be modeled on the writer's own new intellectual confidence after physical success with canoeing over rapids, would occur when Buchan saved the couple on a similar trip over rapids on the Housatonic.

The narrator feels that, besides his own gains from producing a story acceptable to a New York magazine, he may work out a solution that will help Buchan in real life. This sense of the power of the written word completely takes over; by a strange coincidence, Buchan has fallen helplessly in love with just the kind of woman the writer had imagined for him. Although Walsh is not "tightened" by the real-life committee woman as the fictional character was, but rather more disintegrated than usual, the writer's ego causes him to disregard this warning. Buchan is nearly killed in the canoe ride he and the woman take at the writer's urging. Although Walsh announces a new sense of purpose after the scare, even the writer cannot believe he will change. After a few days of euphoria, and a year-long but unresolved affair with the woman, Walsh is drafted, and killed in battle. The writer finds his sergeant, who relates that Walsh actually died of uncommitment. As a corporal, he had to decide whether to turn back or forge through when his squad was ambushed. After ten minutes of thought, he pronounced his own death-sentence: "I guess we'll just stay here." (86)

The story contains only a few inferences that the writer himself was out of bounds in trying to resolve a real-life conflict by using art as a model for life. The narrator seems more disturbed over Buchan's interruption of his story-writing than about his near death in the application of an imagined solution to a real problem. As a whole, the tale concerns the waste of a human life and potential, and the writer's deploring of that. There is a suggestion that the emotional Buchan has more potential than a mechanical social activist would have. Something similar occurs in *The Wall*, as Levinson watches Dolek Berson emerge from a position as "The Drifter" to that of the actual hero of the work.

"The Death of Buchan Walsh" is interesting, too, for its rather memorable portrait of Buchan and its suspenseful use of the canoe ride. The actual death of Walsh, coming as an anti-climax in the reader's expectations, mirrors the senseless and disconnected spirit of the young man and of the war which summoned him.

In a less satisfying piece of fiction, "The Pen" (*The Atlantic Monthly*, June, 1946, pp. 84 - 87), Hersey combines a theme and structure suggestive of meaninglessness with a tone that codemns hypocrisy. Because the outcome of a story that seems to demand closure is left ambivalent, the tale does not seem to work as well as those in which Hersey is clear in both purpose and method. Written on the way to China for his *New Yorker* assignment, it seems to come out of the same fund of anger Hersey felt on the voyage he described in "Two Weeks Water Away," the pair of articles for

the May 18 and May 25, 1946 issues of *The New Yorker* discussed
in the preceding chapter of this book. The chief characters of "The
Pen" are a naive sailor, Charles Silby, and a shrewd, suspicious
passenger, Dr. Curtis. The sailor enters Curtis' stateroom, looks
around, and finds a "gleaming Monel metal fountain pen'" (85)
Hersey uses the pen as a means of self-discovery for Sibley and as
an object revealing Curtis' pride and hypocrisy. The young man,
who—as we later learn—has stolen before, writes his own name on
a sheet of scrap paper in the doctor's room. This seems to unnerve
him; he scratches it out, throws the pen into a drawer, and kneels
with his head bowed for a few minutes.

The purpose of the story seems to be to depict the ruthless
power some people use against the weak and unfortunate, much as
the skipper of the Navy boat had done in Hersey's factual account.
The arrogant doctor traces Sibley, is met by sympathetic officers
who shield the sailor and believe his denial of the theft, and finally
locates the pen in the drawer. Curtis keeps up the appearance that
the pen is gone, hides it in a shoe at the bottom of his suitcase— and
steals a Navy towel. Sibley, tormented by his weakness, talks with
his Lieutenant in an attempt to gain strength against his kleptomania.
When Curtis, after taking every precaution with his locked luggage,
finally looks for the pen in Shanghai, he finds that it is gone.

The implication, perhaps, is that the young man longed to
hold the pen once more, saw the stolen towel, and finally gave in to
the temptation to steal. Unfortunately, the story is not clear enough
on this point; Hersey seems to leave it ambivalent, with a possibility
that someone else stole the pen in Shanghai and the doctor simply
got what was coming to him. The theme—the pursuit of the weak
by the strong, and the hidden, deadly weakness of the proud man—
seems muddled by the reader's unsolved puzzle about whether Sibley
actually takes the pen or whether someone else does. Moreover,
we do not know or care enough about Sibley or the pen, and there is
a false note to the parental care provided the sailor by his officers.
The condemnation of the doctor is sharp, clear and even memorable.
Using the same theme in *The Wall*, Hersey would give dignity, through
Levinson's pen, to the most piteous of the Jewish victims. Even in
this unsuccessful story, Hersey's purpose as a writer appears as a

moral, humane dedication to arousing sympathy and indignation in the reader. A story of the same period, on the subject of the Jewish agony, brings dignity as well as empathy to the central character. Although more sentimental, it is also more believable and satisfying than "The Pen."

In "A Short Wait" (*The New Yorker*, June 14, 1947, pp. 27 - 29), Hersey effectively keeps the reader on a see-saw. We do not know, until the end, whether or not Luba, a young Jewish refugee from Prague, is welcome in her aunt and uncle's New York home. Although Hersey can safely assume that we will want Luba to be welcome, he cannot and does not assume that we will like her. She is cold, stiff, and at times arrogant, yet we are prepared for this by her reflections on the past and her valid fear of rejection. The happy, sudden, almost contrived revelation by her relatives' maid that they had not purposely ignored her desperate letters during the war years does command respect because of careful preparation. As usual, Hersey's solution to human sadness and suffering is the almost too simple device of human communication. Luba's relief, however, is our relief; she is a character close to the reader because of her understandable insecurity. Unlike Hersey's portrayal of Joppolo, the treatment of Luba indicates that Hersey is conscious of his character's limited vision. This more skillful characterization would strengthen the effect of *The Wall*; Stephen Masur, Yitzhok, and Pan Apt would be both attractive and repugnant figures.

Another such figure appears in "Why Were You Sent Out Here?" (*The Atlantic Monthly*, feb., 1947, pp. 88 - 91). Written after Hersey observed in post-war China, the story seems to be an example of his belief that literature has didactic importance. Its form, which contains the question, "Why were you sent out here?" asked by young men of older ones, asks the same question of all Americans. By doing so, it also inquires about the meaning of life itself. One of Hersey's most pessimistic stories—no individual inspires or even really communicates with another, much less with a group—the tale is both brief and haunting.

The story is told from the point of view of an ageing career soldier, Colonel De Angelis. He finds himself being "handled" in an unobtrusive but authoritarian way by a younger man, Colonel

Watson. With some pain, he recalls scenes almost exactly parallel to those he is enduring, in which he had the role of the younger officer, effectively reducing the status and self-respect of an older one. The gap between the generations appears vividly in conversations, but it is even more apparent in the reaction of the Chinese to the two colonels. Watson orders the coolies about, smugly using a few Chinese phrases and confident of his position; they do as he orders them. De Angelis is not confident; he does not even know "why he was sent out here." His coolie whines, shouts and grabs when De Angelis pays him the amount specified by Watson. The older officer knocks the coolie down with his swagger stick, pays him twice the amount required, and with some shame returns to his office hoping no one has seen him.

The interesting contrast in manner of the two officers works as an impressionistic study of ageing and of value placed on wisdom rather than on practical knowledge. It also illustrates the theme Hersey had found for his life work. The older man, for all of his wisdom, has no way to communicate it; he communicates his exhaustion, confusion and vagueness to the coolie. Lacking even a trace of the language, hemmed in throughout his assignment by his own fear, confusion and lack of knowledge, De Angelis cannot help himself, the American cause, or the Chinese. He has good intentions but has given up on following them. This character is sympathetic even in his ignorance, while the younger officer is suavely obnoxious, yet the older man—who should have known better—is portrayed as the true failure.

The fifth story Hersey published during these years, a would-be novelette, appeared in '47, *Magazine of the Year*, an economic venture of several writers, artists and designers.[1] Although the piece is undeveloped and occasionally simplistic, this story, "A Fable South of Cancer," is important for several reasons. First, it indicates Hersey's discovery of a satiric form for his social writing. Although in some ways the tale resembles a parody of society rather than a satire of it, there is a strong display of Hersey's cleverness with detail and perception of human nature. The story also reiterates the persistent theme. This time, Hersey states it directly, and— given the limitations of the work— succeeds in making his point.

The "fable" is a *Lord of the Flies,* of sorts. A Navy ship is lost in the Pacific, and the crew decides to stay on a large, idyllic island. The twenty-six hundred men build a utopian society, but Hersey indicates that the coming of women and of technology bring more complications than the idyll can sustain. A consumer society evolves, but the inhabitants persist in believing they have an ideal state. Significantly, it is an unscrupulous writer, "Watson Manybuck," who blinds the society to its problems by publicizing its peaceful aims without researching its actual problems and flaws.

Another kind of writing in the form of preserved, didactic tradition contains the only hope of the society. The one consistent character, Burlingame, is tattooed with quotations from political history. At the end of the story, he finds that one tattoo itches. It proclaims, " 'Men are not so good as their intentions. They are only as good as their deeds.' " (141) Burlingame insists that he is now " 'going to get busy.' " In the face of hopelessness, he tells his pessimistic wife, who says they can avoid trouble only for a while at best, " 'Well, if you add a while to a while . . . and then if you add a while more to that, pretty soon you have a good long time. And anyhow, a while is better than no time at all. It looks to me as if we have just a little better than no time at all right now. Yes, a while will do very well.' " (141)

The half-joking tale seems, in retrospect, to be a rather clever warning to the newly complacent post-war United States. That Hersey has benefited from his own efforts and experience, and perhaps from the advice of his critics, is happily true. A mental comparison of this story with Hersey's recent prophetic work, *My Petition for More Space,* makes one wish that Hersey would now rewrite "A Fable South of Cancer." In some ways, perhaps he has, in each of the novels that ally honorable survival with human communication.

Although the five short fictions Hersey published between 1946 and 1950 show the promise of serious fictions to come and a preoccupation with the writer's relation to his times, these interesting stories do not hint that Hersey was capable of organizing a vast amount of factual material into a competent, moving novel of contemporary history. It is the long *New Yorker* pieces on China, the spellbinding *Hiroshima,* and later long, colorful profiles of Bernard Baruch, General Marshall, and President Truman, which indicate the writer's talent for eliciting, selecting, and arranging material in a moving way.[2] The fact that *The Wall* is essentially a documentary novel has, David Sanders believes, both made and unmade Hersey's literary reputation.[3] On the one hand, the limitations and also the shadowy reputation of the form affected the book's reception; on the other, the documentary strengths and historical importance of *The Wall* left Hersey's more favorable critics with expectations that his subsequent and remarkably varied novels have not fulfilled because they have moved in the direction of fable and satire rather than documentation.

The criticism of *The Wall* by reviewers in 1950 ranges from accolades for Hersey as a great humanitarian to protests that the novel is a failure as literature—an array of comments that has continued to greet each one of Hersey's books. Somewhere between these extremes, many reviewers grappled with the issue of the empathetic writer and his creation by separating the two in their remarks. Only a few managed to accept *The Wall* on literary grounds while most praised the book enthusiastically as what David Daiches described as the record of Hersey's "noble and almost desperate sympathy."[4] Unlike many reviewers who praised the book only for Hersey's good intentions, Daiches did remark that its form gave the clear impression of a search for truth with a cumulative, powerful impact upon the reader. This critic also noted that Hersey's scholarship was excellent, despite a few errors about such things as Jewish burial customs.

Alfred Kazin and Maxwell Geismar also gave careful attention to the form of the book and praised it, much as Daiches had, in a somewhat lefthanded manner that seemed to say, "It is not like novels of brilliance, but it has something memorable and important we cannot quite define." Stating that the book lacked the depth of actual survivors' accounts, Kazin said that the "astonishing and very moving book has quick, affectionate sympathy and a wealth of love . . . an imaginative act of human solidarity."[5] The chief fault Kazin found with the book was that Hersey had not seen the political implications of his subject, as Koestler or Orwell might have. At the same time, Kazin says that Hersey feels real excitement over the possibilities of individual human beings, and that Levinson is superior to any Koestler creation.

  This critic, who could accept the farm as "an act of human solidarity" and recognize the specific area of Hersey's interest as a writer, really desired Hersey to emulate Silone or other political writers in condemning or endorsing specific systems of government because he writes about events in his century. As Hersey has made more clear in each successive novel, he is really skeptical of all large organizations where the emotions and ideas of individuals are expendable; he has never found political grounds for unequivocal rejection or subscription; he has seen his work as the recording of individual human possibilities in a changing and growing world. Kazin's wish for a political structure to the novel might, if fulfilled, have removed interest from the beauty, pain, and intensity of the Jews' ordeal and partial triumph.

  Maxwell Geismar—in a review he later characterized as "a trifle fervent"[6]—said the book might be judged as an outstanding contribution to contemporary literature. In language close to my own attitude toward the work, Geismar called it "an urgent and remarkable novel on a ground scale and one which seizes our minds and hearts." The words "urgent" and "seizes," along with Daiches' "search for truth" and "act of human solidarity" suggest the book's didactic force and rhetorical structure. In *American Moderns* (1958), Geismar's chapter, "John Hersey: The Revival of Conscience," the most extensive praise Hersey has received from a nationally known critic, indicates that *The Wall* continued to seem Hersey's "best and most solid work." Intending his remarks as helpful advice for future Hersey novels, Geismar said *The Wall* seemed "almost too fluid, delicate, and tender;" it lacked "a final sense of horror and evil."[7] Yet, it had ably met a large moral and social drama, the first American novel of the forties to do so. Significantly, Geismar mentioned that social writers were currently out of style. Edward Weeks, at the time of the book's publication, had placed Hersey in the tradition of Steinbeck and maintained that he had "sensitively enlarged the novel of contemporary history."[8]

  That Hersey had, in effect written a book that was both *nice* and *true*—both compassionate and factual—was, I think, the way he had "enlarged the novel of contemporary history." Differing from the Kazin favorites, Koestler and Orwell, or the Geismar example, Dostoevsky, Hersey had really done something nevertheless quite original and effective, although out of step with ordinary and justifiable critical expectations. Current interest in variant forms offers the most helpful guidelines in understanding Hersey's accomplishment. William Stott's recent *Documentary Expression and Thirties America* (1973), a study of persuasion for which Hersey, along with many others, gave advice, deals with many kinds of factual, didactic forms. Stott argues that true excellence in the documentary genre, as in any other, amounts to "the bursting of a mould" or form. "That the world can be improved and yet must be celebrated as it is are contradictions. The beginning of maturity may be the recognition that both are true."[9] James Agee and Walker Evans, Stott says, "burst" their respective forms in *Let Us Now Praise Famous Men* (1941) when they used them not only to arouse pity and indignation over the situation of the tenant farmers, but also to evoke awe and wonder at the sheer beauty of these human lives. Without the poetic self-consciousness of Agee's writing, and of course without the pictures which are essential to the impact of the whole work, there is room for comparison of Hersey's creation with theirs.

For nearly two years, Hersey lived with the Jews of Warsaw— not as Agee and Evans had lived with the farmers by sharing their quarters—but by sharing their thoughts. He listened to wire recordings of diaries, plays, poems and other documents from the ghetto. The recordings were made by two Jewish translators from Polish and Yiddish into English; both became intensely moved and often added their own reactions to the translated materials. For nearly a year, Hersey worked on a chronological retelling; the manuscript was nearly completed when he found that his narrator had come to life in his mind and would not be subdued, would not remain a mechanical device.[10] He then began the novel again, using Noach Levinson as the central character. Through this sensitive, admirable, yet not exactly heroic figure, Hersey both celebrated the human world of the ghetto and suggested its need for improvement. Using the horribly imposed system of annihilation as a fact in somewhat the way Agee and Evans used the poverty of the tenants, Hersey—as they did—actually expressed something else. By doing so, he made the Nazi madness recede without diminishing. He used his factual materials to create a personal documentary fiction, similar to *The Grapes of Wrath* yet significantly different in its apolitical nature, a departure from the ordinary political or historical novel. Condemning fascism as Agee did capitalism, he celebrated the human beings caught in its grip and showed why a few of them were able to escape it with a beauty of culture worth preserving outside of it.

An important part of the documentary form, Stott argues, is its believability. Radio, for example once enjoyed an extremely believable role; for that reason, Edward R. Murrow, who understood the medium thoroughly, may actually have shaped American entry into World War II through his persuasive London broadcasts. Hersey's part in shaping American attitudes toward atomic weapons had been significant; his reputation as a truthful, persuasive, humanitarian observer infused a special life into *The Wall* which further places it in the realm of "personal documentary fiction." Although the use of Levinson effectively separates it from the nonfiction novel, the act of writing such a book out of such materials, of creating such characters as Levinson, Berson, and Rachel Apt and endorsing their values within the story, places Hersey in a very different category from a writer shaping personal materials only. His own act of response to public materials—the "act of human solidarity" Kazin had come to doubt possible in our century—is the basis of *The Wall* and what we actually examine when we look at the novel.

Hersey's novel, the first American book about the mass murder of the Jews, is not mentioned in the new body of criticism which addresses the problem of reading and writing about the Holocaust. Writers like Elie Wiesel and critics like Alvin Rosenfeld stress that the Holocaust as a historical event resists theoretical and imaginative approaches to it. It is "something else" than World War II, defying analogy to other human experience and generating a literature without antecedants.[11] Certainly Mas'ud Zavarzadeh's theory of a "mythopoeic reality" which cannot be "totalized" via conventional, coherence-building art should apply to the Holocaust as well as to Hiroshima, yet theorists who work with Holocaust literature resist grouping it with any other phenomenon. Hersey's decision to focus on the human community within the ghetto, and on the resistance group (who were never more than 700 of the 600,000 ghetto inhabitants), demonstrates his conviction that the heroic actions of the resisters (survivors) rather than the still inexplicable fatalism and disbelief in the Nazi intention, the frightening reality of the mass annihilation, should be recorded and disseminated. In fact, he rejected his initial intention to write about the concentration camps he toured under Russian auspices in 1946 because he recognized their dehumanization of both guards and prisoners; it was the civilization preserved in the ghetto which made him see it as a desirable subject.

Holocaust critics no doubt dismiss *The Wall* without mention now because it does not tell that story which still defines telling, but an older tale analogous to other human behavior. Moreover, it responds to the atrocity within a framework of ancient values, roughly those of the liberal humanism which some analysts contend caused the Jews to disbelieve in the reality of the Nazi intent. Despite his journalistic approach to the Holocaust, Hersey chose to focus on the one thread of continuity with the traditional interpretation of human life which he uncovered in his research. Such a choice may seem too easy in view of the murdered millions, yet the book tells a truthful story which differs from other hero tales in its depiction of the slaughter of the people its heroes defended. Perhaps, given the role he had already played as reporter of Hiroshima truth, Hersey's choice to be the chronicler of worthwhile human survival is understandable. In the slow unfolding of literature and criticism, he may deserve to be seen as an early and astute questioner confronting the Holocaust as a yet unrealized horror and providing initial, nearly unthinkable truth in a structure his audience could deal with at the time. His interpretation does not gloss over the deaths, the self-deception, or the bestiality inherent in the tale; it does give a complex presentation also of the factors which contributed to the survival of the resisters who emerged from the sewers.

The struggle Hersey may have gone through in his decision to attempt a novel rather than a report, and to find and honestly shape a story which would be consistent with life as he understood it is only hinted at in his discussion of the process of writing the book. His feelings were a combination of outrage and wonder, a conflict of idealism and the palpable.[12] While Hersey's decision to make art out of fact which defined understanding once it was fully revealed makes him susceptible to the charge of facile opportunism, such a charge is irreconcilable with the philosophy of art he has lived by and written from. The choice of fiction over nonfiction for the story of the Warsaw ghetto is linked to his poetic interpretation of the work of writers, to "sing to us of aspiration and make us aspire."[13] In contrast to the actual survivors of Hiroshima, Hersey created in the diarist Noach Levinson a mythical survivor of thousands of years of rich culture. Diaries and papers from Warsaw now in English demonstrate Noach's shaping by Hersey. The archive of Emmanuel Ringelblum, exhumed at roughly the time Hersey was in Warsaw, may have been a model for Noach's diary, yet this archive contains notes for a history rather than a personal account, and it does not mention the resistance despite Ringelblum's key role.[14] Chaim Kaplan's diary (not available to Hersey) gives an excellent social description of the ghetto, but does not record the stories of individuals, other than Kaplan's own.[15] Noach the artist, freedom fighter and lonely individual exists as testimony to the power Hersey thought inherent in the imagination even in the face of atrocity.

The Wall might have a subtitle appropriate to this discussion: "The Writer's Role in the Survival Process." Using, on his own count, a list of nineteen themes and plotting the activities of more than fifty separate characters, Hersey gave a coherent structure to the story of the chaotic destruction of the Jewish population of Warsaw. He focused on a group of people who were to be destroyed, with a handful of survivors showing that both the terrible struggle and the lonely survival had been enriched by personal relationships and often amazing reservoirs of strength. In the form of a serious diary belonging to a scholar respected for his writing on Jewish culture and in the process of writing a history of Eastern European Jews when the annihilation began, the story comes to us only as the writer-narrator is able to present it. Besides his scholarly credentials, Hersey gives Noach Levinson the endorsement of an "Editor," who relates the background of Levinson's archive, buried in "seventeen iron boxes and a number of small parcels,"[16] and located through maps and letters Levinson had smuggled out of the ghetto. Obsessed by the idea that the only legacy of the ghetto could be its history, Levinson collected every personal and official document he could, and yet was really in-

terested "in separate Jews, in people." Hersey's device for verisimili-
tude is somewhat awkward, yet it does serve an important end. The
reader begins the novel with knowledge of its outcome, sympathy for
its content, and interest in the fictional account as a "legacy." Really
using a rhetorical framework similar to that of *Hiroshima,* the novel
thus achieves some of the power of the nonfiction novel to force the
reader to confront reality. Papers from the ghettos actually do suggest that the inhabitants were incessant chroniclers of their fate.

"Levinson" collected all kinds of documents, yet it is his personal account of the ghetto which has been "published," an account
which fuses the personal lives of some friends brought together by
political insanity, and then shows how these lives were pressed only
gradually into retaliation. Political groups within the ghetto, such as
Socialists and Zionists, come to have real meaning only when inspired by the most basic commitment to survival. The writer, Levinson, watches, takes part in, and records the changes as ordinary people are faced with what they finally realize to be a choice between
survival and annihilation, between truth and self-deception, between
rage and fear. Hersey's design emerges as an inevitably sorrowful one;
choice and commitment come almost—but not quite—too late to do
anyone any good. Levinson's interest in choice, commitment and survival—his own, the other Jews', and finally the reader's—is offered as
a testament and warning by Hersey.

Levinson is a reliable narrator. As a writer-recorder he is exacting, thorough, and candid. He does not have time to go over the en-
tries, to eliminate things which embarrass him or seem imprudent
(7), claims the "Editor," who also mentions that Levinson must have
had blind spots. The reader is drawn to trust Levinson when the character acknowledges a few of these, such as his hopeless infatuation
for the pretty Halinka Apt and his efforts to clear her name, efforts
beyond the importance of the rumors about her. Although the small,
homely man writhes at insults he does record them, admits to numerous physical and even emotional problems, and scrupulously searches
out various viewpoints. If anything, Levinson is not only a reliable
narrator; he appears annoyingly truthful and dedicated to his note-
taking. He rules out tact and social amenities to ask personal questions, and scents out the truth even on such occasions as Dolek

Berson's and Rachel Apt's attempt to hide the fact that they have become lovers during the final days of the ghetto.

While Levinson does admit that some other accounts he has received may be lies, he is usually so careful to check facts and to record accounts from many sources, that his credibility is nearly perfect. The entire book is composed of his conversations with ghetto dwellers he knows; he convinces people of the need to record their struggle and of his own sincerity and professional honesty. In a sense, the story is "an act of human solidarity" on the part of Levinson and those he interviews, as well as on Hersey's. The characters, entrusting Noach with their historic survival as well as their personal ones, endorse the future as well as the present, the reader as well as the plot.

Levinson's value to himself, his society and the reader grows as the book progresses. Only by an understanding of this can the reader possibly accept the closing scenes of the book, when Levinson crouches in a sewer pipe with his notebook, "entertaining" the people who must wait indefinitely for rescue, by drawing out their painful stories, purging and freeing them, actually saving their spirits if not their lives, enabling them to believe their lives have been worthwhile. His boldness, freedom, and sensitivity, his rapport with people, come to Levinson the artist during the long struggle from November, 1939 to the eve of escape, May 10, 1943.

Hersey divided the chronicle into six parts, which correspond to the steps of recognition and action by the community. The writer-narrator tells his own story as well as that of the others, with his life a focal point for the narrative. Noach begins as a member of the *Judenrat,* a Jewish committee which by 1939 is actually a tool for the Germans; he remains uncorrupted within this group because his power and prestige as scholar, writer, and record-keeper exempt him from many dangers. Simultaneous with his work on the *Judenrat* is his membership in a "family," a group including the Bersons, the Apts and the Mazurs which his own creative remarks help to form; his joining the underground is the outgrowth of political awareness painfully gained and personal involvement gradually won. As a fighter, Noach is given the job, his usual one, of historian; his "family" group and *Judenrat* survivors have learned the value of his work by his open instruction and their interaction with the process and re- sults of his labors. In a symbolic and even, perhaps, in a physical sense, no one would have survived without Levinson and his work. Hersey seems to have found an excellent subject to shape with his own perspective; the scholarly, timid, intense, intellectual, isolated but warm Levinson seems an adept means of conveying the impor- tance of listening, telling, seeing, and imagining within the process of human survival.

In Part I of *The Wall,* Noach makes the acquaintance of the Bersons, the Apts and the Mazurs, who, with a few others, form the later "family" and remain the central figures of the story. Noach's first act of recording is the dairy excerpt that describes Dolek Ber- son, a strong, young, wealthy man as a "drifter," an uncommitted type common to the writer's experience. He is curious to see what will happen to such people, especially to one like Berson, alive, curi- ous, moody and sensitive. The first episode is an answer to such a question, and an example of the book's structure: the writer observ- ing reality, recording it, and helping to shape it both by his record and his involvement. Dolek and Noach meet in prison because the young man allows the scholar to persuade (or coerce) him into the place to meet a Nazi command. Berson moves from thinking Noach " 'a sharp little fellow in a brown suit, carrying a black loose-leaf under his arm and wearing glasses so thick that his eyes look like two raw eggs' " (19) to overcoming the remoteness of the intellectual by the warmth of his own personality.

The reader, like Berson, learns to view Noach as a firm, sensi- tive guide to events, a kind of student-to-teacher relationship. Ber- son, for example, is awed by the presence of Benlevi, a Nobel prize winner, but Noach has little use for the pompous man. Later, Noach proves right; Benlevi does nothing to help resist the Nazis, and then buys his way out of the ghetto. The writer's voice is unknowingly prophetic as he silences Berson's complaints, asking the younger man how he got the idea that fairness was even a question in their circum- stances.

The enforced intimacy of prison leads Berson and Levinson

into a conversation that includes a discussion of literature satirized by the bitter Dr. Breithorn. This brilliant man, removed from the communication process, is not a survivor; he becomes a suicide during the impossible days of the later ghetto. The prison episode is thus a microcosm of the ghetto experience; those who survive do so through culture and its communication. Noach continues the education of Berson after they are released into what the Germans have threatened will be a ghetto. As the real wall closes them in with their fellow Jews, Levinson leads Berson toward self-knowledge and finds his own tendency to withdraw in dislike from others counteracted by Berson's vitality.

Noach meets and records his impressions of other people in the exclusive Sienna Street courtyard where Dolek and his fragile wife live. In addition to recording Dolek's growth, the writer helps to cause and also records for the reader the new awareness of Rachel Apt. Destined to be a guerrilla leader, the plain, wealthy young woman evolves with and through Berson and Levinson into a major figure in the survival story. Like Berson, she is drawn to the writer because of his wisdom, vulnerability, humor, and somehow inspiring obsession with the archive. Noach's sense of purpose in life, his writing, is thus a main cause of the resistance and survival of his friends as well as a record of it.

Levinson's importance peaks in this section as the Mazurs, Apts, Bersons and others gather for a kind of housewarming for the Mazurs after their flight from the ghetto at Lodz into the soon-to-be-enclosed Warsaw ghetto. Reb Yechiel Mazur, one of the few religious Jews Hersey depicts, invites Levinson as a "learned guest." His speech about home life begins in bitterness about his own childhood poverty. Although he would once have delighted in the horror he could arouse by such a speech, Levinson—possibly because of a look from Rachel Apt—begins to feel drawn as a member into a circle of brotherhood and friendship, into an ordered and longed-for home. He speaks, transported, about the significance of Jewish family and home life, moving his host to raise his drink in a tearful voice, toasting "Life."

Although Levinson regrets that he failed to warn of the danger in an ordered ritual, "the scratching of the rats in the . . . walls" (68), he finds that his speech has powerfully moved Dolek Berson. "The Drifter"—despite the writer's protest that he had not meant to castigate anyone, but to present a valid picture of life—begins to search for the meaning of new, vague, troublesome aspirations. His attempts to become involved and to find a meaning to life as the Jews now have it, inspired by the writer, lead Berson into confrontations with the German menace he can no longer ignore. In each of these, Levinson is his confidant.

The writer experiences pain himself when he inadvertantly hurts Rachel Apt, and questions his own timidity in facing up to the Germans. Berson and he discuss the matter of collective responsibility, with Berson now committed to collective responsibility and Jewish self-help. He wants to find a proper channel for his commitment, refuting Levinson's concept of shadowy borders between personal and public actions. In an exchange that seems to have Berson expressing the kind of philosophy Hersey's life and work have held, Levinson is the means of drawing out of Berson the clearest sense of self he has been able to find:

> 'No,' says Berson 'there's a sharp difference between being *for* something (a set of ethics) and *against* something (the Nazi doctrine).' 'But,' says Levinson, 'what if something is *against* what you are *for*? Must you not go *against* the *against*?' 'No,' says Berson, 'you must be more *for* the *for*.' (254)

Though Levinson is interested in and even a cause of Dolek's and Rachel's growth, both of these characters differ from him in their affirmation of life. The writer moves away from an isolated pessimism through his relationships with others, but he is the first to arrive at the belief that all of the Jews are doomed, and he adheres to this belief to the end. In fact, his pessimism about human nature and the state of the world drives him to keep his account of human tenacity in the face of overpowering evil. He is myopic, as Hersey has been labeled, able to present the meaning of his own life and that of his comrades, but not interested in or able to propose another solution than his chronicle. In caring about his record and preserving it for an audience, Noach does affirm wider human concerns than those of the immediate ghetto, but his main focus is the life he shares daily, and ultimately hopelessly, with other people. Even Noach's inherent pessimism, however, is not equal to the Nazi reality at the beginning of the ordeal. A year after meeting with Berson, he admits that the brick wall around the ghetto is worse than the spiritual one he had feared.

In Part II, December, 1940 to April, 1942, Noach's diary explores the question raised by the reality of the brick wall, ". . . what is this being in a ghetto?" (114), and ends with a manhunt in which Dolek learns harshly that being in the ghetto means choosing which of his friends to protect. As a partial answer to such inhuman circumstances, the "family" draws closer with each attempt of the Nazis to tear the Jews apart. Noach records the means of closeness with the "family" and others: "One of the things that being in a ghetto means is: being in a conversation. We talk, talk, talk, talk, talk. For want of meat we gossip." (116) He finds that the talk itself is his contribution to making sense of the horror. "What a receptacle I have become! Because I listen patiently, because I ask penetrating questions in a sympathetic tone of voice, people have begun, not only to trust me, but also to use me as a vessel into which to pour their anxieties and privacies." (133) Although at times the writer becomes sick of having people trust him, weary of the burden of grief and anguish, he comes to a shocked realization that this period of deprivation, fear and torture has actually brought him more human happiness than he has ever known, even though he is still accused of being a gloomy person.

In contrast to the writer's sense of synthesis, Dolek Berson's definition of the ghetto is "disorder," which he attempts to correct first by joining the Jewish police, and then by working at the *Judenrat*. Each of these turns out to be forms of surrender and collaboration, and he abandons them. It is Levinson who, finding his own delight in rescuing a cache of books from a library beyond the wall, deepens Dolek's commitment to the past and future by causing him to sell a beloved watch rather than books. Better grounded in a sense of Jewishness because of Noach, Berson can stand in a crowded cafe and insist that Halinka Apt finish the Heine song she has started, despite the protests of a few gamblers. In a Sisyphus-like statement,

Berson tells his wife, ". . . I think it's extremely important not to seem degraded, even if we are beginning to be. By appearances, it may be possible to sustain realities, or at least to prolong them. . . ." (154)

There is a sharp deterioration for the group around Levinson when a Mazur son dies of the typhoid killing thousands in the ghetto, when Pan Apt buys his way to the Aryan side after a secret operation to correct his circumcision (a fact Noach cannot learn until the last day in the ghetto, when Rachel admits it), and when small David Apt is placed by Rachel in a children's home because his own home cannot care for him properly. Even while these things occur, Noach also records other patterns of unity and healing: Rachel Apt and Rutka Mazur insist that the pressures of the ghetto will "squeeze things out of us that our thin hides would normally contain, and that we would prefer not to see issue from us." (162) But not only ruthlessness and selfishness would appear; there would be equally strong nobility and selflessness. Levinson, self-proclaimed pessimist, is also a man of extremes grounded in history and tradition. He cannot resist seeing grandeur in the way that human beings meet suffering. His record of the great feast enjoyed by the family during this period is evidence of such a vision. Even though the meal (a horse slain according to Kosher ritual) depresses him personally because it seems an end to any kind of comfortable living, he records the spirit of defiance Rutka and other family members bring to the gathering. At the end of this time period, Berson has emerged with the nobility Levinson believes possible in the ghetto. One of his peers judges that he is the rare uncorrupt man who does not base every choice on self-interest.

During the summer of 1942, Part III, Hersey re-enforces the position of Levinson as the marrow of the group he depicts as survivors of the ghetto. *The Wall* depicts the preserving of culture and community as dependent upon the interactions of the writer and his community. The action is an imitation of the exchange between Hersey and his readers, who, as Stott suggests about documentary readers in general, read about life to learn about life.[17] "Life," as Hersey presents it through Levinson and his community, has a precious quality, a historical richness resulting from years of accumulated wisdom and maintained only by a continuation of input by various members of the community. This point, which Levinson makes with finality in the last weeks of the ghetto when he speaks to a crowd packed into an underground bunker, is made by the members of the community themselves when they understand they will be annihilated unless they help one another.

Partly because of Levinson's accessibility and partly because of his curiosity, he first hears the news a train worker discovers: trains bearing Jews for "resettlement" in the East return to Warsaw within a few hours. Finally overcoming a personality conflict within their ranks, the Socialists—who still believe their Polish comrades will aid them—send Berson's friend Slonim out to follow the trains. On his return, with the horrible truth of Treblinka now spread through the ghetto, he tells Noach that his own decision to return rather than escape was not reached for idealistic or ideological reasons. He felt the strong pull to justify himself to Rapaport, the Socialist leader. Ultimately, both Slonim and a Zionist leader insist to Noach, human decisions are a matter of personalities more than anything else. Life, Hersey intimates also through his character Berson, is preserved and ennobled through authentic emotional choices. Levinson, once the scholar-recluse, becomes the savior of his culture only when he enters into real dialogue with members of the culture.

Personal interaction of the writer-scholar with his community is actually the means by which Berson, destined to prolong and even save lives by his brilliant understanding of communication, is kept "uncorrupt" and deepened in his commitment to the community. During an hour of Nazi terror, he has almost succumbed to the Germans by appearing as their creature. Rachel Apt is furious that he has posed for propaganda pictures. The occasion of Levinson's poetry reading gives them a way to reconcile. Noach—terrified secretly at witnessing a cold-blooded, physically beautiful German soldier randomly shooting Jews in the streets—has expressed his emotion by reciting an ironic revolutionary poem instead of the more aesthetically respected work he had planned to deliver. In the service of himself and his fellows he employs poetry, and finds the written-spoken words effective exhilaration. Berson, records Levinson, was especially affected; he said the poem restored to him a feeling of immense pride in the poet, the Jewish martyrs he celebrated, and the living Jew as well.

Berson's revivified pride meets a horrible test. During a ruthless drive for resettlement, Berson sees Stefan Mazur, who is a Jewish policeman and member of the "family," cruelly beating the sick, ragged Jews being forced into the "resettlement" cars. For a moment, he is filled with hatred both for Stefan and the miserable specimens he herds, but the hatred "surged over the threshold into the place of compassion and became mixed up with compassion and at last was wholly converted into compassion: and he wept. All morning, ever since first hearing the rapid crescendo of the rumors of alarm, he had wanted to cry; for weeks months years he had wanted to cry; and now he did, with great racking sobs." (272)

This emotional scene is the turning point; there is no more vascillation on Berson's part. Noach remarks "I cannot call Berson any more "the Drifter" (275), and the accuracy of this observation appears in Berson's decisive actions to save his wife and those of the "family" he can trust with his own life. With the hardening of Berson, his protege, the writer himself is dependent upon the young man for physical and emotional survival.

During the fall of 1942 (Part IV) survival becomes both more difficult and more desirable. Levinson learns that the writing and preserving of the archive are not enough to make him a part of the real process of living and surviving in wholeness. The reciprocal strengths the writer and community give each other are becoming all that is left to any of them, for even the "family" breaks up in the fear and chaos, and *Judenrat* employment is no longer a guarantee of safety or respect. Levinson, declaring he will kill himself if he fails to move the archive to a place of safety, insists the Jews at least must keep a record of the culture and the atrocity of the ghetto. Heartsick at the apathy within the ghetto even after Slonim's discovery of Treblinka, Noach works despite his fear that the apathy "forever and ever at the untouched ends of the earth, in Melbourne, in Rio de Janeiro, in Shanghai, in Chicago. . . ." (327) will cancel out the desperate record. Much in the way that the survivors of Hiroshima moved in the face of inexplicable all-encompassing destruction to preserve a semblance of human normality and derived strength from that work, Levinson persuades Berson to take what will seem a backward step: to work at the *Judenrat* again in order to help with the burying of the archive. Realizing that he must have work papers to escape deportation and that all work done in the ghetto actually benefits the Germans anyway, Berson becomes excited by Levinson's plan, freed from his fear and despondency about the "Kettle." Berson believes the idea of the archive, the implicit thought that we can learn from our tragedies, is a tremendously hopeful one; with new strength he plunges into underground work and is finally sent outside the ghetto to gather weapons for the resistance.

Noach in a semi-humorous passage describes his more pessimistic reaction to the archive. "My fellows seem to me to be short-sighted, stupid, incapable of unanimity, and really not satisfied to wait for destruction; they seem bent upon self-destruction, in their systematic unwillingness to face facts. Not I of course: I am a rather sensitive and level-headed fellow at all times. So I tell myself. *Nu* I am getting very little good news these days—why shouldn't I tell myself something acceptable?" (384-385) Ironically Berson's reading of the archive confirmed what Noach had said earlier about nobility as well as degradation being squeezed out of the Jews in the ghetto and led him to take actions which would meliorate Noach's sense of bitterness. Nothing could stop Levinson from gathering the record; it was the step between a proud or a craven life, irony, that seemed to the writer the only reason to live. The culture others such as Rabbi Goldflamm speak of as invincible—because it is a system based upon love and respect rather than hatred and contempt—will be preserved only through the archive. It is life for the whole community, it is immortality for the times.

Levinson, like Hersey, cannot stay aloof from the action that feeds his writing any more than he can stop the writing that inspires the action. As Berson, Rachel Apt and other friends move to leadership and service in the desperate resistance movement solidified by the "Kettle" the writer—for all of his scholarly, unworldly, unrobust ways—astonishes himself by joining the resistance. Part V, covering the winter of 1942-3, begins with the writer's certainty that

"death in the ghetto is neither accidental nor evitable" (425)—"mankind must destroy Anti-Humanity before it becomes extinct itself"
(426)—and that he must play a tiny part in resisting despite the apparent hopelessness of doing so. Partly through his dependence on
Rachel Apt, now a leader of the underground and called "The
Little Mother" because of her ability to set a comfortable emotional
climate in any circumstance, Noach is part of a new solidarity with
his peers. He comes to believe in "the simple, one-sentence politics
of Humanity." (426) "The fact that a man is a man is more important than the fact that he believes what he believes." (426) In
the end, survival cannot depend on a political system but on a deep
realization that human life itself is the precious thing. Hersey's
characters unite only when they have abandoned politics and acknowledged their more basic bonds. Noach the writer, always interested in emotions and daily living, never finds true community
until others recognize with him that these are the things worth
fighting to preserve.

Levinson finds that, when the resistance determines to kill a
scholar still active in the *Judenrat* and suspected of being an informer about the underground, his careful weighing of the man's
life against the shady evidence and suspicion used in condemning
him is not in agreement with the real issue. The radical leader is
determined to assassinate the man as an example and a warning to
other Jewish leaders; the resistance has organized beyond the personal. Noach's protest, however, is evidently somewhat effective;
there is a close vote to assassinate rather than a unanimous one.
Levinson finds himself unable to answer the final question of justice;
because of Zadkin's death the *Judenrat* members resign and go into
hiding, a favorable outcome for the resistance. Noach cannot know
whether the action is worthwhile; he must continue to wonder
whether Zadkin was both a genius and a traitor.

The writer and the other underground members do share an
obsession with communication despite these differences. While
Noach lives in the bunker designed by Berson and commanded by
Rachel, he compulsively prepares a monograph on what he knows
are the final days of the ghetto. Rachel commissions him to do
this work. Berson, at this time, uses the brilliant mind Levinson had

noted and broadened to design a secret network of sewers and rooftops through which the fighter groups can contact one another and flee to other bunkers when necessary. Like the complicated sets of human bonds Levinson has fostered and recorded, these channels of survival are dependent upon one mind. Only Berson's curiosity and vitality could accomplish this task, just as only Levinson's curiosity and vitality could compile the archive which inspired Berson.

As the surviving Jews narrow to less than ten percent of the once packed city, Levinson continues to present personal and cultural scenes. Hersey uses the birth (and later, the death) of Rutka and Mordecai Apt's son, Israel, as one of several effective symbols of the horror; Yitzhok, the commander of the underground, strangles the baby to allow the adults to avoid detection in their bunker. Another indication that the end is near is the deportation of Schpunt, the little man who had always been able to make the Germans laugh until he loses this power in the final, desperate days. One of the things which the disintegrating society continues to cherish is the storytelling power Eastern Jews have used in their survival over many centuries. Several times during the years of the ghetto, characters use this power in ways that at once save lives and make lives worth saving. Rapaport, the old Socialist leader, tells young David Apt a story when they hide under a lighted oven. Froi Mazur uses stories to calm and comfort Rutka and Mordecai when she realizes that Mordecai has been ordered to send either his mother-in-law or his wife to be "resettled." The stories, as well as the endless conversations, typify the human warmth and purpose that give returning couriers a sense of joy at being back within the ghetto community.

Hersey's character Levinson sees the writer's role as essential to the communication that is survival. Levinson is not now a receptacle but a beacon in his society. Asked by Yitzhok to give a morale building lecture on Jewishness to the surviving fighters, Noach speaks on the writings of Peretz. Using the slowly fading light in the bunker as a backdrop for his speech, Levinson creates a multimedia form expressive of what is happening in Warsaw. Although the light fails, the voice of the living writer and the creations of the dead artist convey the continuity of a culture which can take its treasures wherever it wanders in search of a home. Hersey has Levinson voice an effective synthesis of the themes of his diary. Made believable and exciting to the reader because of the complex dramatic background of the book and the symbolic circumstances of its delivery, the speech finishes with the Levinson-Peretz-Hersey creed that cultural exchange, communication, and art constitute the survival process and the fullness of human life.

> Ghetto is impotence. Cultural cross—fertilization is the only possibility for human development. Humanity must be the synthesis, the sum, the quintessence of all national cultural forms and philosophies. (550)

Several characters close to Levinson live by this principle and effect their own survival and that of others because of it. Berson, for example, after saving the ghetto inhabitants once by knowing how and where to drain the sewers when the Germans flood them, is also able to lead them out of the ghetto. He makes use of a concertina, playing both Jewish and Aryan music, to communicate to his own group the news that he is alive and looking for them after a courier trip, and to annoy and foil the Germans as he darts from one city block to another through the underground network. When the trucks that take the survivors out of their sewer hiding place leave without him and several others because the Germans have found the hiding place, Rachel, Noach and the rest of the escapees hear the concertina playing the Jewish anthem, the *Hatikva*. Although it might be argued that this is a melodramatic appeal to our sympathies similar to Rose-of-Sharon's nursing a starved man at the end of *The Grapes of Wrath*, involved readers of both the Hersey and the Steinbeck novels can argue in turn that the ways culture and motherhood are used by the respective authors make such episodes effective correlatives of the works.

Felix Mandeltort, another friend of Noach, also embodies and causes the cultural survival of the Jews. Like Berson, he appears in all six parts of the record and dies a hero's death, but he is an extremely late joiner of the resistance. Because of his intense love for his family, his engaging in smuggling to give them luxuries, his early wish to die—a wish denied because Levinson rescues him from deportation—and his closeness to becoming an informer, he is both a sympathetic and an equivocal person to Levinson and the reader. Levinson sees him as an urbane product of Eastern Jewry's emotionalism and Western rationality, and his actions do suggest such a blend. Because he has become—thanks to Levinson—a member of the ghetto community at last, Mandeltort has a vision of a future with his fighter friends that the resigned, defeated, nearly dead Jews sharing his ride to Treblinka do not have. With such a vision he escapes from the train, a reasonable escape Hersey describes as possible to anyone with hope—a hope the unresisting Jews do not have. The escape and return make Felix a wise, respected man within the ghetto and his sense of a future convinces the fighters to contact groups in the forests outside Warsaw for hiding places rather than to immolate themselves in a total holocaust.

The necessity to go ahead, to take oneself into the future despite the ugliness of the present (the Sisyphus theme) exists in the Socialist leader Rapaport as well. He pours out to Noach his sense of lifelong failure and loss of faith in his Socialist creed, yet a few hours later conducts an inspiring meeting of the fighter groups in Noach's astonished presence. Another person who momentarily surprises Noach and the reader, yet who simply remains faithful to the spirit of the book is Rachel Apt. Like her sister-in-law Rutka who is determined to have another child despite the fact that she "has seen what can happen to Jews" when her son was strangled in the bunker because his infant screams threatened the adults' lives, Rachel affirms the Torah's "Thou shalt love thy neighbor as thyself" even though she has chosen to fight to live. Noach asks if her pledge extends to a neighbor who is a Nazi, and she replies "How else cure him of being a Nazi?" (628) The cross-fertilization of Jewish spirit and Jewish culture, it is implied, will not be effected by hatred and revenge, but by the "politics of humanity" Levinson-Hersey have advocated.

On the final page of the book Noach, Rachel, Zilberzwieg and Rapaport walk in the forest camp to which they have escaped. The writer, exhausted and near his death, finishes his record with two observations that effectively suggest the purpose of the book. Noach is immersed in the physical beauty of the surroundings, but he expresses it in terms that convey both concrete facts and wonder at such facts, crystallizing the Levinson-Hersey task: "I pluck a leaf from a bush. It has tiny veins. The leaf is almost a perfect oval." (632) Within his detached hearing Rachel asks "*Nu,* what is the plan for tomorrow?" (632) The living idiom, the determination, and the future are brought by the writer beyond the boundaries of time and space.

Levinson's role as writer, participant and rhetorical device has been mentioned by Sanders and Girgus but not made the focus of their studies. A rather minute awareness of this character "finer than anything in Koestler" (Kazin's remark) is the key to Hersey's purpose and accomplishment. The sprawling novel, not significant for psychological probing, symbolism, poetic prose or stream-of-consciousness, although in some ways it contains all of these and more, is Hersey's baptism as a writer of serious fiction and a true believer in its persuasive power. Within the waters generated by his plunge Hersey would find numerous ways of expressing, intensifying and re-affirming the same faith which led to it.

CHAPTER III

TWO PARABLES OF ANNIHILATION

Three years after publishing *The Wall* and representing human survival as a process originating in, sustained by, and deriving meaning from the process of communication, Hersey produced the first of two slender novels depicting human self-destruction through failure to share a vision and thereby assist others in forming their own. Both *The Marmot Drive* and *A Single Pebble* indicate that Hersey now wished to explore the darker side of the horrors he had witnessed in his journalistic life. In both books, he departed from his proven skill with masses of detail and external reports designed to enlist the sympathy and anger of his audience. In *The Marmot Drive*, he departed almost wholly from his observed, tangible experience; the book is unlike any of his others in that respect, for even memory and consciousness pieces such as *A Single Pebble, The War Lover, White Lotus,* and *My Petition for More Space* derive much of their strength from description of actual places and dramatization of carefully observed or researched events. *The Marmot Drive* seems to have been an attempt to place the horrors Hersey had observed into an American literary tradition of romantic irony. [1]

Although the book is dull, derivative and allegorically unsatisfying, this novel was an important turning point for Hersey. The relatively successful books which followed it, especially *A Single Pebble* and *White Lotus,* seem to combine the sympathetic reportorial eye with the soul-searching fictional one. As Hersey explains in his introduction to *The Writer's Craft,* "every serious new writer must place himself in relation to the literary tradition that has been given him. The writer's craft, immensely supple though it is, and capable of change, nevertheless cannot be invented in a vacuum;

like any other it is handed on." [2] *The Marmot Drive* can be viewed as a link between the "personal documentary" as Hersey practiced it in *Hiroshima* and *The Wall* and the more symbolic yet basically documentary fictions, *The War Lover, White Lotus, The Child Buyer, Under the Eye of the Storm, The Conspiracy,* and others. A canon of thoughtful American novels, rather than one of brilliant essays, has been Hersey's choice despite the unfavorable reception of *The Marmot Drive.* This cloudy allegory about the pursuit of apparent evil rather than constructive actions for survival deepened the message of Hersey's career as a writer. As a refutation of Ahab's self-hating quest as well as an accord with Hawthorne's humanism, the book foreshadows later works which insist that survival and its essential counterpart, communication, are worth pursuing in the face of the madness of Hiroshima and Warsaw.

Consistent with the image Hersey had created in previous works, of the writer as center of consciousness for a surviving society, the form of *The Marmot Drive* and *A Single Pebble* is suited to this point in Hersey's own career when he needed, like Levinson during his Peretz speech, to speak as an oracle rather than a receptive interpreter. The unusual and yet essentially simple stories share the characteristics of the Biblical parable. They have narrative interest, but this interest is subordinate to, nearly irrelevant to, the real purpose of the fictions. They are transparent dramas, held out as paradigms for believers. Part of the appeal of Biblical parables lies in their clarity, with the psychological comfort they bring by unifying the world of daily realities with the hidden, subconscious or spiritual order the speaker professes to know.

Hersey's earliest work had shown an interest in motives. He hoped through fiction to explore the reasons, as well as the means, for human survival. In speaking of the role of the novelist of contemporary history after the publication of *The Wall,* Hersey expressed the belief that fiction is better able to deal with confusion than journalism is; a disciplined writer can turn his own confusion as a citizen and a human being into a virtue, because he may then communicate with his readers, "who are very likely confused themselves." [3] In *The Marmot Drive,* however, Hersey's confusion so tangles the threads of meaning that the parable form loses some of its comforting effect, while the harshness of the prose and unappealing characters do little to meliorate this flaw. The story concerns the pursuit of evil (the marmots and sexual encounter) by evil (the uncommitted townsmen and the inauthentic young woman), of self by the self, of nature by human nature. By turning away from the self rather than accepting it, by treating sex as an aberration, the people fail, as some of Hawthorne's did. But the marmots—the threat to civilization—fail as an analogy to human weakness. Although it is clear that the Puritan and the lecherous view of sex are really identical and fatal, and that a different treatment of sexuality would make it part of a fully natural human life, the woodchucks which threaten Tunxis have no place in the resolution of the parable. Unlike sensuality, which they seem to represent, the marmots which threaten the village are too horrible to be accepted and integrated into town life. The elements of the parable jar the reader's thirst for resolution by remaining unmatched to the philosophical premise of the story. In *A Single Pebble,* Hersey succeeded better at matching fictional elements to a philosophical creed. In *Under the Eye of the Storm* and later novels, Hersey's "confusion" becomes an immersion in the conflict of appearance and reality, with the fictional elements healthily matched to the philosophical. By controlling his fiction in this book, and even in *A Single Pebble,* Hersey corrects his technical failure in *The Marmot Drive.* That novel remains interesting as his link with literary tradition and an enunciation of his values as a writer.

Just as Hersey's earlier books were essentially records of communication and survival or acts of them, his two parables following *The Wall* are both accounts of failed communication and the annihilation which results. In *The Marmot Drive,* Hester communicates with her inner self but fails to accept that self and make it a part of the living, external world. She perceives her own sensual nature but communicates it as a vision of destruction rather than of survival. The number of times in the book that she offers forced, phony conversation is symptomatic of her inability to create a world view in which her recognized sensuality can have an honorable part. The person who seems most capable of sharing an integrated vision with her, Matthew Avered, has only a foggy perception of his own life. Although the fog occasionally clears, Avered is so withdrawn from his fellows that the moments of his clearest vision frighten them and himself as well. Both characters, by turning from the possible wholeness of mind and body an honest relationship might offer them, lose the most worthwhile quality they possess. Hester loses her moral honesty; Avered loses his lonely strength. The town, in rejecting Avered, Hester, and what they offer, corrupts its own honesty and strength. In fact, the hideous marmots Hersey leaves at large in the story really threaten the physical survival of the town.

Hester and Avered do not draw the reader into any kind of sympathetic alliance. Not only do they spurn what they undoubtedly share with most readers, an awareness of and need for their own sexuality, they offer little or nothing in the way of authentic feelings on any subject. In *A Single Pebble,* the engineer's simple, confessional tone is far more convincing than the elaborate twists of the narrative in *The Marmot Drive.* Yet there is a rawness and hardhitting vitality to this novel which cannot be overlooked despite its departure from Hersey's usual process, exemplified in the survivors of Hiroshima and Warsaw, of consoling the reader while accusing him.

The common element in criticism of *The Marmot Drive* is a reaction to the harsh prose and content of the novel. Irving Howe, its severest critic, commented that Hersey succumbs to "Rich Prose and Symbolism," but added that besides being annoyingly poetical *The Marmot Drive* is "clever, caustic, contemplative and philosophical." [4] Although the internal structure might be of interest, Howe contends that the flimsy, borning external structure removes the need or desire the reader might have to probe the allegory. Writing for *The Saturday Review,* Howard Mumford Jones also states that Hersey had probably tried too hard to write profoundly and come down with "symbolism fever." Despite the puzzling, unresolved allegory and the invalid, unlikeable Hester, Jones said he returned often to the book's "pebbled, gnarled, knotted surface" because he was not fully satisfied with his own reaction to the work; if a failure, it was certainly a failure "on a very high plane." [5] Maxwell Geismar felt that the story was saved from failure by the revelation of personal frustration and mass cruelty Hersey pulled out of a plot that at first seemed to be only a return-to-the-soil saga. [6]

Like these critics, Sanders and Girgus devote their essays on *The Marmot Drive* to exploration of the cloudy meanings of the book. Sanders' treatment of the work is somewhat hurried, compared to his commentary on other books, but he sees it as a basically unsuccessful attempt to say something about the rootlessness of modern Americans.[7] Girgus' elaborate treatment of the work draws comparisons of it with Hawthorne's quest-myth romances such as "Young Goodman Brown" and "My Kinsman, Major Molineux." He sees the work as an illustration of Hersey's existential belief that by giving up part of oneself, by establishing a human relationship with others, a person can gain a true sense of autonomy and community.[8] Like the other reviewers, neither Sanders nor Girgus can account for or accept the loose ends of Hersey's narrative, especially the poorly integrated symbolism of the marmots as sexuality.

Part of any analysis of *The Marmot Drive* must concede that its basic meaning and value are undermined by the rather shallow formal attempt to imitate Hawthorne, and by Hersey's acknowledged confusion as a son of the twentieth century. Even with these problems, however, the novel shows an amazing unity of plot, character and theme within the confines of the parable. The total effect of Hersey's book is a picture of a self-imposed human mess; like Sisyphus, the characters do not know their own fates, yet they pretend to know them. In the tradition of most twentieth-century prophets, especially that of Sartre, Hersey advocates both total honesty about the hard facts of the absurd, and commitment to being in the face of this honesty. Acting on this belief, he offered in *The Marmot Drive* a parable comparable to that of the Foolish and the Wise Virgins. Without the ability to explain or dispel the fact of exterior darkness, Hersey illustrates the need for the oil in the lamp, the warmth and light of human communication, his insistent theme. The Hawthornian view of America's Puritan background is a mode suited to Hersey's parable of annihilation; the coldness and blindness Hawthorne criticized became a vehicle for the twentieth century writer's own perspective. In this sense, *The Marmot Drive*'s imitation of Hawthorne seems more important and appropriate than at first glance.

Throughout the story, the main and supporting characters remain unable to communicate with one another; the falseness with which they speak and act results in the final futile beating of Matthew Avered. He does not know why the beating has occurred. Hester cannot tell him; her own words have misled the citizens, and she cannot defend him publicly. After the beating, no one tells Avered they have punished the sensuality they fear in himself and themselves, and he continues to believe he can solve the town's threatened existence by killing woodchucks, by dealing with externals.

Hester, the central consciousness of the book, is the most pitiable creature of all the divided citizens. Her youth, beauty, intelligence and sensitivity can never break through the fog of Tunxis; when she learns the truth about herself, she has no system of values to use in living this truth. Although the intractable Eben, the harsh townspeople and the unseeing Avered are partly to blame for her denial of self and retreat from honesty at the end of the book, Hersey depicts Hester as guilty of her own destruction. The many times she misuses words and symbols indicate that Hester is weak and incapable of true human communication. She has even come to the town under a misconception; she had not known the seriousness of Eben's intent to "show her off" as a prospective bride and to have her understand his background. The woodchuck hunt, improbable device that it is, comes as another surprise to the city girl. The Avereds' failure to inform their visitors that the drive Eben's father had planned for ten years would be this week-end is a strange condition unexplained by anything in the work except the widening distance among all characters which the plot and theme depict.

Both the preliminary meeting and the drive itself are occasions of confusion. No one but Avered seems to believe the hunt will destroy the marmots, and Hester's mind seems to focus on him as a guide through the double confusion of external events in Tunxis and her inner turmoil. Hersey, however, interestingly structures the plot in episodes of annihilation, so that even while Hester is learning, and to some degree communicating with others, the content

of her lessons and encounters is an awareness of isolation, rootlessness and futility on the part of herself, Avered, Eben and the townspeople. The effect of this structure is a completed separation for the
character; for the reader, it is a painful revelation that American
life does not offer a culture similar to that of Levinson's community.
Hersey implies that the tradition closest to a native one, the Puritan,
contains the germ of its own defeat, as Hawthorne and other writers
have indicated. By showing the process of defeat as a refusal to be
truthful in communicating and a denial of imagination and sensuality,
Hersey reverses the structure of *The Wall* and preaches by negative
example the danger to survival that comes when human beings
legislate away vital human traits as the Nazis had legislated an end
to the Jews.

Each occasion that Hester perceives the possibilities
for human love and full survival becomes a denial of these things,
making the work a series of unpleasant revelations and disappoint-
ments. When she observes the village common from Avered's car,
Hester corrects her first dislike for the town as she observed it from
the train.

> She had not conceived the sense of community such a plot of ground,
> necklaced with inward-facing central-hall houses, could give. The homes
> were built with deference to neighbors; the church and the grange, she
> could see, were for the use of all, the prosperous and the hard-pressed,
> the educated and the benighted, the wise and the foolish, who could
> walk with an illusion of equality on the common grass.[9]

This insight makes Hester want to confide the truth about her
feelings for Eben and casual attitude toward the visit which the
Avereds look on as important and decisive, but she responds instead
with a hollow social remark, " 'It's better than Eben described it' "
(13)

Avered's definition of a "Yankee" as someone who remains
an idealist even after coming to see how hopeless life is, is offered
within the same ironic framework of false communication. Hester,
still stifling her discomfort at being on trial during her visit to Tunxis,
to impress the Avereds with her curiosity or good breeding
(she is not sure which, if either, they admire), asks "What is a Yan-

kee, anyhow?" in response to Avered's statement that ". . .folks in
Tunxis can be real Yankees when they put a mind to it." (16)
Avered's answer is the core of the book, for he emphasizes the
annihilating aspect of the "Yankees' " idealism, their attempts to
be "decent" and to legislate the conduct of others without the
"politics of humanity" Hersey had depicted in *The Wall*. Without a
belief in human worth, the "Yankee" code is absurd and lacking the
comfort even of the Sisyphus myth.

> The folks here in Tunxis know the whole situation is rotten right to the
> core. They know their private dreams'll fail, sure as night follows day;
> they have a sneaking idea God's mostly a hailstone-thrower. They hate
> each other, they feel good when somebody goes to pot. And yet they
> go on living with straight backs and high hopes as if they could make
> everything better. . . . they know how bad things are, but at least they
> keep *trying* to be decent people. . . . (16 - 17)

Avered's description of the "Yankee" as one who remains
an idealist in the face of hopelessness is contradicted by his expanded
definition, "They hate each other!" Yankee idealism thus described
is the antithesis of the humanism Noach Levinson, Rachel Apt and
Dolek Berson attained. None of the characters of *The Marmot
Drive* apparently are meant to see the contradiction in Avered's
words, even though Hester comes close to doing so during the whipping, and at the time of the remark reminisces about Eben's similarly
vague concept of "decent people." She does not pursue her own
question about what "decent" means.

Avered's fellow townsmen do seem full of the contradictions
Avered described, although their "idealism" and "decency" are hard
for Hester to see and the reader to appreciate. They, like Hester,
discover their real meaning in conversation; the teacher Mrs. Tuller,
for example, hints about the characters of Avered and another
politician, but is too cautious to speak openly. The citizens seem to
resent any probing, questioning or other forms of rational discourse.
They despise the Harvard student, Pliny Forward, for his meta-
physical implications about the marmots and have, according to
Eben, isolated Avered because of his normal school education.

Unlike the rustics of Thomas Hardy whom the Tunxis folk

bring to mind, they display little empathy or joy. Their folk wisdom, in fact, seems pointless and unconnected to events in the story. Avered himself tells Hester a long tale about Dorcas Thrall's fear of birds, apparently in order to minimize Hester's fear of the marmots. He shares the town's fear of open or ultimate truth, telling Hester he prefers not to know about such people. "Half-knowledge makes me fierce and self-reliant." (39) Although he warns Hester of his habit of pulling away from people before becoming deeply involved, Avered seems about to offer Hester the deep friendship she longs for. Again the book crackles with the denial of what had seemed momentarily possible.

> Then, looking in Hester's eyes again, so openly and cleanly returned from his daydream that she felt for a moment on the verge of true communication with another human being, he said, 'I don't want to try to manage anybody's life;' whereupon she realized, with an inward shudder, that he was after all thinking mainly about himself, not about her or even about his son, and the ribbons that she had fancied about to run from his mind to hers and from her heart to his were suddenly grayed at the ends and now blew altogether away over the stone wall. (40)

This incident closes the first part of the book. In the second, and longest section, Hersey portrays a series of abortive encounters of Hester with Avered and Eben. Each time the characters seem about to know one another or themselves, they snap off the current. During the first of several talks Avered and Hester have in the woods on the first day of the drive, he begins to tell her about his loss of communication with his wife, who is " 'calm as a pond that doesn't have any inlet or outflow; some call it stagnant. . . ,' " (89) but breaks off his self-revelation to question the young woman about herself. Although he seems to think her an appropriate bride for his son, he hints ominously about marriage. Never does he discuss with Hester the reputation Eben attributes to his father for womanizing; his dislike for marriage and apparent blame of Mrs. Avered seem hypocritical to the reader, but not to Hester, once 90-year old Dorcas Thrall relates his sexual excapade of several years back.

Hester is beginning to think Avered's sexuality will answer her own needs, despite the warnings that Avered has not accepted this part of himself as anything but an evil. During their next encounter in the woods, he asks her intimate questions—is she a virgin?—and then moves into teasing without an indication of his real meaning. "She could not tell whether he had been turning over in his mind the possibility of some harmless woodland toying, or meant what he said and truly and selflessly wanted her for a son he loved and had set a canopy over his feelings in the Yankee way; and because the ambiguity tortured her, she felt maladroit, wordless, shy." (112 - 113) There is another ambiguity which Hester does not seem to notice. Avered believes she has "a feeling of confidence" (112) partly because of her sexual experience. He does not see that she shares his own problem in being unable to justify her pursuit of sexual fulfillment even though she continues the pursuit with Avered, Eben, and the townsman Roswell Coit. The real issue of the book is the inauthenticity of the culture which refuses to supply a full acceptance of human nature and which therefore blocks saving communication among people. One year before Masters and Johnson began to publish their work, Hersey used the "sexual hangups" of Americans to dramatize a deeper problem. Not to imply that Avered and Hester should have become lovers, but to show that the old creed of rugged individualism and Calvinistic self-hatred is fatal, Hersey depicts these characters at the mercy of culture rather than saved by it as the survivors of Hiroshima and Warsaw had been.

One vivid scene shortly after Avered's "Yankee canopy" involves fairly effective symbolism of what Hersey sees as the corrupting element in the American dream, the unnatural rush to acquire material goods at the price of knowledge of self and others. Caught in the tangled vines over a woodchuck path, Hester sees the "dry, whited skeleton" (117) of one of the animals. Imprisoned, as it were, by the quest first to find and then to drive out the marmots because Avered has so decreed, Hester has a sudden memory of the dry, white shells on the beach where she allowed herself to be seduced by a corrupted business man. Her experience had made her despise him and renew her love for "her sweet Yankee character, Eben Avered;" neither sex-without-love from that encounter nor love-without-sex from Eben has seemed enough however. Within the skeleton of the woodchuck, Hester finds a jewel-like stone which she struggles to reach; she then answers Matthew Avered's shouts of rescue rather than Eben's.

The stone, defined by Pliny Forward as a lucky bezoar stone produced by a woodchuck in coating indigestible materials to protect himself, seems to promise Hester that she will attain the whole relationship she desires, perhaps with Matthew Avered. Hersey is careful to show her clutching the stone jealously while once again pretending interest in conversation, being a "phony" in much the same way Mandeson had been. Hersey seems to imply—though too much is happening to allow a one-time reader to appreciate this— that Hester does not know how to coat her hard, rough, and elemental desires with a nourishing and protecting sense of community. She wants to belong, yet despises the group around her; as she sees later, her inability to love is a symptom of her self-hatred. She loses the stone while falsely arousing Roswell Coit, and tells herself after Matthew's beating by townsfolk that she had never really possessed the power to love. Yet, Hersey implies she had that power for a time and did not know how to use it in authentic communication.

Part Three is the turning point of Hester's tragedy of isolation. Still in possession of the stone, potentially on the verge of knowing herself, Eben and Avered and sharing her life with Eben, Hester disregards the example of Dorcas Thrall—who has acted out of love and in spite of fear, killing a chicken hawk that attacked her kitten— and who seems to be a symbolic model of equilibrium. The old woman actually relishes Hester's crude attempt to shock the dinner table in order to reach Avered. She also has a humanistic view toward religion and toward death. Although she tells Hester the story of Avered's being caught in adultery, she seems able to tolerate his failing as simply a fault charcteristic of "soft-hearted people." (195) The old woman agrees that "Nobody trusts anybody any more," (197) yet by her actions appears to trust both Avered and herself. She is a true contrast to Hester, who has refused to be honest with Eben about her feelings for his father, and at the same time accused Eben of false communication. She senses that she has lived through a day of lost opportunities, yet does not know why. In Part Four, Hester—now without the bezoar stone and unable to find it—tries desperately to seduce Matthew Avered. She abandons hope for anything fuller, and by misreading the townspeople's questions, essentially causes Avered's whipping.

During this final section, Hersey depicts Hester more ill at ease, quicker to mistake meanings and to respond falsely. She perceives her own confusion, but insists that Eben and his father have "lonely courage," the quality she most admires, but which really involves a divorce from self and others, a removal from society rather than a participation in it. It is the quality which causes Avered to accept the whipping for a public failure instead of the private one the people wish to punish, an idealism which thwarts itself because it lacks the element of human sharing. Avered's final plea for help as he tries to kill the marmots alone and his persistence in thinking of such a drive again display both the helplessness of the "lonely courage" and its removal from the reality of human concern.

Hester is mistaken in her reasons for admiring the Avereds. Their search for meanings rather than their blind isolation is their true strength. Because she has shut herself off from a search for meaning, Hester fails to attain authentic being. She cannot show "lonely courage" or any courage when Avered is whipped. She lacks community with him or the townspeople. She has not really been present to them, and cannot rely on any bond with the others to explain that Avered is not guilty of seducing her.

The complex and somewhat unsatisfying novel contains, like *The Wall* and later Hersey books, several interesting motifs. One of these is the direct invoking of cultural objects or art works and authors to suggest the meaning of the story. Avered and Hester both represent the broken, fragmented American culture. Like the woodchucks in their "senseless, sun-struck flight," they know only parts of who they are and where they are going. Avered knows smatterings of poetry, philosophy and literature and likes to show his knowledge, yet he cannot bear its deeper implications. He calls Eben "young Hamlet," but tells Hester rather sharply not to tease that Avered himself is "the king of Denmark." He refers piously to the Patmore marriage poems and their disillusion, yet does not allude to the basic issue of fidelity they concern. He has absorbed only part of a whole world view, and his shallowness or insufficiency as a father, friend, and leader comes from this. He personally rejects the idea that love, including marital fidelity, is possible and even necessary for human survival, and yet he laments the "breakdown of ordinary, everyday love." With all of his learning and experience, he can promise Hester nothing more than that she and Eben will have to "scrape by" on what little they can find for themselves in the way of ethics.

The culture has failed Hester as well as Avered, and she has failed it. She knows she speaks glibly of plays, books and music without any real knowledge of them. She equates her sensuality with a step "Backward and downward from the arts!" (99) emphasizing the split between body and spirit preached by the neo-Puritan country. Hersey implies that Hester and others like her are responsible for their fragmented vision. In turning his back on the progress made by Eben's generation in spite of its barren heritage, Avered—as displayed in his cavalier treatment of Eben—fails to connect his world with his son's, knowledge with practice, tradition with contemporary life, body with mind and spirit.

Although Hersey has never stated that his novel is a reaction to the McCarthy hearings of the fifties, the fact is that Whittaker Chambers did mention Hersey as one of several reporters who had praised Communist China. Lillian Hellman, a close friend of Hersey, has written in *Pentimento* of the extreme anger, pain and anxiety felt by writers during this period of witch-hunting. Arthur Miller, who wrote *The Crucible* in protest of this period, ranks with Hellman as one of Hersey's most admired authors. *The Marmot Drive*, coming after the Chambers remark and Hersey's public support of Adlai Stevenson in 1952, reflects Hersey's obvious disgust with the limits to freedom and truth imposed at home after the horrors of the war, Hiroshima and Warsaw had indicated the need for open exploration of better ways to form societies. *The Marmot Drive* has some of the ugliness of its subject matter, much like the long prodding sticks used by Puritan beadles to keep their congregations awake.

As a contrast to the frenetic American culture he felt compelled to criticize, in *A Single Pebble* Hersey created a beautiful smooth-flowing parable about oneness rather than fragmentation. This novel attempts to supply a few of the solutions *The Marmot Drive* declined to give—in fact, nipped in the bud each time they seemed to appear. The stunning, senseless death of Old Pebble and the renewed, admirable life of the engineer are at once more shocking and more memorable than the exercise in Hawthorneian irony.

A Single Pebble concerns not only the annihilation of a person, Old Pebble, for failing to trust in the richness of his culture, and the annihilation of a friendship between East and West because of falseness on both sides, but it also concerns the threatened extinction (as in *The Wall*) of a "primitive" culture by a "progressive" one. The engineer and Su-ling, however, as representatives of their cultures, succeed in creating an alternative to this by their integrating through communication the values for survival that both can offer. The engineer's superior technical knowledge is shown to be dependent upon the more basic human ingenuity for survival, and the ending of the novel depicts him surviving as a mature person through human values shared with Su-ling and Pebble rather than those intrinsic to technology. The engineer, like Levinson, accepts his humaness as Sisyphus accepts his burden; Hester and Avered refuse to carry theirs.

The form of *A Single Pebble* differs in significant ways from that of *The Marmot Drive*. The parable itself has integrity; no massive symbol such as the marmots remains inapplicable to the suggested meaning. The river as source of life and challenge to it in the story can comfortably signify both the flow of experience and the collective response of human culture to this flow. The limited friendship of the engineer with the Chinese and the violent death of Old Pebble effectively depict the problems of cross-cultural exchange and unquestioning acceptance of tradition without true self-knowledge.

Unlike the contradictions of character and situation in *The Marmot Drive*, the structure of *A Single Pebble* has a smooth flow similar to that of its central metaphor, the Yangtze. The source of the flow is the engineer's memory, which constantly affirms for the reader the idea that human nature is more a shared potential than a shared weakness. Without omitting or underestimating human weakness in the form of the destructive self-images of the young engineer and Old Pebble, Hersey seems to argue effectively in this parable of annihilation for the possibility of worthwhile survival through communication. The special perspective of *Hiroshima*, the writer's empathetic attack on the idiocy of the human massacre, appears in this work as well. The book seems truer to Hersey's beliefs than does the bitter one preceding it, and is a more effective example of the writer's power to shape attitudes. Nothing in *The Marmot Drive* equals the empathy Hersey brings to and gets from the death of Old Pebble and the waste of human lives the engineer relates. Although there are passages of graceless obviousness and open preaching in this work, the story has an effective combination of strangeness and plausibility. Hersey seems to know what he means and to have found a pleasing, memorable way to say it in especially careful language.

Critical attitudes toward this work are important in a final analysis of Hersey's position in American letters. They generally praise the form and the style of the work, but a few reject the meaning or intent of the author. Hersey's earnestness and moral mission, his conviction of the writer's ultimately didactic role and decision to urge survival through communication as his central literary pattern and thematic principle, seems to jar literary sensibilities in the age of alienation. In one sense, this reaction to *A Single Pebble* is deserved. In isolation, the work seems to affirm only a terribly obvious truth in a way that Frye suggests devalues an author in our culture. [10] Hersey's didactic message seems to lack the idiosyncratic insight of truly imaginative artists. Nevertheless, the cumulative impact of his writing, the numerous ways he has depicted and examined and urged human communciation as the reason for and means of survival, is really quite inspiring and in some ways original as well. My discussion of Hersey's use of this theme and its resultant forms thus answers some of the exasperation Leslie Fiedler, for example, has expressed at Hersey's unexceptionable sentiments in *A Single Pebble*. [11] Although the concept of human cooperation and endorsement of varied cultures might seem too simple to some readers and lacking in precise definition and direction, the excellent prose style and the appealing story help to clarify the generalized philosophical meaning; Hersey clothes an ordinary idea with detail and precision, affirming a belief he sees as threatened, but not absent,

in American culture. Sanders and Girgus have recognized the beauty
of the book and another critic, Samuel Beckoff, thought enough of
the work to include it in an anthology of short American novels he
prepared for the New York City public school system. It appears
in *Four Complete American Novels,* Globe, 1960, in company with
The House of the Seven Gables, Benito Cereno, and *Washington
Square.* Beckoff explains in his introduction that all four of the
novels share an interest in the American personality, or even in the
American soul, rather than in social or economic issues. [12] He sees
all of the authors as didactic in the sense of the parable, allegory or
fable, and justifies the rather startling inclusion of Hersey by referring to the "quiet indignation, a moral fervor and enthusiasm for the
pure, the basic elements in American life" he sees in this and in
Hersey's previous books. (9) Beckoff admires Hersey's "bias in favor
of human values." (627) Since all of the reviewers—even the disgusted Leslie Fiedler—praised the language of the book, and since
several scholars have endorsed it totally, it seems in order to view it
as one of Hersey's more successful didactic novels, especially as one
of several ways he has found to plead as a brother for the preservation
of a traditional value he believes intrinsic to life itself.

A *Single Pebble,* constructed as a simple, direct confessional
monologue is, like *Hiroshima* and *The Wall,* an obvious act of communication with the reader. Like these books and unlike *The Marmot
Drive,* it assumes an audience of well-intentioned comrades from the
outset. The "I" of the opening sentence "I became an engineer"
engages the reader by beginning a recurrent series of references to
the theme that he has something to impart of value to the reader,
and that he can trust the reader with the story of a mistake he had
made. In nearly poetic prose suited to the regretted but fruitful
experience, the narrator draws us into the stream of powerful
memory by describing this young, eager self preparing for his meeting
with the Yangtze. The description of the river contains a synthesis
of the actual novel, setting up expectations about the meeting of
the young, raw life (and culture) with the powerful, dreadful and
honorable one of the Yangtze:

> I spent a year preparing myself for the trip. I applied myself to
> spoken Mandarin Chinese and got a fair fluency in it. I read all I could
> find on the Yangtze. I learned of its mad rise and fall, of the floods it

loosed each year, killing unnumbered pwople and ruining widespread crops; of its fierce rapids and beautiful gorges, and of its endless, patient traffic of hundreds of junks towed upstream and rowed down by human motive power. [13]

With this preparation for the conflict between two ways of dealing with a natural force, technology and tradition, change and co-existence, science and huamnism, Hersey develops the failure of tradition when it refuses to acknowledge its own worth by engaging the force of change in mutual dialogue. The novel endorses the gift imparted to technology by a reverence for culture in the form of ritual, myth, poetry, song and story, and shows that the two become more valuable by uniting scientific knowledge of the world with the inner world of mind and spirit. Rather than a simplistic plea that Americans respect other cultures and learn from them, Hersey offers a demonstration of the waste of human potential when technology is shunned or allowed to operate without the informing values of humanism. In this way, the novel is a logical outcome of the experiences Hersey had in writing *Hiroshima* and *The Wall*. It is the parable of the new tragedy and the new hope that can result from the most devastating mistakes of the century. It is a vivid example of Hersey's equating of survival with communication, and of the saving role the artist, story-teller, scholar, poet and sincere lover of words and of all modes human beings use to share their perceptions with one another, have in his vision of life.

This powerful meaning is offered to the reader through the story the survivor, the engineer who communicated and reached a high awareness of life, tells of his journey on the Yangtze and the relationships he formed or tried to form during it. Hersey employs an effective symbolic structure to move the reader and the story through time. The four parts of the book express the main external events of the narrative, the internal structure of the conflict between technology and humanism, and the solution Hersey endorses for the conflict. The parts, simply labeled "The Junk," "The Rapids," "The Dam," and "The Path" have appropriate concrete names for the outer and inner experiences they describe. In "The Junk," Hersey describes a miniature society moving its members through the challenges and beauties of life. With some of the differeces among the members already depicted, "The Rapids" shows the tremendous contrast of the threat of death and the will to live. In "The Dam," the engineer proposes an answer to the threat of death from the river that fails to include the truly powerful antithesis to the river, the human will to survive in a meaningful way. At the same time, Hersey shows that the engineer's dream comes out of that same concern for meaning his own culture has forgotten in its euphoria of power. In failing to recognize a concern for meaning, the engineer's technology could wipe out the cultural life of the society, and that is death. In "The Path," Old Pebble's annihilation is made to seem both accidental and inevitable. Just as the engineer had fallen ill in "The Junk" because he was devalued by the society, Pebble—the object of his proud, manipulative and humanly deficient engineering dream—is the victim of devaluation. More clearly than he conveys this in *The Marmot Drive,* however, Hersey indicates that devaluing by others is never so fatal as devaluing by the self. Pebble was strong, immersed in a life-giving tradition. He failed to trust that richness, and died spiritually before his physical death. As is clear from the engineer's confession, his technological dream was inadequate to solve the vast Yangtze-life's ageless problems. Yet, with the humanistic wisdom and reverence for culture the twenty years since Pebble's death have reinforced in the engineer, he continues to believe "The dam is still to be built." (181) The skillful ending of the novel evoked both the passionate wish to add meaning to life rather than to end it by blind technology and the implied solution, a cooperation of science and humanism evidenced by the whole personality of the older engineer. The narrator describes his first night after parting from the Chinese in terms that suggest his added, saving humanism, his poetic rather than technical attitude toward experience. The words imply a world beyond the apparent, one which informs external events and actions.

> I lay wide awake, aching and wishing I could hear the buzz of the citizens of Wanhsien through the paper-paned window of my room. I heard an itinerant story-teller pass by with a crude shadow-scope, a kind of stereopticon that I had seen in towns downriver, and I heard him wail out his advertisements of famous things to be heard and seen at the modest charge of one round copper coin. Through distant streets wandered a time-keeper, beating on a gong the hours as they fled. All that night the Great River climbed the steps of the myriad city. (181)

The tone of appreciation and wonder, the unity of the world he describes, and the peaceful evocation of the beauty of human destiny, make final the wholeness the engineer began to learn on the river. "The Path" itself is a focus for the painful conflict. The way carved so persistently out of rock suggests the Sisyphus-life of humanity and its saving sense of dignity and cooperation.

> . . . he (Old Pebble) endured his Sisyphus life with the same patience as a tree its growth. . . .
> . . . I thought of debased men I had read about, but I could not imagine any more enslaved, more doomed, than the trackers who transversed the tight path, with a mountain of stone pressing on their shoulder-blades and death off the edge to the left. Yet what a broad grin Old Pebble had used to wear at night, who had trudged through that horrible path a hundred times; what devils of happiness in his eyes sometimes! (140)

For Old Pebble, the path in the rock, and the stone steps on the opposite side of the cliff, suggest both pride and a horrible sense of despair at the slow, small ways humanity has tried to improve its condition. The Great River, with its wealth of tradition and history, is actually a killer, a force of death one cannot ultimately overcome. Not hope but shame and despair at his limitations come to the tracker when he views the path. Although the engineer's daring, presently impossible dam offers an alternative to the painful life and early death the wisdom of the river people has taught the tracker to endure and even to enjoy, he refused to engage in "the politics of humanity." His death is a clear result of his refusal of cross-cultural fertilization. He builds his own ghetto and is swallowed up, not led outward, by his vital culture. Because the tracker is an appealing, almost mystical figure in comparison with the more ordinary engineer he enriches, Hersey implies that the loss implicit in refusal to trust and to share visions is just as destructive as the blind technology and artificial self-affiramtion which gave the world the atom bomb and the Nazi party. Like Dolek Berson and even like Buchan Walsh, the wasted dreamer in Hersey's early story, Old Pebble has the greatness of humanism as his strength. His shutting out of the engineer from his own life resembles Hester's inability to affirm her own nature. He cannot face the chaos technology must bring to religion, philosophy, and other traditional modes of interpreting human experience.

Instead of attempting to build new ways of dealing with the world, he chooses annihilation when he denies the fundamentally human process of communication from which religion, philosophy and art proceed. Pebble actually cancels out his own culture by refusing to trust the strength it imparts. Threatened by the engineer's dream with the wiping out of his own interpretation of life, he retaliates by cancelling out the engineer from his conversation with Su-ling and the cook. By cancelling out his shared humanity, he answers fire with fire and dies.

Whatever simplistic overtones there may be to Hersey's insistence on communication, the structure of the tale has a complexity and a seriousness that lend weight to his conviction. The death of Pebble is precipitated by a shallowness the engineer senses in his own culture and evidences in his actions. His failure to win the tracker as a friend because of his condescending, immature ways and his overbearing description of the dam which would wipe out society as Pebble knows it, stem from his need to compensate for his own culture's humanistic emptiness by exploiting its scientific skill. Early in the voyage, he senses his lack of a rich tradition similar to the magnificent one Pebble and Su-ling share. Hersey uses an effective example to convince the reader of the hollow, disjointed aspect of a culture which rejects and demeans the communicative arts. The engineer cannot remember more than a line or two of poetry. In response to Su-ling's beautiful stories and poems, he can offer only a line or two of "When lilacs last in the dooryard bloomed." He has no adequate explanation for the beauties and horrors of the river, and finds himself caught up into the rituals and myths the crew employs.

Knowing himself an outsider in the society of " The Junk," the engineer encounters and safely guides himself through dangerous obstacles to communication (and his ultimate worthwhile survival) in "The Rapids." Aware of his separation from others, the young man recognizes in the owner of the junk a person who remains stubbornly unwilling to learn from and depend upon others. He is bitter over losing a junk earlier, but that loss was caused by the owner's failure to understand his pilot's signals, as well as by the pilot's deception of the owner. On this voyage, he pretends solicitation for the engineer, but actually puts him off the junk as it crosses the rapids because he is superstitious about the foreigner's presence. Accompanied by Su-ling and the cook, the young American learns the sadness of blocked communication, but by recognizing at once his own mistakes and the beauty of the river culture, he begins to move toward wholeness. At a place called The Scholar's Restaurant, Su-ling shows him a room papered with poems from English textbooks. He laughs at the stilted prose, the effect of Chinese writers using English, and laughs also at the letter from one friend to another chiding a young man for neglecting to look at the river covered with snow, ". . . I regret to see you continue in those bad habits of indifference to beautiful views which may shorten your life." (70) As he translates this seemingly funny sentiment for Su-ling, she laughs too. The wisdom of experience has taught the narrator that Su-ling was laughing at his awkward translation, not at the absurdity of the idea.

> . . . I realize that the real gulf between us lay in the fact that I, who was so proud of coming from the swift-winged world of science, was laughing at an old world where it was possible seriously to believe that men die young of the bad habit of failing to go out on a dangerous river to gaze at the earth when it turns overnight into silver. (71)

The words of the narrator here indicate the closing of that gap. Hersey does not, however, construct a cut-and-dried conversion story. The reader, instead, is told that the young man actually is deficient in the understanding of people; he forces his vision of the dam upon the Chinese without regard for their human dignity and aspirations. Even after the death of Pebble, the engineer does not perceive the clash between his culture and that of the river people as final. With a well-intentioned but clumsy earnestness reminiscent of traveling Americans in novels as varied as *Daisy Miller* and *The Ugly American* he invites his friends to a Western-style party that is a failure. There, the Chinese are as ill at ease and out of place as he had been when he boarded the junk. Hersey portrays the young man as one who spends the rest of his life motivated by the memory and idealism of his trip on the Yangtze. The delicate, complex but necessary union of technology with human values is a passionate dream for him. He communicates the sympathy and reverence for humanity he learned through the river trip and, it is suggested,

through his aloneness after it, to the reader. His position is analogous
to that of Strether in *The Ambassadors*. The only way to make
sense or utility out of his wholeness is, as Hersey sees it, to share this
invaluable vision by directly describing it. He must create a community of whole Americans.

The condition of the engineer in his middle life, the
vantage point from which he narrates, makes him a teacher and trans-
mittor of culture in the manner of Noach Levinson. In the continuing
stream of experience and communication that his narration makes
possible, the humanistic scientist plays a role similar to Su-ling's
part in his own education. Her amazing knowledge of river culture
and aesthetic appreciation have become his, and now may become
the reader's. By retaining belief in the technology American culture
offers, but cross-fertilizing it with a sense of history, tradition and
art, Hersey's engineer affirms his own heritage while acknowledging
its limitations in space and time. In this way, Hersey points out the
advantage Americans have. Pebble and Su-ling were confounded by
the overpowering force of technology. Like the atomic bomb, it
has the effect of destroying their civilization. Yet the engineer's
dam, like technology itself, proceeded from the same fund of human
self-preservation that the path and the steps above the Yangtze come
from. It is part of the mystery and sadness of the work that the
engineer cannot communicate his sense of hope about technology
to the Chinese. Hersey insists that the basis for communication,
a humanistic tradition, is fragmented in the world the young man
comes from. Only when he learns this from Su-ling's culture does he
learn to look for it in his own and see that his own must depend on
the past of other nations. The American soil has a brilliant layer
which can produce monstrous growths (like the bomb) because it
is not in touch with its humanistic roots. The Chinese soil is rich and
fertile, but in the reality of the twentieth century it cannot sustain
its people. Hersey, despite his portrayal of the insufficient education of the engineer and the joyful river culture, makes his affirmation of technology rooted in humanism by poignant descriptions
of the trackers and the well diggers.

The description of the well diggers is particularly interesting,
for it describes the actual process Hersey's work preaches.

> At the wells I was greeted by the sight of hundreds of naked men toiling up and down the spiral interior paths of the enormous brine pits. I began at first, seeing these figures that reminded me of Blake and Dante and Milton, to feel some kind of shallow theoretical distress, over men like these who were forced to do the work, not merely of animals, but of most primitive machines, and this tripped off, as it made me think first of our trackers, then sharply of Old Pebble, a very strong feeling of waste; cringing back from the brink of one of the huge conical pits, I was overcome by a sudden rage. (164 - 166)

The engineer draws from his Western humanistic tradition, as well as from his technological background, in arriving at the rage which will motivate his life. The catalyst for unifying his knowledge of poetry and of machinery into an active force is his relationship with the Chinese workers. One after another, Hersey characters follow this process; Boman and the narrator of *My Petition for More Space* are examples, people who unify the layers of technology and tradition by the deep spading process of self-knowledge through knowledge of others.

This agonized urge of the characters he creates earns Hersey the label of "do-gooder." Although the works are not shallow moralistic fables but interesting and complex didactic structures, the fact that Hersey's engineer, for example, lives in the work not primarily as a representation of interesting (and therefore inspiring) human life, but as a spur to the reader, brings to the book a built-in artistic problem. Hersey always seems to care more for affecting the reader's conduct than for creating a work that just "is." Unlike Bellow's Herzog, for example, the engineer is not really important or memorable for himself but for the example of his experience and what it may enable the reader to do and be.

Beckoff has described the early Hersey as "a more empathetic Daniel Defoe," [14] a comparison I thought of also when I began to study his work. In a sense, since Hersey too writes "survivor" tales and employs realistic reporting to advantage, and since he shares Defoe's ambivalent literary reputation as a "journalist," the comparison appears quite useful. As Ian Watt has argued, however, in *The Rise of the Novel* (1967), Defoe's position as moralist is questionable. Watt suggests that Defoe failed to unify his avowed moral aims with his artistic ones. He wrote ethically neutral novels "because they make formal realism an end rather than a means, subordinating any coherent ulterior significance to the illusion that the text represents the authentic lucubrations of an historical person."[15] Hersey, linked with Hawthorne, Melville and James by Beckoff, and with Silone, Malraux, Dos Passos and Steinbeck by his own appraisal, has benefited from a long tradition of morally effective novelists.[16] But, as the evidence of Hersey's work attests, especially in his two parables of annihilation, he is off beat as an artist. He uses his stories, he uses art itself within the stories, as a means to an end outside of them. He is quite different from Defoe as Watt sees him. He has more in common with the author of *Rasselas* than with Defoe or even the modern writers he has had as models. The difference between Hersey and Johnson is the moral position from which they write. Hersey is a part of the chaotic twentieth century, and never denies it. His work may seem ineffectual partly from the fact that he urges readers to search out new values even as they use older models to sustain themselves in the search. Without resting in a tradition in the manner of Jewish or Southern American authors, and without depicting the real texture of human life out of sheer delight in the manner of, for example, Nabokov, Hersey offers an abstract, though appealing, promise rather than a full-blooded presence. Yet, seizing on what does seem to be the central preoccupation and potential for his age, an intensification of human communication, Hersey's work seems both appropriately timely and, as a record as well as a directive, a historically and aesthetically valuable creation. After the parables of annihilation, Hersey continued to experiment with ready-made fictional forms to document contemporary life, always amplifying the saving role of the writer and of communication.

CHAPTER IV

HUMANISM, OR DEATH

Hersey's first two "parables of annihilation" offered harsh lessons. Hester's fragmented understanding of herself and her culture, and Pebble's suicidal rejection of himself and his culture, were mitigated only partially by the humanly wise voice of the engineer describing his own survival. Without altering substantially the message of *The Wall*, Hersey next created another pair of works to impress it on the collective mind of his audience. In a now familiar pattern, he shaped his books more deliberately to suit a moral purpose than an artistic one. *The War Lover*, critics agree, is heavy-handed with all of Boman's insistence that Daphne uncovers an important and startling truth about Marrow and men like him; *The Child Buyer* is a clever imitation of Swift, but not a truly unique artistic creation. Hersey's war novel and satire seem more valuable than this, however, when we observe their relationship to his other work and their development of the communication-survival theme into first, a realistic picture of humanism as a viable alternative to destruction in the novel, and second, a memorable glorification of humanism in the satire. These works definitely mark Hersey as a virtuoso in the sense that Webster suggests: an experimental philosopher, an empiricist. Moving from one historical concern to another, Hersey continues to play with outward form as he examines the idea that has been his passion.

The forms Hersey chose for these two crusades to preserve humanistic values reflect the role he assumed in *The Marmot Drive* as a serious critic of American life. Still moving like a reporter from one catastrophe to another, Hersey turned his attention to the second World War and to the American educational system to apply the philosophy hinted at in *A Single Pebble*. The war book portrays the modest but important triumph of a person in conflict with himself; ironically, the work based on the educational system of the country depicts the crushing of human ingenuity. Although on the surface these plot descriptions sound ordinary—heroic war novels and criticism of institutions are plentiful enough—both of the works evidence Hersey's sense of what is timely while treating issues that seem timeless. *The Child Buyer* received criticism from B. F. Skinner himself; *The War Lover* anticipated *Catch-22* in its portrayal of a life-loving bomber pilot.

Unlike *Catch-22*, Hersey's war novel is in the first person; Boman discovers that he is his own deadly enemy, second only to his death-seeking pilot. *The Child Buyer*, a story of life at home, written in the distant third person of transcripts, is actually closer in spirit to *Catch-22* than is *The War Lover*. The important difference is that Hersey stubbornly refuses to indict a system as the ultimate cause of human destruction. Each person abandons potential for a different choice than the one offered by the child buyer. In an era when most serious art has been negative, it is not surprising that an author would attempt to write in affirmation of human possibilities. Popular writers repeatedly affirm that the individual is capable of good, of course, but Hersey's complex war novel and stinging satire do not offer the tidy comfort of the traditional best seller. The surprising element in Hersey's work is his ability to walk the thin line between didactic and sentimental writing with consistent success, shaping a form appropriate to each issue he treats.

In choosing a traditional war novel as the setting for an expanded definition of the saving humanism proposed in *The Wall* and dramatized in *The Marmot Drive* and *A Single Pebble,* Hersey selected an effective teaching device as well as an occasion to use his talents for description, suspense, and detail. Using transcripts of hearings to illustrate the death implicit in a world which abandons belief in human achievement is a simple trick which effectively parallels Hersey's rhetoric in *The Child Buyer* with Swift's in *A Modest Proposal*, who also wrote in a political form common to his day. That the transcript is a cold record, seemingly devoid of authorial prejudice, shows Hersey's ingenuity as his characters indict themselves in much the same way Swift's pamphleteer indicts society by having a common political medium act as a mirror for human cruelty.

The war confessional and the satirical work followed Hersey's work in various public forms. After completing *A Single Pebble* (1956), he worked briefly for Adlai Stevenson, trying to restore to his speeches the intellectual and idealistic content admired in 1952. Thus, Hersey may have been indirectly responsible for the nuclear test-ban agreement with the Soviet Union after Stevenson's memorable speech on the subject. [1] Hersey also visited Hungarian refugee camps and wrote a narration for a United Nations film about them during this period. Since 1954, he had been working actively as a member of the National Citizens Commission for the Public Schools. [2] Although Hersey has stated in an interview with me that his "life as a man is peripheral" to his life as a writer, it is obvious that *The Child Buyer* and his next book, *Here to Stay* (1963) were influenced by these activities. During this same period (1958) Hersey was divorced and remarried. *The War Lover*, the first of his books to depict a full-blown, two sided love affair and the first to place rhetorical authority in the voice of a female character, is dedicated in turn to his mother, his publisher, and his children.

Personal relationships become integral to the new, broadened concept of survival-in-community the later books treat. Levinson's hesitant friendship with Dolek Berson and Rachel Apt is quite far from the passionate humanism Boman discovers in himself through Daphne. Hersey, with a dignity and discretion he seems to cherish, has kept his family life out of the public eye. He apparently believes that his creative work is almost a separate dimension of his experience. Since his tenure at Pierson College during the student revolution, however, Hersey has stated that his work has become more directly personal. [3] *The War Lover* may represent Hersey's own humanizing. Boman's pain at the possible loss of Daphne and the powerful portrait of Marrow's terror that he cannot love, are important in convincing the reader of the value of a full human life. Whatever their source, they are welcome elements in Hersey's work. They are, in fact, needed to supplement Hester's search and the engineer's vision with concrete evidence that the quest and the dream are tied to basic human experiences, making high achievement possible as well as desirable.

The War Lover received the usual mixed reviews praising Hersey's moral sense and skill with realistic narrative, but objecting either to the oversimplified idea that war is caused by a Freudian neurosis or to the earnest tone of the novel. In addition to such reviews, *The War Lover* has received some scholarly criticism of a favorable tone. Not all readers dismiss the work as simplistic in its interpretation and portrayal of war, for Robert N. Hudspeth, in a 1969 article for *The University Review-Kansas City*, argues that *The War Lover* is an extended definition of nihilism. He states that Hersey is "a humanist aghast at humanity's self-abasement," [4] and constructs a definition of nihilism as a world empty of value in which humanity is thrown back upon itself and its traditional values of love, self-respect, and humility. Writing in *PMLA* in 1972, Randall H. Waldron uses the term "humanist" to define Boman, the narrator of *The War Lover*. [5]

In order to explain what has been taken for bad planning on Hersey's part, the sudden sexual involvement of Daphne with Marrow at the end of the book, Girgus interprets Boman's hero worship of his pilot as a form of latent homosexuality which Daphne must overcome but conceal from Boman. [6] Yet only once does a character—and not Boman—allude to Marrow as a "Charles Atlas" type. The superficial friendship of Marrow and Boman could suggest a homo-erotic theme similar to that found in other American works, but nothing in the work reflects that Daphne has any such awareness. Instead, Daphne seems to be a humanist herself who has learned from a former lover the insanity of killing. She is further advanced in love and self-knowledge than Boman is even at the end of the book, but she has recognized and developed in Boman the life-loving and life-giving qualities of another humanist.

Hudspeth states that Boman's inability to acknowledge Daphne's individuality prevents him from achieving a successful confrontation with Marrow's nihilism. [7] In devaluing Daphne to an adjunct, Boman blocks his own development and powers as a human being. Seen in terms of feminist criticism, Daphne's attempt to free herself from total dependence upon her affair with Boman, her search for another love relationship, and her willingness to sleep with Marrow as a sign of her right to a full life rather than one delineated by her uncommitted lover, typify the fully human and prophetic interpretation Hersey has given to his times. Daphne's sexual freedom and moral integrity, her courageous self-acceptance and defence, seem perfectly plausible now, despite the dislike some reviewers in 1959 felt for Daphne's willingness to accept other sexual partners than Boman. That Hersey's woman character could love a man without surrendering love of self is more a sign of universal vision than of mechanistic plot construction. Subsequent women characters in *White Lotus, The Conspiracy,* and *My Petition for More Space* have had this refreshing wholeness.

In the development of Boman's final ideal of selfless love, Daphne and another character, Kid Lynch, act in exemplar roles analogous to those of Levinson and Su-ling. Boman, true to Hersey's insistence on individual potential and responsibility and also true to his depiction of American culture as available though unassimilated brings to his tour as a flyer a heritage he defines as "basic decency" and a sensitivity to art, poetry, architecture, history and music. Hersey has the character mention directly his appreciation for such things as Turner paintings, but Boman's speech communicates an idealistic, sensitive and imaginative perception of reality from the first sentence he speaks: "I woke up hearing a word break like a wave on the shells of my ears; *Mission.*" [8] Throughout the narration, Boman uses metaphors, similes, and references to cultural symbols or works of art in a way that is original without being cumbersome. His education and sensitivity are two of the reasons Marrow claims Bo cannot be a good fighter pilot; Hersey clearly portrays the humanistic, liberally educated view of life as incompatible with and threatened by the anti-intellectual, stereotyped masculinity and personally isolated existence of Marrow. Like Pebble, Boman at the start of his tour has not fully accepted himself nor understood his culture. He stands in danger of annihilation of self, as well as of physical death, from the pilot, from himself, from the enemy fighters, and from the destructive urge that a whole civilization seems to embrace.

That Boman has, at the end of the novel, survived these

threats to his wholeness and begun to work toward the highest possibilities of his human nature, is partly due to his background, his personality, and his interaction with Daphne and Lynch. In fact, his entire narration takes place after all of this interaction. Although the narrative structure is cumbersome, Hersey employs it prudently. The uninitiated Boman could not have spoken with even the limited authority his experienced voice has. Because the flashback accounts, as well as the more immediate description of the final raid, come from a narrator enriched by Daphne's knowledge and Lynch's idealism, the entire story rather than simply its outcome exemplifies the life-loving attitude Hersey posits as a condition for survival. A certain amount of confusion and frustration for the reader result from the alternation between the "tour" and the "raid." It is easier to assume that Hersey knew and intended this, than that the author of *Hiroshima* had ignored the needs of his audience. Hersey wanted to depict chaos, not order. The limited sense Boman can make of the experience as he narrates it during the final, decisive mission, is all of the sense the audience is permitted to make, although we add our own compassion or impatience as we read. Unfortunate as Hersey's conscious or unconscious habit of working harder for moral than for aesthetic strength may be for his critical reputation, this work seems to survive stoutly as an effective defense of traditional human values.

Daphne and Lynch, like Marrow and Boman, contribute to the reader's sense that this novel is more an allegory than it is an adventure or romance. Both seem present in order to change Boman. They exist in an intricate way within the narrative, which ostensibly is Boman's tale of discovery about the reasons for war and the means of preventing it. Daphne, who is Boman's lover and teacher, ironically is the object of his self-delusion. He uses her as a receptacle for his fears and hopes, as a mirror for his vanity about his "separate peace" with the enemy. There is a parallel between Marrow's use of his flying to obtain sexual pleasure, a use of the sky which Boman describes in terms of a mirror for Marrow's imagined self, and Boman's inconsiderate, even destructive use of Daphne to prove he is a loving human being. He sees the relationship in terms of himself, much as Marrow perceives the actions of bombing cities. Boman's image of himself as a lover is distorted, until he sees that Daphne's needs are as real as his own. Only then does he have the compassion-ate, hopeful and humble voice of a humanist. The distorted sexuality in Marrow's love of war has a more subtle and convincing aspect when Hersey uses it as an image of inhuman, selfish, conduct through Boman's unwittingly empty love for Daphne.

Although Daphne clearly is as much an expedient for Hersey as for Boman, she is an intriguing witness for humanism. She is the moral authority within the work, exacting an idealism in action Boman may never attain, yet capable of inflicting pain on Boman because she owes herself more than she owes him. Beyond this, she seems to stand for England itself and the yet unproven American commitment to its English heritage. Daphne is Boman's goal in several ways. She serves as immediate physical satisfaction through-out the tour, but she is more than that almost immediately. Boman's relationship with her affirms his liberal education, his love for history, his conscious attempt to avoid stereotypes and develop uniquely. Hersey's knowledge of Cambridge, gained as a student there, serves to create a background for Daphne as both source and goal of the humanist in Boman, paralleling the complicated American relation-ship with the mother country.

More than once, Daphne undercuts simplistic idealism in Boman and in the reader. There is no clear explanation for the war, but she also consistently refutes acceptance of it on idealistic grounds. Once she tells Boman, " 'Darling, you're so American! You get what is and what you want all mixed up together in your head.' " (388) When Bo recites sentimental verse to her, she answers with Eliot's lines about the Phoenician Sailor. Boman realizes that she is simply answering his verses with words she likes, but he recognizes the cultural gulf; "Naive sentiment; powerful irony. A nice cleancut American boy; a woman on the edge of a Europe in agony." (166) Through Daphne, as through Pebble and Levinson, as through the fragmented Puritan culture of Matthew Avered, Hersey calls for the cultural cross-fertilization intrinsic to survival. Boman's remark that the American war novels depicting alienation in youth had little relationship to actual American belief is a part of Hersey's didactic structure; the writer ought to affect the audience, teach it, lead it, not express a view peculiar to himself and assume that all share it. Boman's statement, "We were ready to die to the last man for Dinah Shore, rare sirloin, a cold beer, and a Caribbean cruise," (225) is a throwback to the "blueberry pie" of *Into the Valley* and an image of the shallow cultural innocence of the raw young country. Immersion in the past and valuing of the individual are the two remedies humanism offers through the symbolic character of Daphne. Bo's longing, as he brings the plane home from the raid, is for "England," as well as for Daphne, an England he defines in terms of "Bacon, Ben Jonson, Cromwell, Milton, Dryden, Newton, Pitt the Younger, Byron, Darwin, Thackeray," (399) as well as in terms of loved topography and familiarity. The longing for England and Daphne expands into an idealistic lyrical longing for the best of his own past and "another chance at life. Couldn't a man try again, and get it right this time?" (399)

Kid Lynch, like Daphne, forces Boman to see more than he wants to see. Hersey used this typically alienated intellectual as another potential humanist whose death, Daphne points out, frees Boman from a didactic influence he had begun to resent. The poetic, satirical Lynch, whom Boman describes as "a marvelous half-trained mind" (27), a "lover of sounds," a "prophetic spirit," appears briefly in the story but acts as a truth-teller long before Daphne is finally able to unmask Marrow. In a curious way, Lynch's relationship with Boman is analogous to Hersey's with his readers. When Lynch dies—his prophetic, poetic brains smeared around the radio room of a bomber—Boman perceives the two-faceted relationship he had with his friend. Talking with Daphne, he illustrates his instinct for self-preservation as he talks himself out of destructive, total grief:

> As I talked about him my praise of him gradually shaded toward a
> slightly whining tone. 'He had such a good mind, I almost never had to
> think when I was around him. He always had suggestions of what to
> do. . . " (309)

Lynch had "worked on" Bo to change his actions toward Marrow and Daphne. As a custodian of culture, but one limited by his lack of education, he performed an important but somewhat unpleasant service for his friend. Like Hersey's many appeals to imagination and emotion, Lynch's attempts to awaken Boman had a clever rhetorical framework.

Like Dolek Berson, Lynch used a communications network, the broadcasting set at the base, to save and to infuriate his listeners. He recited poems such as Yeats' "An Irish Airman Foresees his Death" as well as doggerel, limericks and wisecracks. The set, which Boman describes as "the voice of doom," becomes a voice of life, a reminder of originality and of potential. Lynch satirizes the myth of the pilots about their kinship in heroism with enemy fliers and the love for war Marrow and, by extension, followers of Marrow, had. Hersey has this sympathetic, prophetic, but unfulfilled voice use his knowledge of German folklore and poetry to construct a fable of a war-loving "Black Knight" on the German force, a fable that actually satirized Marrow and others like him. Since this artist contributed to the fear which ultimately killed Marrow, who had nothing outside of himself with which to confront fear, and con-tributed to the maturity of Boman, whose saving compassion and understanding Lynch nourished, he is directly at the center of the work. Boman's grief for him, with Daphne's help, becomes the hero's first experience of the selfless love which is lacking in his own vague "sense of decency" (the Yankee idealism Hersey rejected in *The Marmot Drive*). Like writers in Hersey's view of things, Lynch would contribute to the worthwhile survival of others:

> As I began to think then of other parts of Lynch, of the best of him, I experienced a new kind of grief, one that was centered on him rather than on myself, a sadness which, like my sobs, had a pleasant aspect, but this pleasantness, too, had to do with Lynch and not me. This sadness was his memorial, his life after death. Through its growth in me he would help to keep me going; I would remember him and so give him a little immortality, not very much, but more than some people get. (310)

Although Boman narrates the story and other characters are seen only in their relationship to him, there has been a tendency to refer to this book the way the cover of the Bantam edition does, as a novel about "the ecstacy of war," focused on Marrow. The real difference between the work and its reputation may have its cause in the popular reputation of Hersey since World War II, and also in the problems of form and characterization which keep the book from a critical audience that might admire the complexities it contains. Marrow is a flamboyant stereotype, but Boman is a unique individual. The book's only true meaning lies in his account of survival through a humanism that leads to community. Everything in the work leads to and supports the final chapter on the raid, when Boman becomes the nucleus of an authentic group on board the ship. The myth of Marrow's heroism dissolves, but the co-pilot is there, enriched by a full culture, painfully thrown at emotional and physical levels onto his own deep resources. Unlike Pebble, like Levinson, he can meet the challenge. Hersey's skillful writing of this section, which one reviewer described as "remarkably sustained," is more than that . Its form reflects its essence. Boman's last flight and vision of home has a rich merriment at times, reflecting the love of life the humanist has. The scene with Max contains the heightened experience of human community the book urges.

Hersey leaves unsaid the outcome of Bo's commitment to life. For Daphne, selfless love in its truest sense would mean an abandonment of the war. The men on the crew must fly one more mission, and the issue of Boman's going with them is simply left open. The evidence of his love for his "brothers in life" suggests he will see them through the tour. The question of how one must act to live in a fully human way is left to puzzle the reader, a parable to mull over when the preacher is gone. Hersey's posing of this dilemma shortly before the war resistance of the sixties indicates, like most of his work, his sensitivity to his times; it may also indicate that he, like Lynch, is a disturbing truth-teller and effective exhorter.

With *The Child Buyer,* Hersey made an experiment in form away from the traditional novel. Like *The Wall,* the work uses a documentary form to capture the author's vision of a contemporary matter, and to sway the reader's opinion of it. Hersey's abrupt departure from novel writing to satire has helped to thwart critical studies of his work. Students adhering to a generic interest in fiction, for example, have not found him an exciting author. In a study of Hersey's moral commitment and contribution to American letters, the author's delight in varied forms, represented by later works such as *The Algiers Motel Incident* and *The Conspiracy,* seems courageous and suitable rather than a symptom of inferior intelligence or artistry. In yet a new way, *The Child Buyer* contains a memorable dramatic portrait of human potential and of the death implicit in a denial of that potential.

It may be only a coincidence that *The Child Buyer*, destined to be compared with *A Modest Proposal* and *The Shortest Way with Dissenters*, should bear a dedication drawn from Hersey's eighteenth century studies. The quotation dedicating the book to his mother, Grace Baird Hersey, is Addison's, in *The Spectator*, May 17, 1712: " 'Cheerfulness keeps up a kind of daylight in the mind, and fills it with a steady and perpetual serenity.' " The child Barry Rudd has a special daylight in the mind, a delight in the world accompanied by confidence and serenity, almost wholly imparted to him by his mother and Dr. Gozar. When these two abandon him through their respective forms of mistaken pride, Barry longs for the child buyer's forgetting chamber. The book, like the dedication, champions the beauty of an individual human mind, but dramatizes the dependence of such a mind on support of a loving community.

Hersey created in Barry a walking symbol not of genius alone but of the liberal humanism and affirmation of life his other works advocate. *The Child Buyer* is a bitter work which shows a suicidal culture defeating its ends, yet in the reader's mind, the child sold to "United Lymphomilloid" outlives the unbelievable scheme. Barry is alive with enthusiasm and desire to learn, capable, Hersey implies, of re-aligning man with nature in the devastated twentieth century. In addition to amazing knowledge and motivation, Barry has the kindness which comes from wisdom. Despite his own suffering at the hands of educationists, politicians, and his own parents, he speaks of them with perceptive tolerance even when criticizing them. One example of this is Barry's response to "Senator Skypack" during the hearings:

> I must say, Senator, for a so-called educator, Mr. Cleary has an odd way of grading mental abilities: A stupid person is one who lets himself be victimized; a gifted person is one who's shrewd. He thinks intelligence is cleverness. Since he thinks he's a "realist," thinks moral values are nothing but cant, he has the great advantage of not having to decide what he really believes—his morality is the cops, his golden rule is don't get caught. Yet, I've got to admit the G-man's honest; I mean to

says he sees himself as honest and other people see him as honest. Perhaps the two views make him practically speaking, honest indeed, though
they aren't the same. . . ." [9]

In Barry and in Dr. Gozar, his mentor and the person who,
with Mrs. Rudd, has developed Barry's mind, Hersey presented
norms for the satire. Both Barry and Gozar are natural and verbal
artists. Everyone else in the work, including the fumbling, well-
intentioned Mansfield, is reduced to absurdity. Gozar's capitulation
to the child buyer has also seemed absurd to some readers; she is so
magnanimous, original and strong that her betrayal of Barry is an
artistic incongruity. Hersey's didactic intent, of course, outweighs
concern for form, and Gozar's sudden defeat by the child buyer is
necessary to his thesis, that neither gifted children nor humanism
itself can withstand a culture that blindly succumbs to technology.
The similarity of *The Child Buyer* to *Brave New World* is obvious;
to understand the Hersey book, it is helpful to look at the difference
from it.

Hersey's persistent label of "journalist" is a clue to our understanding of *The Child Buyer*. Unlike Huxley, and unlike Swift in
his description of Laputa, Hersey did not trouble to construct a
new world for his satire. Orwell's "Ingsoc," for all of its troubling
likeness to modern systems, is still imaginatively new and distant
from our experience. Hersey's approach is really not that of the
typical satirist, even though *The Child Buyer* is good satire. His
approach is similar to that of the documentary reporter, and is consistent with his conviction that his own ordering of the facts at
hand will convey a valid truth and effect a change in his reader.
Like a Walker Evans or a Margaret Bourke-White, he orders ordinary
reality authoritatively for a purpose beyond the artistic delight of
doing so. *The Child Buyer* is a distorted, carefully arranged portrayal of facts and experience the reader already shares with the author.
It is a slanted way of looking at reality similar to *Main Street,* a
clever attack on the readily observed but seldom seen environment,
with Hersey's special emphasis on saving humanism.

In *The Child Buyer,* as in the early journalism, Hersey seems
to share too much with the reader, bringing a record instead of an

interpretation of experience. Paradoxically, of course, this is intrinsic to Hersey's role of moralist and culture critic. The far-fetched
concoction of his satiric plot really has shock value in pointing out
what may be obvious, and also dangerous, in American life. The
criticism which greeted this work is a mixture of praise and disgust,
but it may be a more perceptive mixture than Hersey has usually
received. The five reviewers engaged by the editors of *The New
Republic,* especially, give instructive responses to the question of
Hersey's importance as a writer. They also provide keys to a rhetorical analysis of *The Child Buyer* consistent with its form.

Stating that the work is obviously controversial, the editors
recognized that Hersey's book needed to be judged not only on
literary grounds, but also on cultural ones. [10] They hired an American satirist, Margaret Halsey, a poet with political interests, William
Jay Smith, a controversial educator, Carl Hansen, a behavioral scientist, B. F. Skinner, and a literary critic, Robert Gorham Davis, to
review it. It is interesting and perhaps significant that the artists,
Halsey and Smith, praised the work, while the literary critic (whose
interest lies in textual criticism) rejected it vociferously. The educator, who had fought for a "track" system allowing children to be
educated with their intellectual peers, defended individual educators
but agreed that Hersey had asked a challenging question and left a
sense of "unfinished business" as a mark of the greatness of the
book. B. F. Skinner, whom the editors describe as the possible villain
of the book, rejects the book without admitting that it is an attack
on behaviorism; as Girgus points out, Skinner triumphs in the work
when everyone, even Dr. Gozar, proves to be a product of environment. [11]

The strong and divided reactions of these authorities symbol-
ize very well Hersey's relation to his age. He is a gifted trouble-
maker, but he wears the white hat of his establishment background
and beliefs. He is bold and naive, taking on any adversary; in *Too
Far to Walk* he again employs a literary device in a way that seems
simplistic and unbelievable, and yet seems consonant with his whole
moral and artistic position. Halsey recognizes that *The Child Buyer*
is a tract, but she defends it as "a tract at its superlative best," (21)
and implies what Wayne Booth asserts in *The Rhetoric of Irony,*

that the convention in which an author writes can cancel a need or claim to reflect reality accurately. [12] Hersey's wild abandon in attacking the culture seems, from Halsey's point of view, an "unself-serving" piece of moral leadership, and she wishes for more of it:

> This is the pure, clear, wrath of the righteous man; and so far from being intimidating, it is exciting. Mr. Hersey in writing this book has done something intelligent and brave, and by implication he asks his countrymen also to be intelligent and brave. So clear is the impli-cation that more than one reader of *The Child Buyer,* in this autumn of 1960, is going to think what a pity it is that the author is not running for President. (22)

Except for Davis, the other reviewers share Halsey's admira-tion for Hersey as a person. Skinner is the least admiring, but he refers to Hersey as a writer whose anger is obvious though not helpful to his book, and—apparently attempting sarcasm—lists Hersey's seven different involvements with local, state and national educational groups in a way that effectively raises Hersey in the estimation of all but the most cynical readers. Smith gives strong testimony to the truth of Hersey's work, quoting from educational journals which actually group gifted children, under the heading "exceptional," with the handicapped. He recognizes Hersey's book as a needed attack on behaviorists and educationist gobbledygook in a sentence which also focuses on Hersey's brilliant portrayal of Barry as a symbol of human potential:

> . . . Mr. Hersey is attacking not only the present deplorable state of education in this country but also the major remedies that have been proposed for it, remedies that grow out of a complete misconception of the role of intelligence in a free society. (25)

Smith makes a perceptive comment about *The Child Buyer* as a work of art. He seems to use originality as a criterion when he says it is not entirely successful as art because its caricatures of education-ists are so true to life. (26) Widespread impatience with educationese and disgust with the American public school system existed in 1960 and exist now. Hersey's view of education is not a private one, not a unique one, and he does not have to work to convince his readers to believe him. Whatever freshness and strength he possesses as a writer do not lie in creating new values but in reaffirming old ones in startling ways; Skinner refers to this same process when he says Hersey clings to the myth of the intellectual hero. (22) Barry is the ideal and symbol Hersey unabashedly offers to the reader. He is the old Renaissance man, not perfect, but better than the alternative of computer rule. None of Hersey's work offers another solution than a return to humanism.

Robert Gorham Davis offers a precise example of the kind of scrutiny Hersey's work cannot withstand. Davis applies ahistorical textual analysis, in which originality as well as traditional measuring-sticks for the novel, unity, coherence and development of plot, character and theme, are his operating criteria. He makes no generic distinction between satire and the novel. He does not mention Hersey's actions in the field of education, nor his apparent didactic intention. He does not mention the intellectual content nor the extrinsic relevance of the work, except to imply that they are outside of his sphere; "Of the ideas in *The Child Buyer* it is not my place here to speak." (24) He accuses Hersey of stealing from *Brave New World*, but compares the book to *Advise and Consent*, rather than to any kind of satire. He condemns it as a work of the imagination.

Literary criticism that rules out a discussion of the "ideas" in a work and cuts it off from its historical milieu is, in its extreme, a type that very few works can withstand. Wayne Booth has shown its particularly devastating effect upon didactic works, and in *A Rhetoric of Irony* provides some suggestions that can build a more favorable case for *The Child Buyer*, although Booth would not count Hersey among the world's great writers because his work is not always constructed well or in an original way. (216) Booth's interest, however, in rhetorical criticism and his idea that hundreds, even thousands of different "genres" (works similar in effect, shape and beliefs) exist (209) do give Hersey more credibility as an artist than most critical approaches afford him. Davis himself describes the form of *The Child Buyer* in structural terms that hint at the rage or disappointment Hersey's book evokes in the reader:

> In a detective story all the principle characters except the detective have to be unpleasant at the beginning, displaying enough resentment or greed so that any one of them may be supposed capable of the crime. *The*

Child Buyer moves in the opposite direction. During much of the action—or talk, rather—some characters, mostly women, appear to be working in the interests of good, humanity, non-conformism, free intelligence. But then at the end, everyone sells out to the agent, this after the corporation will destroy the bright boy as a human being by the most repulsive methods straight out of Huxley's *Brave New World*. (24)

The death which comes with a denial of individual freedom and potential is indeed a controlling force in *The Child Buyer*. A careful study of the work reveals that the capitulation of Barry's teachers and parent is to be expected. Not even Hersey will argue that one magnificent individual, Dr. Gozar, is a match for an entire age. By making the sale of Barry absurd, painful and inevitable, Hersey satirizes an immediate reality. Within his work, which is a form we might call "documentary satire," the writer effectively shows the reader much that is stupid and wasteful, and even tragic, in contemporary life.

Arthur Burton, an existential psychologist, sees Hersey's book as an authentic description of both the educational system of the United States and the anxiety of contemporary man. [13] The educators in *The Child Buyer,* Burton argues, live a non-creative existence, parasitically feeding upon children rather than providing them an open existence. They seem incapable of a fully human life of awareness and communciation. Burton views Hersey's portrayal of Barry and Dr. Gozar as an important model for educators, who ought to possess the fullness of human personality. To move away form the quality of "presence" in a teacher, the teacher's standing personally for all that is human in culture, is to move toward a denial of life and a surrender to the death instinct, a longing to escape the burden of Sisyphus. Burton implies that the characteristic which designated a child as "gifted" is really a fuller endowment of the creative, communicative intelligence all people have. (257)

Burton demonstrates that Hersey is able to dramatize an essential stand of a major contemporary philosophy. Barry and Dr. Gozar represent the joyous, open questioning and integrating of the free human mind and spirit, the qualities of a life and culture worth perserving. Burton's article, like Hudspeth's discussion of *The War*

Lover, is a sign of Hersey's importance as a writer of thesis novels of distinct relevance and universality.

Given its justifiable praise as contemporary satire and tract, with their special conventions and liberties, how does *The Child Buyer* make its didactic appeal to the reader to champion humanism over behaviorism? As Davis noted but did not appreciate, the work is structured mechanically as a reflection of the machine which will remove sense and memory from Barry. As each witness is bombarded by external stimuli in the form of the child buyer's crass consumer temptations (themselves a paradigm for the "blueberry pie" syndrome), the person—Cleary, Perrin, Mrs. Rudd, Gozar—loses awareness of other ideas. Without the supportive humanism Boman carried within himself and saw in Daphne, these people find nothing of themselves in the world outside of the child buyer's offer. The culture has failed to meet the terrible needs they feel, as it failed Marrow. Cleary's need for power, Perrin's for economic security and freedom from a system she has never believed in, Mrs. Rudd's longing for refinement, are distorted versions of needs technology exploits. Power, money, and even the arts are subsumed by it.

Gozar's capitulation, deemed unconvincing by Sanders and other commentators, actually captures the danger Hersey sees in humanism's opposition to behaviorism. The brilliant woman fails to know the child buyer as a formidable threat to herself. She laughs at his challenges and absurd demands, secure in her wide knowledge and free-ranging mind. She does not seek a true understanding of "United Lympho;" she is guilty of the Renaissance sin of *hubris.* This is apparent in her assertion that Barry can withstand the machine; she compares him with Aristotle and—by implication—herself with Plato. Not just at that moment, but throughout the book, Gozar is an isolated person, almost contemptuous in her recognizable greatness. She is a humanist, but she neither seeks, finds, not provides community. Barry, abandoned by her and his mother, capitulates too; without community, his more brilliant mind perceives, United Lympho can offer him far more than the town of Pequod. Hersey, as in previous works, offers an image of the world as it seems, a vivid documentary rather than a work dramatizing new possibilities for man. The reader is told, in effect, to reject inauthentic cultural trends in favor of the threatened but treasured values of the humanist. Although we might wish Hersey could make a brilliant new synthesis of human experience, he carries out his role of agent for old beliefs in a convincing manner.

In *The Child Buyer*, Sanders notes, the author of *A Bell for Adano* proves himself a capable ironist. [14] It is this irony, including the defeat of Dr. Gozar and of Barry, which makes the work an effective piece of Hersey persuasion. Booth notes that not all satires are equally ironic; it is possible to attack without the kind of twisting or reversal found in, for example, *A Modest Proposal.* (48) Some satires, such as *The Shortest Way with Dissenters,* are less interesting than others because they lack the strange, sudden "consistently inconsistent ironic mixture" Swift often employs. (117) Although it is possible that Hersey (or someone else) could have written a more original, more humorous, or more coherent work than *The Child Buyer,* it bears up well under rhetorical analysis because it is "consistently inconsistent" in demonstrating the absurdity Hersey wants the reader to see in his surroundings.

Hersey's use of ironic satire to make his point has sound precedent in the work of other moralistic writers. As Booth states, irony furthers community. (29) The title page of *The Child Buyer* draws the reader into a half-joking allegiance with the writer; aside from the shock value of the actual title, the sub-title's teasing archaic form and alternation of italics with ordinary print convey notions of officialese and inefficiency along with an appeal to the reader's assumed disapproval of child-purchasing:

The
Child Buyer
A Novel *in the Form of* Hearings *before the Standing* Committee *on Education,* welfare, and *Public Morality of a certain* State Senate, *Investigating the conspiracy of* Mr. Wissey Jones, *with others,* to Purchase *a* Male Child.

The opening page of *The Child Buyer* continues this archaic officialese. A hint that the "State Senate Standing Committee on Education, Welfare, and Public Morality" is on a fruitless quest may lie in the name of the town where the situation has developed, "Pequod," with its Melvillean appearance. Hersey, like Swift, gives a date for his document, but implies that he is satirizing an age rather than an event by dating the hearing "October, 19   ." At first, the absurdity of the "transcript of hearings" does not appear, except in some provocative Senatorial names: Mansfield, Skypack, and Voyolko, and in the counsel's name: Broadbent. The reader is startled shortly, however, by a transition from legal jargon to the vernacular when Skypack breaks into the counsel's opening remarks by asking "Was the deal completed?" (4) From this moment, the reader is on a new level of awareness. Not only official jargon and procedures, but the conduct and personalities of those who practice them are under attack. The absurdity of Broadbent's presentation becomes clear as he tells the committee they will have to decide whether the purchase or sale of persons should remain illegal, and Wissey Jones is to be distrusted because he is "a very unusual type of individual." (4)

Within a few pages, Hersey uses virtually all of the clues ironists, according to Booth, supply. Direct warnings, including the solemn-humorous title, the hint of "Pequod," the use of transcripts directly after the McCarthy hearings (and, with Hersey's usual prophetic touch, before the Nixon scandals), cliches and dialect from supposedly august officials, long descriptive passages and other irrelevancies masking the official form and tone, dodging of work and responsibility by the investigators, open questioning of one another's reputations, maudlin fear of publicity unmasked as hypocrisy and self-interest, and, finally, a clear conflict of belief between the values of the reader, the famous author, and the work. (73)

Hersey's immediacy, the sense we have of seeing familiar events in his work, creates a curious double edge for his irony. On the one hand, he builds community at once with those of his readers who regard committees, transcripts, educators, and technology with mistrust; for those who see these same things as blessings ("My Country, Right or Wrong") there are infuriating but condemning instances of stupidity, greed, inefficiency, and inconsistency to undermine them for the reader who has valued them. Although some readers—Hansen and Skinner for example—have rejected Gozar and Barry as norms for human experience, no reader has been known to like the senators, educators, or child buyer as Hersey presents them, nor even to disagree very strongly with the assumption that politicians, school people and wheeling-and-dealing businessmen deserve this unfavorable image.

One way that Hersey balances ironic closeness and distance and wins readers to his point of view is by an intriguing use of names. This, a mark of his allegorical intent in many works—is Levinson the "leaven" of his community, is Poynter (*My Petition for More Space*) a "pointer" for others?—is especially apparent in *The Child Buyer* although, as usual, not all of the names in the book seem to play with meaning. "Mansfield," the name of a prominent contemporary United States Senator, belongs to a well-intentioned but ineffectual pseudo-humanist, who—ironically—chairs the record of Barry's purchase by the child buyer. "Skypack" is a human rocket ship, ready to soar at the faintest mention of incendiary words like "national defense," "morals charge," "atheist," or "communist." "Voyolko" is a yokel, an amoral idiot. "Luke Wairy" is the chairman of the Board of Education who announces that he is a shrewd Yankee; "Sean Cleary" is the guidance counselor who refuses to include Barry in his "Talent Search." Indeed, Hersey makes it impossible for the reader to miss his point.

To get the reader to care about his point, Hersey creates the two norms for the work, the magnanimous Dr. Gozar and her brilliant pupil. If the chief pleasure offered the reader in *A Modest Proposal* is the awareness of duplicity (Booth, 41), then something similar occurs each time one of these humanists takes the witness stand. Hersey, and the reader, view with satisfaction the free-ranging minds which cannot be made petty or foolish by the questions of the committee. Although Barry appears pompous and boring to a few readers, he is an important creation, and Girgus remarks that he is the result of Hersey's own cultured and free mind.[15] It is interesting that one of Barry's soliloquies about nature has been used in a college writing text as an example of fine descriptive writing, in company with passages by Ralph Ellison, Saul Bellow, Willa Cather, James Baldwin and other noted writers.[16]

One of the chief ironies of *The Child Buyer* is that Wissey

Jones has an intelligence which modestly approaches that of Barry, Dr. Gozar, and Mrs. Rudd. Like these characters, Jones has keen observational powers; like them, he ranges over the universe of culture for examples in his speeches. Giving a two-sided picture of Miss Perrin, Jones compares her to a character in *Anna Karenina,* a reference which seems absurd when directed at the committee members. The difference between Jones and the humanly free characters is his all-encompassing commitment to U. Lympho. Where they are questing, open, exploratory scientists, he works toward a preconceived goal which allows for no deviation or surprises. The child buyer's coldly rational, frighteningly true account of the gifted child's outcast state is effective irony for the reader, who must agree with the child buyer's appraisal of the culture, an appraisal so perceptive it leads almost to acceptance of the solution he proposes.

> . . .I hardly have to tell you that the culture in which we live is riddled with inconsistencies, from the point of view of a child with a quick mind, who sees that he is punished more than he is rewarded for his brilliance. A bitter inharmony results. . . . Our system at United Lymphomilloid is to get the brain early and eliminate this conflict altogether. (34)

One other solution for the misfit genius is conformity. Hersey gives an example of this in Barry's mother, who succumbs to ordinary but voracious reading habits, stifles her potential, lives through Barry and finally betrays him when he no longer perceives her as his idol. Her misfit status will disappear when she can plunge into artificial "culture." Mrs. Rudd is not an alternative any reader would wish for Barry.

Once the third path, joyous individual humanism, is shown to have its trap of proud isolation when Dr. Gozar is tricked into capitulation, the reader is again brought to the ironic point of agreeing that the child buyer's proposal is all that is left to Barry. Indeed, Hersey constructs the work skillfully to let us continue seeing Barry as the authority. After losing parents, teachers and government, Barry's wise childhood has no guide but his own love for learning and experience. His agreement with Jones that "a life dedicated to U. Lympho would at least be *interesting*" (256) is one of the brilliant "consistent inconsistencies" of the work. That Barry remains a child although he is our leader in the work, that he is the victim of an enormously foolish and terribly real social order is a final twist reminiscent of the child's soliloquy at the end of *Hiroshima.*

The ironic structuring of *The Child Buyer,* with its movement through potential-killing conformity to the final science of death, the loss of individual experience and imagination, is really quite effective for Hersey's purpose. There is no survival without love and community; a life without these is doomed on individual and group levels. As a successful ironic satire of the documentary mode, *The Child Buyer* stands as a valuable humanistic protest to a tendency Hersey is not alone in fearing. Hersey's subsequent works have explored other forms of protest, warning, and possibility in the face of annihilation.

CHAPTER V

COMMUNICATION AS A MEANS TO FREEDOM

Between *The Child Buyer* in 1960 and *White Lotus* in 1965, Hersey published only one book, *Here to Stay*, in 1963. Because this work is a collection of previously published journalism, including *Hiroshima*, it might not seem of much importance in Hersey's career. There are, however, biographical and literary reasons for studying the book. Like much of Hersey's writing, *Here to Stay* is ordinary only if the writer's moral commitment and documentary inventiveness are judged unimportant. As the focus for a public action of Hersey, as a collection of his brilliant journalism, and as a source for *White Lotus, Here to Stay* is a significant volume. With *White Lotus,* it suggests that Hersey's concern with the quality of life in the twentieth century extends beyond the basic question of survival, to the individual's means of effecting and dignifying that survival through responsible acts and moral choices in a society veering toward the annihilation symbolized by its marmot drives, war loving, and child buying.

In June, 1965, Hersey took part in the White House Festival of Arts, an occasion its director Eric Goldman had conceived of as "an outgoing, warm, colorful White House salute to the Americans who were building up the museums and symphonies in the local communities, organizing reading and discussion groups, staging their own arts festivals."[1] Goldman devotes a chapter of *The Tragedy of Lyndon Johnson* to this festival, a chapter he entitles "The President and the Intellectuals." Because first Robert Lowell, and then other artists, refused to participate in the festival in order to protest against intervention in the Dominican Republic and bombing of North Viet Nam which the Johnson administration engaged in during the early spring of 1965, Hersey's choice and manner of participation dramatized the didactic message of his writing in a historically significant way.

Goldman chose authors respected as craftsmen in different genres to read from their work; besides Hersey and Saul Bellow as "novelists of contrasting types," he selected Mark Van Doren, Robert Lowell, Phyllis McGinley, Catherine Drinker Bowen, E. B. White and Edmund Wilson. White refused graciously, Wilson brusquely, but the other authors accepted at once. Lowell, however, reversed his acceptance, explaining in a letter to Johnson that he feared eventual nuclear ruin for the United States and so had to take a painful, public step. (Goldman, 427) Because academics and other intellectuals had become increasingly vocal in their criticism of Johnson's foreign policy, Lowell's action threatened to align with the administration all of the artists who took part in the festival, and to make the festival itself seem a political maneuver on Johnson's part. Some artists, including Saul Bellow, tried to separate politics from the occasion; others, including Jack Levine, followed Lowell's example.

Hersey chose to attend, but by reading from nonfiction rather than from his novels, to make his reading a protest. He told the press, " 'Like many others, I have been deeply troubled by the drift toward reliance on military solutions in our foreign policy. . . . It has been my intention to attend the festival because I felt that rather than by declining or withdrawing, I could make a stronger point by standing in the White House, I would hope in the presence of the President, and reading from a work of mine entitled *Hiroshima*'." (Goldman, 449) In addition to passages describing Miss Sosaki's pain, Hersey selected "The Big If," his brief introduction to *Hiroshima* in *Here to Stay*. This selection provides statistics about the power of new weapons "two thousand nine hundred times as powerful as the bomb that did to a city what the following pages described,"[2] and warns of a weapon large enough to "render six entire states—Idaho, Montana, Nevada, Utah, and Colorado—incapable of supporting life of any kind." (244)

Although Hersey was permitted to read these things only after Goldman persuaded Mrs. Johnson, and indirectly the President, that stopping him would amount to a crude form of censorship, Hersey extended his message by an added statement which he knew would further inflame the situation:

> I read these passages on behalf of the great number of citizens who have become alarmed in recent weeks by the sight of fire begetting fire. Let these words be a reminder. The step from one degree of violence to the next is imperceptibly taken and cannot easily be taken back. The end point of these little steps is horror and oblivion.
>
> We cannot for a moment forget the truly terminal dangers, in these times, of miscalculation, of arrogance, of accident, of reliance not on moral strength but on mere military power. Wars have a way of getting out of hand. (Hersey in Goldman, 465-466)

Hersey did not get his wish to confront President Johnson, but he did look at Mrs. Johnson occasionally as he read. No other artist who attended the festival chose to make a direct statement there, but Dwight MacDonald circulated a petition in favor of Lowell's stand. Goldman's account stresses his respect for Hersey as well as his disappointment over Lowell's politicizing the event and his anger with MacDonald's open rudeness. In assessing his pride and his sadness over the festival, Goldman regrets the President's absence from the readings. Meeting Hersey's eyes when he spoke his haunting words might have offered the kind of helpful criticism Johnson needed.

Seen in connection with his moral stand at the time of the festival, *Here to Stay* emphasizes the particular contribution Hersey has made to his times. Nothing that he has done or written conveys his concept of his role as a writer more eloquently than his lonely and painful cautioning of Johnson at the White House. His writings had made him the ideal spokesman for the liberal intellectuals. He had immortalized the concern of his fellow artists for their government's morality; unlike Lowell, and unlike such writers as Lillian Hellmann and Arthur Miller who dissented from the administration but who had not been invited to read from their works, Hersey's long public career of empathetic journalism and morally committed novels had placed him in the role of trusted prophet-preacher. His impressive work in education and in politics had, in fact, probably kept the Johnsons from withdrawing their invitation or censoring his remarks. Hersey's action at the time of the festival, differing from the "I am an artist, not a political expert" creed of Bellow and also of W. H. Auden, and differing from the alienation of Lowell and MacDonald, indicate that he has provided—like Noach—a special "leavening" effect within our culture.

Hersey's conviction that he is a leader and exhorter, that he possesses moral authority, ties together the varied reports in *Here to Stay*. Dedicated to Alfred A. Knopf, the book seems designed to give Hersey a forum, or pulpit, for his moral concerns. In the preface, Hersey states that the book is about the will to live, the synthesis of the great themes, love and death. Affirming his stubborn humanism, he writes:

> I believe that man is here to stay in spite of the appalling tools he invents to destroy himself, for it seems to me that he loves this seamy world more than he desires, as he dreads and flirts with an end to it. Moreover, he has astonishing resources for holding on to his life. . . . (vii)

In exploring such resources for holding on to life as chance, flight, a sense of community, and strength from without, Hersey insists that he is offering his readers not a narcotic, but a draught of adrenalin to put us on guard "against blunderers, tyrants, madmen, and ourselves." (vii) He admonishes the reader to "Drink deeply. . .of the adrenal wine" (viii) because the threat to existence comes from man's "capacity to act on the worst in his nature." In spite of his own exposure to disaster and violence, Hersey retains an almost clinical interest in man's drive to survival and the forms it takes. Not all the forces for survival are noble, he states, but all of them are interesting. Working from his assumption that human life has a unique and mysterious value, Hersey prefaces each article with brief remarks centering on the particular means to survival depicted —luck, altruism, courage through community.

The tone of the prefatory essays is deceptively light, pointing with some pleasure toward the inexplicable and variegated shapes that human life can take. The accounts include a tale of an old, sick and poor woman who so loved life she hand-crawled across a chasm on a rope to survive a flood; the story of P-t 109, which Hersey uses as an example of survival through a sense of community; and stories of people who survived war camps. The reader is given vivid, concrete details to emphasize shared humanity with the subjects of the articles. Old Mrs. Kelly protects herself with her winter coat; Kennedy struggles to forget tales about barricuda that attack genitals, as he swims all night through infested waters; Stirner contrives a series of ways to obtain extra bread rations.

In the preface to "Joe Is Home Now," Hersey compares his journalistic technique with the process of "cannibalizing," building one flyable airplane from the parts of many. (108) Because he has not invented the story, Hersey insists, it is not a "fictionalized" account, although, as in the case of *Hiroshima,* he has arranged its parts with a definite purpose in mind. The reader must trust the author with the use of facts. In the case of the returned veteran, Hersey wanted to show love as a mortal enemy of death, especially of "living death." (107) With concern for the subject—Hersey "dovetailed" many stories into one to protect the veterans—and concern for the reader who will now share Hersey's energy and confidence, the accounts convey the conscientious and realistic moral tone the author had assumed since, and even before, *Hiroshima.* Many reports refer to the ideas basic to Hersey's work, ideas shared with him by human beings threatened with annihilation. One Hungarian refugee, for example, muses that "a political system is nothing more, in the end, than a system of human relations. . .freedom is the sense of being treated well." (72) Hersey writes John F. Kennedy's story with an emphasis on his saving sense of duty toward his men, noting that he held on to a heavy lantern as a symbol of contact with his fellows, while he drifted in a trance during a long night in the water. Friendship and the finding of self are other survival techniques the book depicts. Leading up to, in this collection at least, the momentous *Hiroshima,* the works seem to explore the question of whether a human being can will to live toward utter uncertainty.[3]

Sanders has pointed out that *White Lotus* benefits from the fresh survival tales Hersey knew. Not only the factual relationship is important; *White Lotus* flows from the same activist, moralistic

stance which led Hersey to his White House podium, and its greatest
success lies in Hersey's skill at "cannibalizing" history to convey a
truth. In the preface to *Here to Stay,* Hersey remarked that the collection left out references to the important survival stories of "the
Royal Air Force that saved Britain from Hitler, and the struggle of
the Negro in the United States for a proper share in what is called,
sometimes without irony, 'the American Way'." (viii) The important civil rights struggle of the sixties and earlier apparently was
an issue Hersey wanted to write about in the same spirit as he offered the readers of *Here to Stay* the "bitter draught of adrenalin."

Sanders and Girgus view the novel with respect and admiration. Sanders notes with some bitterness, "If Hersey's story had
been set nowhere and had undertaken to say nothing, it would have
had a good chance for critical approval."[4] In contrast to Sanders,
the problems of character and believability do not trouble Girgus.
He argues that Hersey offers an impressive experience of doubleness
in *White Lotus,* with the reader identifying with the oppressed whites
and also with the oppressed yellows.[5] He also contends that the
book clearly depicts the conflict inherent in a slave-owning society
which has cultural roots in the Enlightenment. Girgus' discussion
can be extended to include that suicidal tendency of American culture, the denial of its true identity and accomplishments, which
Hersey dramatized in *The Marmot Drive, A Single Pebble,* and the
later books. The denial of human identity to slaves is characteristic
not of feudal societies but of "liberal" ones.[6] By tampering with
her idealistic roots, the United States had created a sick society
which had however, the built-in capacity to recover. White Lotus,
left suspended on the edge of violence, is thus an effective symbol
of stalemated communication and another haunting warning from
Hersey.

The value of this work is its didactic, labored, intricate witnessing to the cruelty, hypocrisy and self-destruction of a pseudo-
liberal racist society. Hersey only partially overcomes the problem
inherent in a "true" and "well-known" story, the becalmed sense of
expectation the reader must have. His attempts to lend story interest
include bizarre descriptions of American society at the time of
White Lotus' capture by slavers, and skillful descriptions of the

yellow world, especially the Shen home and lifestyle. For the most part, Hersey seems to depend on the reader's willingness to review black history.

The story is a compressed account of the slaves' capture, toil, emancipation, repression, and demand for civil equality. My first reading of *White Lotus* impressed me with the moral dedication and the skill at invention Hersey showed; my second reading of the work seemed an endurance test; my third, after I had completed much of this essay, offered nearly the pleasure of a first reading. These sub-jective reactions may not be valid critical data, but they do support my thesis that enjoying Hersey's work often requires a willingness to be taught and even reprimanded slightly. Experiences I have had with students tend to confirm the amount of admiration Hersey evokes in people whose moral values he expresses and challenges. One young idealist, a worker in both the McCarthy and McGovern campaigns, recommended the work as "an excellent political novel everyone should read," in a conversation outside of any classroom work. A black student, who had missed classes and refused to take part in discussions of other works such as *The Last Hurrah!* and *Darkness at Noon,* not only attended my class on the political novel during the week we discussed *White Lotus,* but also expounded with enthusiasm, earnestness, and insight about the meaning of the book. He was disappointed to learn that Hersey is white. If Hersey's only role had been to support and encourage these two people who identified with the philosophy of *White Lotus,* he probably would have counted himself a success. Not only Girgus, random students, and I have found the book worthwhile; the reviewer in *The New Statesman and Nation* actually called it "one of the most remarkable books to come out of the present vigorous phase of the American novel. . .John Hersey's most creative and rewarding novel."[7]

Externally, *White Lotus* resembles *The Wall.* It is a detailed, first-person narrative describing the history of an oppressed people and their movement toward community. Internally, the book differs from the early masterpiece because it lacks both the richness of a treasured culture and the painful but triumphant movement toward escape which lends urgency to the many pages of *The Wall.* The dramatic force of *The Wall* is not present as a decisive factor in

White Lotus. Although the enslaved whites are beginning to have a sense of "white power" which would make it possible to confront the yellows on their own terms, and which Hersey depicts in the prologue and epilogue, the body of the work is an artificially structured, capsulized ("cannibalized") account corresponding to the history of blacks in the United States.

Since the body of the work has for dramatic interest only Hersey's parallels of Chinese (yellow) culture with American and of white (slave) mentality with African, the heart of Hersey's contract with the reader is the rhetorical structure of the book. Hersey once again creates a documentary novel whose purpose is to move the reader through the careful presentation of factual matter. In a more massive and less direct way, Hersey works in a mode similar to that of John Howard Griffin in *Black Like Me.* Instead of a real experience, however, he presents an imagined one constructed clearly of real facts. The dreamlike abstraction on which the novel is based—that the captivity of one race suggests the captivity of another—is a simple idea on the surface, but one which effectively threatens the reader with sharing the fate of both oppressor and oppressed. Stott argues that the redundant and obvious become virtues in social documentaries.[8] If Hersey's long work is understood and accepted as a variation of the documentary form, it will need no apologetic dismissal as a simplistic, boring and too explicit fiction. *White Lotus,* for the readers willing to participate in it, is an impressive piece of rhetoric. Its effect is similar to Alain Resnais' "Night and Fog," a documentary film in which the viewer gets the sudden impression that he is sharing the fate of the Jews burned in the ovens of Auchswitz. The camera virtually sweeps the viewer into the death chambers. A conviction of guilt, a fear of the future, and a recognition of reality are evoked. *White Lotus* goes a step beyond this with its obvious plea for an understanding of the oppressed race in the United States, an understanding based on historical and cultural facts as well as on the kind of psychological reality offered by *Black Like Me* and "Night and Fog."

Hersey's preface to *White Lotus,* a clear indication of his didactic purpose, explains also the fluidity of time and circumstance within the novel; it is meant to be an "extended dream" of something which might have already taken place, rather than a form of prophecy.[9] The transient, surprising and shallow parade of events in a dream is a suitable metaphor of the book's unrealistic side, but it also names the experience Hersey wants us to have. We are to imagine that we have been taken from our home and forced to live as slaves in an alien culture where we will have no memory of our roots and no control of our future. As a figure in a dream, the character of White Lotus is more acceptable than as a protagonist in a novel. Things happen to Lotus, and she initiates some action, but she remains faceless, unexplained, and bland. We learn next to nothing about her through other people in the book; if Hersey intended—and there is evidence that he did—to create a form and character which imitates the absence of identity and individuality, then this narrative and this narrator are extremely successful.

Given the distinctive quality of its form as combined dream, slave narrative, and historical parallel, *White Lotus* can be discussed profitably as the story of yet another communicator and humanist. Hersey provides a certain amount of creditability when he uses a single person as the continuity figure for his story of the white (black) experience. Lotus begins and ends the narrative in solitary, non-violent protest. As the reader learns her history, he finds that the young woman has not simply hopped into the "Sleeping Bird" stance without motivation and preparation. The figure who can voice protest and lead communities rather resembles Noach, Boman, and Hersey himself. Like Noach, she has intellectual gifts which fit her for leadership; like Boman, she has learned to live with herself and to love others; like Hersey, she feels compelled to work for her beliefs.

White Lotus tells her story as she takes part in a non-violent demonstration which is a natural outgrowth of the Oriental philosophy she and her fellow whites adopted in slavery. It is significant that they have worked with existing and viable communal beliefs rather than going outside of their present language and society to get them; Hersey views human systems in terms of potential rather than in terms of fixed values. It is significant, too, that Lotus is alone in representing the whites. Her life in slavery has, in many ways, been passive and imitative. She has watched a succession of lovers—Nose, Peace, Dolphin, and Rock—engage in various forms of protest against slavery. Now, with the classical education which has been her one independent and distinguishing trait, she is eminently capable of the long vigil. At a time when she is most alone, unsupported by any kind of protective or escapist relationship (Rock is present, but remote), Lotus is most responsible and most effective. Backed by her living culture, she seems to possess the "lonely strength" of the Avereds in an effective medium.

The reader completing the prologue has two important concepts in mind. The confrontation takes place because of skin color, not because of genetic inferiority or economics; the confrontation is the outcome of and the answer to the memories which occur to White Lotus as she perches on one leg in the "Sleeping Bird" position. The likeness to Martin Luther King's methods and the correspondence to black history are of interest; the reader understands the allegory. At the same time, the idea of whites in slavery to yellows is intriguing as well as obvious, an invitation to read on.

Lotus begins her tale of being kidnapped and shipped to China from Arizona with a reference to Kathy Blaw, a woman from her strange, tribal village. (The Americans have resorted to primitive ways since losing a war to yellows.) Blaw seems to be a prophetic, troublemaking storyteller. She becomes a mother-figure for the fifteen year old girl at the outset, but she is crushed and killed by slavery. Her purpose in the story seems to be to supply the first example of protest for the young girl. She is wild-eyed and erratic, prone to telling strange stories at strategic moments. On board the slave ship, she pronounces a cathartic funeral rite for the Jewish woman who dies of, among other ailments, humiliation at having to swallow pork. Her moral, " 'All the different forms Death takes are just the one Death' " (75) serves to calm the maddened slaves, and also to give them the beginning of white "numbness," which is their answer to the horror of their lives. It is, however, the least effective of the protests slaves can make. It requires nothing from the masters in the way of dialogue, because it requires little of the slaves. It is the most primitive survival technique for them, a freezing of life until it can be lived.

Hersey's satirical gifts are evident in this work, despite its surface simplicity and obviousness. Although he depicts a society different from the readers' own, an America in a crude condition of feudal or tribal isolation, there are enough touches of reality to cut into our complacency about what happens in the work. Not the helplessness of Africans centuries ago, but the emptiness of Americans now, is the justification for depicting the whites in slavery. Hersey shows the slaves forced to abandon their clannish and divisive religious differences. In an effectively detailed passage, he shows them moving, at crisis, toward community. As well as their doctrinal differences, the slaves must forget absurd class differences. A wealthy Episcopalian, for example, had resorted to the "uncivilized" behavior of biting the ship's doctor; Hersey portrays her caught in the miserable group, and his words mock the whites' values in a way that attacks the readers, not the imaginary slaves.

> . . .Still another Californian—the soil of that state had been, for religious revival as for vegetables and fruits, far more fertile than ours in Arizona, and among the California captives there seemed to be numerous divines— called to his upraised hands all Methodists. And soon about the deck we were gathered in more than a score of clusters of worshippers. . . . Catholics, Presbyterians, Methodists, Lutherans, Jews, Northern and Southern Baptists, Episcopalians (I heard the good lady who had bitten the physician genteelly trilling: "Let the sea make a noise and all that therein is. Let the floods clap their hands. . .") Congregationalists, Mormons, Quakers, Seventh-Day Adventists, and numerous sects on the near and outer fringes. The yellows thought we were all one, merely white, but we were many. Many voices, that is; the extraordinary thing was that we were of one mind. (76)

The slaves' religious spirit leads them to yearn fiercely for a murderous storm to end their lives; this is the hope the old culture brings in the face of the new conditions. Some reviewers have felt Hersey's assumption, that the slaves must become fully integrated into the master society, harms his book. The white culture disappears; no "back to America" movements occur. This is due in part to Hersey's white liberal view of his own country; it is due also to his didactic purposes in this work. Not only is it impossible to preserve the old ways under the conditions of slavery, but it is also undesirable. The old ways were not good enough to keep the community together; the new yellow culture is also flawed, but it is viable for a huge mass of people and contains a saving idealism. The whites have no future unless they live within and help to create this society to which they have been brought by force. Human beings have much to contribute in any time and place, but no group can cancel out another; slaves no more than masters can oppress.

After numbness and its alternate, the death urge, another form of protest appears as a model for White Lotus. A youth from her village, renamed "Nose," parades his degradation as a slave. In contrast to the brave insolence he displayed on the auction block, Nose now offers the stereotype of the "bad nigger" discussed in *Native Son.* By being bad, he feels, he becomes worth less money and thus fights the slave owners. Nose has chosen a path of protest that leads to his death as a criminal, but his beheading does give a moral advantage to the slaves. The drunken and degrading community Lotus finds through her affair with Nose is actually the beginning of her self-preservation and leadership. She becomes obsessed with the memory of the "chalk circle," the game of defiance Nose originated at a tavern for whites. Girgus has pointed out that Lotus uses her sexuality as a means toward self-affirmation. Unlike Hester, she is not ashamed of her humanity, but she does stand in danger of living without the necessary "Yankee idealism" typified by the Avereds' and Boman's quest for a decent life.

Lotus senses the deficiency of Nose's form of protest. She never entirely makes it her own, just as she cannot be satisfied with numbness or suicide as effective protest. A third model, the Nat Turner-like Peace, contributes to her development without fully answering the needs of his fellow slaves. In his fanatical claim to a "vision" of bloody triumph over the yellows, Peace appears too remote to be an effective leader. The girl observes that he is "inwardly deaf," (287) possessed by his vision but not by a saving sense of community. The single-minded Peace, however, recognizes the freeing power of White Lotus' intellect. His disciples begin to teach her to read, write, and remember the fragmented white culture. Because she knows that Peace's revolution failed when he could not adapt to his real environment, White Lotus seizes the opportunity she finds under her third set of owners, to learn to read, write and remember the dominant yellow culture. Her seemingly useless and pretentious classical knowledge becomes the best form of protest she can find. Eventually, she uses it in her "Sleeping Bird" protest.

A third lover with a fourth kind of protest educates White Lotus to readiness for dialogue with the yellows. Dolphin is the antithesis of Daphne's ideal of selfless love. His violence and stubborn, vain dream of "going to the mountain"—escaping alone to live in the wild—lead to his death, just as the protests of Kathy Blaw, Nose, and Peace led to theirs. Lotus feels herself succumbing to "white numbness" after Dolphin's escape and death remove the sense of self her marriage with the defiant slave had meant, but her own form of defiance, the secret learning of reading and writing, is the catalyst for her freedom. An abolitionist contacts her; he knows her to have intelligence and courage because of her insistence upon learning. In a sharply satirical depiction of the yellows' fanaticism and guilt, Hersey speeds White Lotus through an Oriental Underground Railroad to a "freedom" which proves hollow.

The whites belong nowhere. They become citizens in name only, blamed for the war being waged among the provinces. Lotus, as usual, finds a defiant lover. This time, she and her lover—aptly named "Rock"—seem to share a number of important qualities. Both are cynical, warmly sexual, and determined to better themselves and their race. Their attempt to survive as sharecroppers is doomed by the same maddening cycle of economic deprivation which ruins their first attempt to survive as city dwellers and laborers. Lotus starts a school for white children, defying the law which decrees that whites shall learn only the rudiments of knowledge. Her work is crushed by "The Hall," a group of Oriental Klansmen.

Hersey's need to pack all of black history since the Civil War into his account of Lotus and Rock's history makes these sections of the book wearying as well as predictable. The two experience various forms of white (black) humiliation: infidelity, hunger, homelessness, near prostitution, drugs, knife fights, and vain attempts to emulate the master race. Rock and Lotus, as weighty symbols of endurance, lose some creditability, yet their turning in their desperation to Runner, the selfless leader they have dreamed of, seems plausible to one familiar with *The Autobiography of Malcolm X.*

   With the philosophy and religion of Runner, White Lotus seems to attain both individuality and community. Toward the end of her second period in an urban ghetto, she finds herself doubting her own memories of what has happened to her. Other white storytellers repeat the tale of Peace's war, removing the horror of the storm and the whites' feeling of having been abandoned by their God. The secularized myths attribute the whites' failures and bondage to their own treachery and weakness. Yellows, not God's wrath, continue to hold them captive. The confusion White Lotus feels between "art" and "truth" underscores the large task Hersey takes upon himself in this work. Although the secular accounts of history may well express his own philosophy, he creates a narrator whose experience embraces the myth-making tendencies of humanity, and who can draw on the collective ego of her people.[10] Lotus' self-doubt when the old explanations are challenged is an additional device to compress the history of a race, but it is interesting to watch her move through a series of realizations that she does not know how to be true to herself.

   While involved with a yellow man, Lotus recognizes a sweating coolie to be Rock, whom she has not seen for months. This seems to be the final push she needs to join Runner. The story of his "Sleeping Bird" protests has reached her several times, and she has watched the hidden admiration the whites feel for this new, strange method of protest. When she and Rock lead a crowd of agitated whites in non-violent protest, repudiating the violent confrontation urged by another white leader Hersey depicts as an exploiter of his race, Lotus achieves a joy she describes as dignity. The "sleeping bird" position makes the whites "peaceable, vulnerable, utterly reproachful." (669) As a huge crowd of whites breaks free from the tyranny of their selfish leaders and joins Runner, Lotus, and Rock, Lotus says that she shouts with the realization that she is free at last.

   Somewhere in these confused actions I had come to realize that
   freedom could be felt at best only for moments: that even for the

powerful, even for yellows, it was inconstant, elusive, fickle, and quickly flew on. It turned out to be an experience rather than a status. Ayah, much needed to be changed in our lives, to give us, not freedom, but mere humanity. Freedom was not to be bestowed but grasped—and only for a moment at a time. (670)

Watching Rock, with his history of quarrels and roughness, return to the "sleeping bird" posture after yellow policemen knock him down, Lotus is confirmed in her belief that the whites can attain both full humanity and freedom.

For Hersey's hero, the attainment of full humanity lies not only in the power of a community of peers, but also in that community's recognition of the qualities shared with others outside the community. The author of *Hiroshima* depicts White Lotus, who has participated in the yellow culture more fully than other whites, as the person who begins creating a new society posited on the full humanity of both whites and yellows. Knowing herself free and human, she moves beyond the passive protest of Runner and challenges the governor to a mental endurance test, then breaks the whites' rule of silence by yielding to her overwhelming desire to speak as an equal, to draw the two sides together. Her opening words, "Virtuous wisdom, gentle hand," show her able to read the arch above the parade grounds where she stands; they also add to the reproach inherent in the protest. They are, moreover, a conventional form of address for the yellows. Lotus is taking the rhetoric of one culture and both shaping it for and sharing it with another. Her ability to create a new confrontation through speech symbolizes her ability to create community through it. Although the governor refuses to answer her, she knows that she has found a means to retain both freedom and humanity.

> I look at him, wanting to engage his eyes again. Now I am really convinced that if the deeper impasse that today's look represented is ever to be broken, we must speak to each other, I to him and he to me, whites to yellows and yellows to whites, openly, in such a way that eventually nothing is held back, each having the courage to hear the most dreadful truths that the other may harbor, for the present, even from himself. I cannot blame myself for feeling that the debt of speech,

as of everything else, is very great on his side. (682-683)

As White Lotus is surrounded by police, Hersey ends his work with
the raw question, "What if someday we are the masters and they
are the underdogs?" (683) The reader is left abruptly to mull over
an inside-out Golden Rule. Like his participation in the White House
Festival of the Arts, *White Lotus* is a memorable act of moral reproach by a writer. It may seem to lack the beauty of *The Wall*
because it tells an uncomfortable truth, not about remote, inhuman
Nazis, but about ourselves.

CHAPTER VI

BEING, SEEMING AND THE AFFIRMATIVE CHOICE

In the five-year period following *White Lotus,* Hersey produced two novels and two nonfiction works which probe skillfully at contemporary issues with authority and insight. There is, however, something picaresque in Hersey's moving from the issue of race in *White Lotus* to that of student rebellion in *Too Far to Walk* (1966) and then grappling with the mysteries of nature and the human psyche in *Under the Eye of the Storm* (1967). The essential question he raises in these novels—how, and for what purpose, can man survive in the twentieth century?—then becomes the subject matter of two non-fiction works. *The Algiers Motel Incident* (1968) is part of Hersey's personal means of survival, a voluntary profession of faith in his own moral vision, a humanistic and existential leap in the dark similar to the ones he depicts John Fist and Tom Medlar taking. *Letter to the Alumni* (1970), a long essay written for the alumni of Pierson College at the end of Hersey's tenure as Master there, ranges over the three topics of youth, racism, and the nature of reality he treated in the two novels and the journalism and ends with an unabashedly melodramatic picture of the humanistic community the author insists is possible because he has not only imagined it but participated in it. These prolific years, filled with actions as much as with artistry, put a deeper stamp on Hersey's reputation as a brashly didactic moralist albeit a genuinely concerned and talented writer. The first of the novels conveys this impression as effectively as does *Letter to the Alumni.*

In some ways, *Too Far to Walk* is an outrageous book. Without any attempt to be subtle, Hersey employs the legend of Faust to explain the torment and disorientation of students in the sixties. Many reviewers objected to the obviousness and apparent carelessness of the work. No serious discussions of the book have appeared, except in Girgus' chapter on Hersey's view of education. A close examination of several reviews, however, indicates that many readers relished the humorous, realistic texture of the book and the explanation of rebellion Hersey makes. Granville Hicks, one of those who objected to the use of the fantasy although he commented "This took nerve,"[1] was intrigued with the story of John because he knew students like him. Hersey's reportorial, documentary style had impressed him. The use of the legend seemed damaging to Hicks, for with it Hersey appeared not to trust his own story of the alienated youth, feeling it needed more significance by being related to legend, fable, and symbol.

Although the use of the legend is glib and obvious, Hersey's bravado or "nerve" in using it is quite understandable, both in the context of his other work and of the book itself. In fact, the boldness of the story is part of its charm as the offering of a writer convinced of his truth-telling mission and ability, and able to hold an audience to hear his message by very skillful rhetorical means.

The use of the Faust legend, as well as a few dream sequences, stems partly from Hersey's activist sense of his role. Just as he presumed to reproach President Johnson and all of his white readers in the two previous works, now he assertively cautioned the young and reassured the old that their apparently new concerns were ancient and well-comprehended ones, rooted in the questioning of individualism of Western culture, in the debilitating aspects of Puritanism, and in the conflicting desires of human nature itself. The forceful intrusion of the Faust myth and the dream sequences have their primary source in Hersey's didacticism. Because they are related to Hersey's insistence upon art and story-telling as a means to survival-in-community, the devices continue the important pattern, born in the early journalism and exemplified in Noach, Su-ling, Daphne and White Lotus, whereby a major character draws from and gives sustenance to a rich cultural heritage. They are Hersey's way of using culture to prolong and to enrich the life of his readers, and to support the "communicator," Professor Orreman, as a figure of strength and worth in his passionate belief in humanism. Just as Orreman revels in myth, poem and legend, so Hersey—and with him, the reader—can savor the appropriateness of the Faust story and the dream visions. The form of the book—forced as it may seem otherwise—thus causes the reader to ponder the answer the book proposes. We must practice the role of "communicator" by drawing upon our culture to comprehend the present. At the same time, Hersey's documentary skills make the work a new expression of that present.

Orreman himself is an example of the empathetic, documentary approach Hersey takes to the subject of youthful rebellion in our times. His erratic grading system stresses individualism and potential, so that John cannot escape the fundamental question of personal responsibility. Orreman, a famous and challenging culture figure, contradicts modern notions of alienation and hopelessness. The attraction John feels for such teachers as "Gutwillig" (Hersey's fun with names is especially noticeable in this work) is due to the younger man's audacious search for new understandings appropriate to the times. *Too Far to Walk*, written before Hersey's stay at Pierson College, stresses that John must learn from Orreman before he can hope to emulate or surpass Gutwillig. In *Letter to the Alumni*, Hersey insists that, if budgetary matters make it necessary to trim the curriculum at Yale, the old must not be retained at the price of the new. The way to see contradiction in this is to ignore the complexity of both works, as reviewers have often done. John's salvation lies only partially within Orreman's classroom; it is more likely to come from his own free-ranging quest for knowledge and experience, a quest that can spare him from becoming a replica of his compromised father, another brilliant student of Orreman. He will make the culture his own, then re-make it, or re-understand it as Hersey asks his readers to do within the work, and as he later describes the students of Pierson College doing in their seminars and art displays. Rather than holding up John's return to the classroom as a lesson in conduct or advocating the abandonment of tradition in his essay, Hersey conveys his open, tolerant, and affirmative humanism in both books.

In addition to the powerful message and clever reportage of *Too Far to Walk*, Hersey creates a comic tone in this work which helps to unify the various elements of legend, dream, and journalism it contains. The familiar, rather trashy image of teen-agers speeding in a car which opens the book has hints of necromancy about it. Breed drives as if the wheel were a "ring of sleep;" hemlocks appear to be "running in a pack, dark gowns flying."[2] The implication that Breed causes the death of another driver adds to the sinister effect, yet points out the cynical smallness of John's reaction. The next view of John, aimless in his cluttered college room, effectively describes his style of life and state of mind, then helps to account for it by his mother's letter. Its salutation, "My darling Johnnycake," and closing, "Snuggles and Hugs," have the effect of caricature. They also help the reader to understand, even participate in, John's alienation. Hersey continues this process, using details and events to render absurd both the young protagonist and the adults. It is clear, however, that John's ridicule of parents and friends comes as a result of Breed's influence. John's emergence from his L.S.D. nightmare brings a return to the real, which seems anything but absurd or devalued:

> He shaved, and took an endless shower in steaming jets of water, and put on laundered linens, and then he went to Emil's and gorged: a tall juice, squeezed as he watched, and two eggs scrambled, and grainy Canadian bacon, and sweet rolls studded with currants, and four cups of Emil's coffee. . . . (238)

Breed, at the end, is left to do the laughing. For John and the reader, there are the small, serious comforts of an honest conversation and the complexity of the poetry Orreman quotes. Very briefly— perhaps too briefly—Hersey displays the difference between two states of mind.

Although John's needed recovery (the rape of his mother by the devil in his final hallucination is the ultimate horror, yet a comical put-down for John's stuffy Puritanism) comes late and briefly, the moral is clear. In addition to John's disappointment in the "breakthroughs" promised by Breed and his return to home and classroom, Hersey's use of the Faust legend makes Breed a stable villain, a character who remains evil after John's hallucinations end and his cynicism abates.

Breed is a good example of the mental attitude Hersey sees as a danger to his age. The naivete and missionary innocence critics cite in Hersey's work, which are actually intrinsic to his role of prophet-preacher, clash directly with the kind of negativism depicted first in Marrow and now in Breed, the very "devil" himself. He is master of the perpetual sneer, a sophisticated underminer of affirmation who had "hooted at the Mississippi volunteers." (15) Breed's offerings of sex and drugs as "breakthroughs" in sense experience are less interesting than John's final adventure before using L.S.D., the night he robs a poor black woman of "everything that mattered to her"—pictures, a sewing machine, a diaphragm, her savings, her Social Security card. To Hersey, the ultimate crime is the destruction of an individual's dignity, pride, and freedom, and it is the nattural outgrowth of the attitude which refuses the affirmation his novels endorse.

Hersey, of course, does not see himself as a simplisitc defender of a dead world view, "on the side of the angels," as Fiedler puts it.[3] John's release from Breed's power is characterized by self-determination and a return to the dullness of ordinary events; reviewers disliked this ending to the story, contrasting it to the wild frenzy of Marlowe's Faustus at the end of the play, but Hersey is too much a man of his own times to suggest passionate extremes of heaven and hell, good and evil. The open quest he advocates in all of his work is closer to negativism than it is to positivism, yet it clutches at the search itself as the meaning of life. Hersey has described his philosophy, in an unpublished speech, as "lively skepticism" rather than the stance of Marrow and Breed, scoffing.

Speaking at the 1963 graduation of his son Baird from the eighth grade at Browning School in New York, Hersey advised the young people to be skeptical of facts and aware of the illusion that can exist even in such apparently objective records as photographs; he used the example of pictures in a news magazine purposely arranged by photographers to show Darien, Connecticut teen-agers drinking outside a tavern. He defined the skeptic as " 'one who seeks and never finds,' " a humanist who rejects dogmatic arrogance. Such a skeptic, beneath flashy feathers, had "the awkward skin and bones of an idealist," and avoids the numbing withdrawal of the scoffer. "The true skeptic wants to stand aside and criticize life; he also wants to plunge into life to make his criticism effective."[4]   Hersey notes that each new discovery or breakthrough reveals another barrier; wise human beings must be seekers, inquirers, doubters.   In order to avoid the extremes of the scoffer, the skeptical humanist needs patience, modesty, reticence and "When the drift of society is toward pessimism, this balance requires memory, for memory is the power to gather roses in winter."   Hersey's measured prose, full of contrasts and examples, is a simple but effective description of a simple, yet carefully balanced, course of survival.   The comic tone of John Fist's search is Hersey's own skepticism, questioning the young while believing in them, dramatizing with the Faust myth, the dream sequences, and the Hawthorneian orgy the illusion which veils reality and makes it acceptable, twists truth and makes it ugly.

The unsolvable conflict between truth and illusion, being and seeming, dramatized in earlier works by Boman's consciousness and Pebble's mysterious death, is the chief problem of the humanist in the quest for community, for it is possible to arrange objective reality to suit one's mood, desires and fears.   What Hersey seems to propound in his works of the sixties and seventies is the consciously affirmative ordering of reality by human beings who have another choice, the consciously negative arrangement of the elements of life. This is the truly creative potential of the humanist, the work of the story-teller, the artist, the reporter and the lover, the option to read life or death into humanity's future.   "Choose life" is the lesson Hersey teaches, because he sees this as the only one worth teaching, although not the only one possible.

The danger to survival, the threat to the choice of life, is the elusive nature of reality itself, the quality Hersey calls "the b.s. factor" in *Letter to the Alumni*.   When Breed defines himself as "The Spirit of Playing It Cool," (46) he is expressing the nihilistic possibilities of the human being, the withdrawal into scoffing which is the logical danger in skepticism, the logical philosophy of twentieth century man.   The scoffer who cannot bear to stay alive will escape confrontation with mysterious reality, abandon the quest which is life, and deliberately avoid the truth, such as it is.   *Too Far to Walk* has an episodic structure which depicts John's retreat from unsatisfactory actuality through progressively more contrived re-orderings of his existence. These experiences remove the elements of chance, luck, community and the other honest, natural experiences Hersey described as survival factors in *Here to Stay*.

In Book One, John describes his longing for "breakthroughs," experiences which, ironically, include knowing truth and achieving community.

> . . .instants when everything would fall away and naked perception and feeling, truth, the pure only thing, would be right there: all the walls would come tumbling down that most of the time shut John away from other human beings, from trees, from sea water, from light, from air to breathe. . . . The ineffable would in those moments come clear. . . . Genuine feeling, openness, impulses right out in the open—until you'd share with another human being a perfect moment of really complete acceptance and understanding, with no part of the self held back, till giving and taking would become a single motionless force: a full stop of simply being. (42-43)

Although, at the end of the work, John knows that no "breakthrough" ever will afford ultimate truth and permanent community, the distortion of his quest by his contract with Breed (almost a metaphor of artificiality, which is the very thing spurned by the young) gives more pain than joy to every event. The contrived sexual encounter with Margaret affords its only pleasure through the self-righteousness of its failure; John is too much a part of his culture to relish lust.

In Book Two, John sheds the cultural community which seems to hinder him from ordering his life toward ultimate experience. After taking a prostitute "home for the week-end" to torment his parents, and rejecting Orreman's advice that it is impossible to break natural laws, he is told by the Dean to leave Sheldon for a year. Breed claims that, only now, freed of the conflict between the real and the ideal, and between life and death—in fact, floating, bored, and withdrawn into apathy, can John experience the present without care for the past or worry about the future.

The "dizzying edges" Breed offers in Book Three include the

robbery, which is John's final separation from the society in which he was raised; like the other events, it is a deliberate distortion of the act of robbery itself. The final distortion Breed supplies is L.S.D. Hersey moves from describing an exalted experience to a "bad trip," then shows John in a string of backgrounds: a hippie commune, complete with satire of hypocrisy; a battle, with his father as the slain commander; a hospital in which John is judged insane; and the midnight orgy in which his mother is "raped" (she seems willing) by the devil. The reason John gives Breed for not renewing his contract is that he "can't go on living in a world that's on a knife-edge between hallucination and objective truth;" (241) he wants the "real world, crummy as it is." (241) This "real world," however, retains the quality of imagination, the recognized "dreaming up" of experience which does not masquerade as objective truth. John defines reality as friction between human beings. The artificial removal of friction imposes stagnation and death.

When Breed points out, "Who's to say what's real?" and John replies that friction between human beings constitutes reality, Hersey is telling, not showing, the habit that gives a flatness to this work despite its real merit. *Under the Eye of the Storm*, one year later, is an effective dramatization of this dialogue, while the dialogue provides insight to the puzzling qualities of the second novel.

The friction between human beings aboard the ship *Harmony* is reality for Tom Medlar, yet it is a reality virtually impossible to comprehend because of his isolation. In Medlar, Hersey depicts the weakness of contemporary American culture more dramatically than in previous works such as *A Single Pebble, The Marmot Drive*, and *The War Lover*. Medlar, more than the engineer, Hester, or Boman, is a recognizable, acceptable, yet flawed "self" for the reader. Tom's anguish and self-consciousness clash with the outward liveliness and superficiality of Flick Hampden, whom he sees as a rival for the attention and regard of his wife, Audrey, and Flick's wife, Dottie. Hersey's use of a point of view limited to Tom confines the reader drastically; we never learn the minds of Audrey, Flick and Dot because Tom is incapable of drawing them out. This aspect of the work may prevent it from being a very fine novel, but it shapes it as an effective allegory consonant with Hersey's vision. Using the third person rather than the first, Hersey controls our attitude toward Tom. We will find him a comrade, yet will deprecate him; we will learn not to trust his lonely mind. Hersey sets up this conflict between our identifying with Medlar and our belittling him early in the tale:

> Look at him! The right side of his face is creased with the impress of the cloth folds of the pillow case against which it has lain in a hard morning sleep following two waking hours in the middle of the night. The expression is pinched, chary, and cautious—of a man trying to keep track of small points at a time when the large drift of events is unthinkable. The source of his income and dismay: the slippery mass of the human liver. . . . This already famous hepatologist is here on his boat precisely to put distance between himself and diseased livers. The best way to escape thoughts of livers is to pay undeviating attention to the myriad details of his awkward vessel, *Harmony*. His wife calls him, sometimes, Dr. Meticulous. What an impeccable tool chest he keeps aboard his yawl! How tidy his log book is!. . .[5]

Medlar's effectiveness as an example of the reader's self comes from Hersey's knowledge and use of contemporary cultural analyses. In a sense, Tom and Flick represent the clash of Reisman's "inner" and "other-directed" men, yet Hersey succeeds in showing a person caught between these categories; the comfort of inner-directedness seems to be Tom's goal, yet it is his bane as well. He suffers excruciatingly from the imagined opinion of others, and needs to be a part of his own times as well as an independent spirit. Medlar seems, therefore, both a type and an individual, an interesting protagonist for the sea narrative and a representative cultural figure as well. Although no reviewer has made the analogy, Hersey seems to have offered a cultural critique and dramatization in the style of his onetime employer, Sinclair Lewis, yet marked by his own gifts and ideas.

The reviews of *Under the Eye of the Storm* are, rather surprisingly, less warm than those of *Too Far to Walk*. Most describe the book as allegorical, but none examines in depth the nature of the allegory. Edward Weeks' review in *The Atlantic* is similar to most of the favorable criticism Hersey receives; he speaks first of the writer's character, sympathy, and openness, then discusses the novel as an example of powerful, believable narrative.[6] One critic, however, notes that the work is a morality tale, "one almost lacking in the comforting clarity of a medieval morality tale."[7] Although this comment was intended negatively, it demonstrates that Hersey is working in a modern, not a medieval, philosophical framework. The reviewer, James F. Fixx, recognizes the involvement of the reader in the issues the story raises; he says that *Under the Eye of the Storm* is an impressive piece of work which haunts the imagination. The unfavorable comments complain of cardboard characters and too much symbolism, a reaction which seems to judge the didactic intent rather than the work itself. The book drew extremes in criticism of its style; Richard Sullivan, in *The Critic,* thought it reminiscent of Homer and Conrad,[8] while J. C. Pine, in *Library Journal,* thought Hersey's prose "a towering slag heap of bad English."[9]

Although the characters, and even the plot, depart from ordinary critical expectations—the storm is a kind of deus ex machina for the action—this book is among Hersey's most entertaining works. Tom, his problem, and the storm itself, are engrossing reading material, and Sullivan's comment about the style seems much closer to the truth than Pine's. Less original in form than some of Hersey's other books, the work is a compelling fiction of ideas. It dramatizes the scoffer's reaction, "What is truth?" with the special barriers our times create for the skeptic who is also a humanist. Poor, crippled Medlar is a brave figure, an Odysseus of sorts in his daring, limping return to wife and home. Faced with the knowledge that he cannot know truth, Medlar chooses one of two possible routes, the one affirming rather than the one negating his life and hopes, the one leading to the survival and self-acceptance all of Hersey's work advocates.

Basic to the novel, supporting and confirming the survival and acceptance themes, is the true keel of the tale, the existential concepts of being and seeming. The secret flaws of the ship's dry rot and the man's inner doubt make it impossible to distinguish with any absolute certainty between appearance and reality. This idea grows into the most well-developed one of the story, proceeding from incidents early in the trip to the loss of relativity on the towering seas, and allowing the hero to choose affirmation when he realizes the impossibility of, or limitations upon, final truth.

On the first morning, while Audrey and Dot sleep, Tom waits on deck to talk to the old Portuguese garbage woman. He sees her as a sturdy, enduring figure, one of the strong people of the coast-line's past. Her high, weak voice shocks him. He cannot share with her his love for the sea, his boat, and the zest of braving the elements. She is not what she seemed, not part of the sea-going tradition he associated with *Harmony* and, thus, with himself. Flick Hamden, computer expert, destroys another illusion: Tom's "aesthetic" appreciation of the air and canvas, working to move the ship through walls of water. "You talk about canvas! Lab stuff. You can't turn the clock back just by pretending it's cotton cloth." (35)

One of the most significant incidents in the development of this theme is Tom's momentary idea that Dottie, waking up, appealed with her eyes for a sexual encounter. He turns to see if Audrey and Flick are still asleep; they are, but as he looks at Dottie and nearly touches her cheek, he sees goose flesh spreading. The wind on the deck is too cold for her in her bikini. She is appealing for physical warmth, but not for his body. Later, at the height of the double storm, dealing with his fear that Audrey is having an affair with Flick, Tom acknowledges that he has had an arbitrary wish for extra-marital sex for a long time.

> It was he who had been unfaithful to Audrey, not the other way around. . . . The whole world had become one great eye-fooler, and suddenly a large number of things—opposites that had dissolved into each other, paradoxes, lies that were truths, troughs that were crests, wests that were easts—struck him as funny, and he began to laugh. . . . He threw back his head and roared at the big joke of Esme, and what it was doing to his beliefs and perceptions. . . . (185)

Tom's feeling about the difficulty of true communication with and of the self is underscored by Flick's constant orations on electronic communication. The more insistently the other man raves about mechanical possibilities, the more do events—the arrival of the storm, Esme, contrary to weather reports, and the mysterious collusion Tom senses among Audrey, Flick and Dottie—confirm him in his isolation and unprotected struggle. The double strength of the storm becomes the only reality, and he thinks he may sense whatever truth he can know under the enforced calm and brightness of the eye of the storm.

When the ship reaches the dead center of the storm, the human beings interact according to pre-storm patterns. Audrey forces Flick out of his silent trance and goes below to get the slicker Tom had bought for him but the blowhard had refused to wear. Dottie, too, ministers to "the lump" and belatedly offers coffee to the skipper at the wheel. Then Dottie looks below, gives Tom a frightened look, and enters the cabin very quickly. After he forces Flick to take the wheel, he looks down the companionway.

> Dottie was killing Audrey. . . . He had a glimpse of blood lapped by water on Audrey's styrofoam-white face. . . . Dottie was bending over her, hitting or clawing, partially blocking Tom's view of her. . . . Gentle Dottie, helpless Dottie—she was taking her dark, dark revenge on Audrey: murdering her. (204)

Tom goes below, but there the thrumming sound he had barely heard up on deck overpowers him. The action of trying to push Dottie away from Audrey trips open the memory which he had felt blocked out by the dead calm of the storm's eye. He had forgotten to tighten the keel bolt before the storm, forgotten to check Harmony's possibly fatal flaw. He wades across the cabin and desperately jams the wrench under the floorboards so that the keel bolt would have to tear the ship apart before moving further. He cannot tell if the bolt has slipped or even if it responds to his wrench. The sunlight of the storm's eye floods his panic:

> He had got everything all wrong! All that about the loosening of the nut had been a seeming; there were two human beings in a death lock back there in the cabin. . . . "Jesu, let her go down! Let her sink!" (209)

Unable to tell the real from the unreal any longer, Tom does not know whether he has shouted or not. On the way back to the wheel, he wonders why Dottie has left Audrey propped up on a settee, and the thought flickers that Dottie had not been trying to kill her at all. Once he has this realization—not of the truth, but of his own inability to perceive, the eyes of Esme and of the inner storm have passed.

Hersey does not narrate the second half of the storm. The characters discuss it when they have passed through. Then, still aware that what he has seen is not a certainty, Tom realizes that Audrey, Flick and Dottie are recounting a very different trip from the one he remembers. Flick is emerging as the hero; Tom recalls only that Audrey and Dottie pumped until they were exhausted, then forced Hamden to take over. He had seemed, Tom thinks, to pump wildly, without knowledge of what he did, still in the same shocked trance he had had during the first half of the storm. Yet he had pumped them through the second half of the storm, when *Harmony* was filling much too fast. Then Audrey and Dottie warmly tell of Dottie's having pulled Audrey out of the water in the cabin after the fall in which she injured her shoulder. Tom is asked what he was doing below—why hadn't he helped Dottie? Before he can attempt an answer, he goes below again—and there, yes, is the wrench, still straining the floorboards. It is a sign of negligence, a nearly fatal mistake of carelessness, which had almost canceled out the foresight and wisdom of his other actions. He cannot, in the face of it, insist on his own truth, on infallibility. He cannot even judge who is making a distortion and who is not.

> . . .could there be a no-man's land somewhere between what he thought he had seen and others' "truths"?. . .
> Was one doomed to see all of life in one's own way, only to have to adjust his vision after each livelong day according to the likewise distorted visions of others? (240)

There is no way to know how far he had lost his head. He longs for certitude, but receives instead "a thought that had struck him like a hearty clap on the back, of congratulations." (240) As he had misread and misjudged other signs, he may—of course—have misread and misjudged Audrey's feelings for Flick. With the replacement of the wrench in its locker and the rearrangement of the floorboards, Tom makes a pact with himself, decides to keep his sorrows private. No one would know the ship's flaw; she appeared sound, and would pass for that. No one would know of his inner storm, either, for that is becoming as much a confused, unreliable memory as the other events of the storm. He aches to be different, free of the agony of his uncertainty, but the clear skies and returning world suggest only "perhaps."

The ending tersely relates what good conversation *Harmony* and the storm made at dinner parties, and how people told Tom he was lucky to have a wife like Audrey. The reader has shared Tom's distorted, anguished view; Tom has been proven wrong about many things, but right about the flaw in *Harmony*. The question of Flick and Audrey is not settled directly. The reader must take the same answer Tom has to take, for there is no other evidence. "We cannot know; we must go on, must build, must try," is the Hersey-existential response to despair and annihilation. One of Tom's reveries during the storm had concerned his hero, Camus, and it is as Camus' Sisyphus that Hersey creates Tom and ironically admires him. His intense love for details, with his attempt to order his life through them and thus escape futility, is his labor and his joy.

> This universe henceforth without a master seems to him neither sterile nor futile. Each mineral flake of that night-filled mountain, in itself forms a world. The struggle itself toward the heights is enough to fill a man's heart. One must imagine Sisypus happy.[10]

To assume that Tom learns nothing from the ordeal would be to give a bitter interpretation to the entire novel. It would be completely alien to Hersey to write about the storm simply to express futility. The work itself demands another reaction. We distrust Medlar enough, and are sufficiently glad to see him distrust himself, to accept with relief the choice he makes to continue his life. The problem of the ending is its apparent artificiality, its seeming falseness, yet what is Medlar to do? What seems false may be true, and vice versa. The reason that Tom cannot come closer to truth is, of course, his exasperating distance from the other characters. He cannot know them, despite his belief that he is a humanist. He is crucially different from Levinson who, out of the richness of his culture, can ask for others' versions of events and conceivably hope to depict reality. His situation is comparable to Boman's misreading of Daphne and Marrow, but Hersey does not permit him an awakening. He does not even have the confidence of Lotus, on the brink of arrest, that she will elicit truth from the yellows and herself. Yet Medlar can live with the version of reality he creates in subsequent years. The flaw in *Harmony* does not remove her from the sea, nor does the flaw in his nature remove Tom from life. He suffers too much from his lack of community to be a positive model for the reader, but he is a singular negative one, an example to be followed only in the interests of basic survival. His is the choice of the slave, but it is the choice to endure, and his slavery is not one from which anyone can be wholly free. His life on the ship, filled with decision and purpose, may seem admirable, but his life on land is the dull reality John Fist learns to accept and hopes, occasionally, to transform. The reader who ponders the tale may well believe that Tom's final choice is not only prudent but "true;" although we know little about his crew, we know much about the captain.

The reader's skepticism about Medlar's ability to perceive truth is an aesthetic effect similar in kind to the one Hersey brings about in *The Algiers Motel Incident* when he again presents a situation in which appearance and reality seem hopelessly blurred. Hersey maintains that a true difference in nature separates journalism from fiction; journalism must contain nothing imaginary, even when it uses novelistic techniques.[11] Despite the criticism he has received for presenting what was called a "biased" account of the murder of black youths by Detroit police officers during the 1967 riots, Hersey insists that everything in the account is true, "though indeed colored by sympathy." In effect, Hersey is the "Medlar" of this book; his version arranged and explained, is the one the reader is given, and this time, asked to believe. Like the fictional character, Hersey moves beyond the knowledge of "dry rot" in himself and in society. He acknowledges his own weakness: ". . .I was deeply chagrined to discover that stereotypic thoughts lurked in corners of my own mind. . .and that some of my own fears had been tinged by the irrational in our history,"[12] but explains that his immersion in the work of black writers had helped him to gain the trust of the black community. (35) He does not claim to be objective, but admits and accepts his own bias as a necessary part of the account. "There is no such thing as objective reportage." (34) Very much in the manner of Levinson, Hersey asks for the trust of the reader; a person who does not give this trust would, we assume, have to discontinue reading or read with a mounting rage and confusion which, if Hersey's case is strong enough for him, could be resolved in an awakening.

Throughout the work the reader must rely on Hersey's point of view, with his empathetic bias for the black community based on his observations in Detroit and also upon his own sense of liberal guilt; he has accepted the premise that racial discrimination had infected American society, and all that he sees must be colored by that premise. In judging Hersey, the reader can use the evidence he presents, the urgent tone of the book and the soundness of the original premise; he can (as reviewers often do) recall Hersey's honorable life. Even for the reader who rejects the unconditional premise with which federal legislation since the fifties has repeatedly agreed, the book is decidedly moving. Hersey's role as "medler" must evoke a response; the likely one is a form of agreement.

In summarizing the proceedings against the three white officers and the black security guard arraigned on a number of charges after three young blacks were shot at the Algiers Motel, a University of Michigan Law School professor points out the ironically effective "medler" role Hersey plays in the book and in the case. Noting that the defense attorney said he won the case "thanks to John Hersey" because he succeeded in having the trials moved to all-white suburbs after Hersey's book appeared, Yale Kamisar adds that Hersey probably came closer than the ineffectual state prosecutors to proving beyond a reasonable doubt that some or all of the charges were true.[13]

When I questioned Hersey about this book during our interview, his body language was memorable. To use an old-fashioned phrase, it can be said that he "reared up." The image of a wild stallion is appropriate; his eyes flashed, his expression became stern, and his words were quick and sharp. His self-image as a moralist seemed to fill the room as he shook his head, "Everything in the account is true, though *indeed* colored by sympathy." Such sympathy and its deliberate use seems to be a matter Hersey views as natural and honorable. He trusts himself; in this instance, at least, he seems to have attained the ideal his characters pursue. Like the humanistic skeptic he described to his son's class, like the involved communicators of his novels, the essence of life for him is to share his version of reality with others. The sharing is essential for other lives as well.

> The assassination of Martin Luther King, Jr. which occurred during my writing of this book, demonstrated that white racists had learned nothing from that great preacher of nonviolence and less than nothing, even from the instructive violence in the summers in the cities; and it gave me, along with a sense of despair, a sense of great urgency about the completion of this book. I am not so foolish as to believe that my telling of these events will change the course of history, or even of justice in this narrow instance; but I do believe that every scrap of understanding, every door-crack glimmer of illumination, every thread that may lead not just to survival of the races but to health—all should be shared as soon as possible. (35)

The version of reality Hersey offers includes the assumption, here more than elsewhere in his work, that he is an authority because of the kind of life he has led (and must lead) as a writer. As in the case of *Hiroshima,* Hersey accepted no money for this story. (35) His writing it is a response to his own conscience, a conscience which seems to impel him to be a voice in the wilderness, to judge and to warn. He had declined to work on the President's Commission of Civil Disorders, because he did not want to participate in a report which he could not be certain would reflect his own convictions. (31) When the document appeared, it was "remarkable for its frankness;" to this judgment, Hersey adds that Lyndon Johnson's behavior "was not only disgusting; it was positively inflammatory. . . ." (36) Although he commends the report, Hersey conveys his personal conviction that sex is at the core of racism, an issue left out of the report. His book deals with this issue as well as with the thesis that unequal justice exists for the black community. He exhorts his readers to view the people caught up in the case as nearly tragic figures who cannot fail to evoke pity and terror in their minds. (37)

In universalizing the event as an artist acting according to his deepest convictions, Hersey seems to have sacrificed the possible outcome of the case in order to use the time for the larger purpose of changing the system which is at fault. As a working journalist, he was aware of the issue of pre-trial publicity; his book calls for emotional reaction as the catalyst for reform. Even before the work was published, according to Hersey's account, the police and the courts did their best to spare the accused. In the aftermath of the Nixon scandals, especially of the trial in Washington of Mitchell, Haldeman, and Erlichman, the change of venue in the Detroit case seems less a result of Hersey's urgent book than of a system eager to spare its own. To ask why Hersey published his account at once is to ask the role of intelligence in a free society. For Hersey, power belongs to the individual, and he uses his own considerable power to summon into action the dormant powers of his readers. A story of human beings which would otherwise have been lost to all but historians is, in his book, accessible and unforgettable.

Long before he wrote *The Algiers Motel Incident,* Hersey had spoken of the "hooks and snares" which lie in wait for the reader in every piece of prose, and which are the proper province of critics.[14] No work of his seems more strewn with devices of persuasion than this; its structure seems to be nothing more than a dramatic plea for belief and rage, embellished with small dramatic tableaux, objective evidence with affective captions, and frequent comments from the committed writer. The chief skills of social documentary, the contracting to reprimand and to reveal, are used with remarkable obviousness and confidence. Hersey's selection of material, as well as the material itself, seems to create a drama of opposites in the style of *The Glass Menagerie;* his authority and sympathy endow the black English of the young men's friends with a richness of life the self-incriminating statements of the police lack, especially as they are sprinkled with his comments and captions.

The theatrical tone of the work is reflected in its first chapter, which Hersey entitles "Do You Hate the Police?" The reader enters the horror of the Algiers Motel at once, watching the surviving youths leave under threats from the police officers: " 'Start walking in the direction you're going with your hands above your heads. If you look back, we'll kill you, because we'll be following you all the way home'." (7-8) Hersey depicts the families of the dead young men as they receive the news from the survivors. (The police never notified them officially of the deaths.) The families' accounts establish all but hardened readers' sympathies; Carl Cooper and Fred Temple are described by their mothers, and Auburey Pollard's father relates his impressions of his dead son. In the second chapter, Hersey discusses his reasons for writing the book and his sense that he is only beginning to understand the racial situation. Armed with the two means of persuasion—the evidence he arranges and his reader's knowledge of his good will—he proceeds into a kaleidoscope of testimony and interviews, the most startling of which is the statement of Carl's mother that he had been castrated. (56) No doctor had stated this directly, but Carl had received " 'a number of punctate wounds in this abraded area'." (56)

The second section of the book is an interesting contrast to the first. Hersey is very subtle here; he allows the three officers to speak for themselves, interspersing their monologues about the riots and their attitudes toward police work with vignettes from the black youths' families. He places first the account of David Senak, the policeman he believes capable of the sadistic killings. Senak's long monologue describes his hatred of prostitutes and pimps, an arrest he made while drunk, and his ironically suitable insight that police are " 'propagandized by their surroundings' " to be racists. (102) Hersey labels a section describing Senak's shooting of a looter as "Senak's First Killing." (114) He elicits from Senak the story of another officer's death during the riot, and the admission that after this "everything just went loose." (155) Hersey's interviewing skills met a formidable test; he apparently had the easy confidence of the white officers, and the difficult trust of the black families. The long sections in which the policeman speak alone make it clear that Hersey's idea about what happened is not based solely on the rage of the black community. Senak, for example, seems to characterize himself with his words as the "snake" he is nicknamed by his family.

In Part IV, Hersey announces that he wants to convey the life of a young black man in a city; he sees Auburey as "in the middle," between Carl Cooper, who had a police record, and Fred Temple, who had none. He also seemed midway between his older brother, in the Marines, and his younger brother, in prison. The accounts of

Auburey's family and friends, which include excerpts from the two brothers, is lively, emotional testimony to the problem Hersey says all black youths meet, the fork in the road between a form of accommodation to the system and open alienation from which only Malcolm X seems to have found a return. (168)

Part IV is brief and succinct, "Confession." After denying that he shot anyone, Patrolman August rescinds his statement and admits to one killing during a struggle for a gun; Paille also confesses to one killing; Senak is silent.

Part V, following a loose pattern of narrative, recollection and synopsis, depicts "the Algiers Motel Incident" as a tragic, confused, brutal racist nightmare. Hersey defends the recalcitrant black youths who are difficult, frightened witnesses for the prosecution; he eventually got one of the youths to admit firing a starter pistol in the motel, which may have been the "sniper fire" the police responded to. (An F.B.I. witness, a black woman, later testified that some firing took place, an important factor in acquitting the police.) The presentation is replete with Hersey's opinions; for example, he calls the brief visit and retreat of the state troopers to the Algiers "the most inglorious" chapter of the narrative. The black youths— four or five of them—give an account of brutal beatings which change to sadistic killing games once the white prostitutes become their targets also. Instead of accusing the youths of being snipers, the police call them pimps, and tear off the girls' clothing. At least two of the killings, according to the witnesses, were performed at Senak's instructions.

Part VI, "Aftermath," includes the feelings of blacks and whites involved, and the court proceedings. Hersey selects a few incidents which show that even the prosecutor seemed halfhearted; for example, he states of the policemen, "If they kept quiet, they wouldn't be here today," effectively winning sympathy for them. This last part is floating and open-ended; the white officers seem to adjust to new ways of earning a living—though Senak becomes involved in knifing a prostitute, evidently on a voluntary citizen patrol. The black community organizes a People's Tribunal, and the Pollard family disintegrates, displaying one of Hersey's reasons for depicting

Auburey's life in detail. The book ends with Hersey's account of postponement at the death of Robert Kennedy, a postponement he is not certain will end in justice. Like *White Lotus,* this book ends with an "inflammatory" query; "What is wrong?" (397)

Two brief essays from the late sixties reflect Hersey's confidence that the writer can and must propose answers to such questions, and explain his audacity in publishing his open, candid and zealous exhortations to the Yale alumni as a book relevant to the concerns of a wide public. The warm, vulnerable tone of *Letter to the Alumni* seems less an attribute of a naive, unthinking sermonizer and more a specific artistic and moral medium when we examine the definitions of the writer's role and process which Hersey formulated shortly before he published this work. In an essay for *Yale Daily News,* Jan. 18, 1967, "The One Without Whom. . . ," Hersey speaks of writing in terms of quest, search and mission.

> The quest for a superb sentence is a groping for honesty, a search for the innermost self, a self-discipline, a generous giving out of one's most intimate rhythms and meanings. . . . The underlying and sustaining impulse is. . .to *tell* someone something—to offer, almost as to someone to whom a letter is being written, a set of *appeals* to the sense, of pictures and sounds and smells and tastes and palpable tactile feelings, and another set of *appeals* to the mind, subtle and keen, and finally, binding the rest together, a set of *appeals,* unsentimental yet compelling, to the emotions. He must want to pierce reality with his personal vision and tell someone else what he has seen.[15]

The writer's credentials as a moralist seem intrinsic to Hersey's view of art as questioning, seeing, and telling. Speaking at the dedication of John Hersey High School in 1968, he asserted his intention to "go on writing about controversial matters because I believe that somewhere in the body of controversy must lie the heart of truth. . . ."[16] His belief that he can perceive that truth, or at least a life-affirming version of it, was evident in the text of the speech, a defense of the student protest movement. His audience gasped when he referred to Spiro Agnew as a "third-rate man;" on the whole, Hersey's vivid speech was unsettling and provocative for his adult and conservative audience but inspiring to the young people and liberals present. His entire visit to the school, in fact, had the aura of a visitation from "on high" of a being endowed with special powers to interpret and explain who nevertheless seemed accessible and utterly sincere. As an extension of his own presence and a rather daring act of trust in his audience, *Letter to the Alumni* records, in its epistolary form and its earnest content, both the good will and the effectiveness of this writer.

Early in the book, Hersey establishes his purpose in writing it. He is leaving Yale, and wishes to express his own version of the events which include Kingman Brewster's statement on the Panther trials, the Mayday demonstrations of 1970, and Hersey's experiences with the students of Pierson College. Using techniques similar to those of *The Algiers Motel Incident,* Hersey dramatizes, reproaches, and finally prophesizes. His stand that the protest of the young can result either in a "survival that is worth it" or in "American repression" is the consistent theme of the essays.[17] Published in the same year as Reich's *The Greening of America*, a work which also grew from events at Yale, *Letter* is simpler and less hopeful than the best-seller, an attempt to persuade by personal contact rather than by extended analysis. Like *Here to Stay,* it is a podium for an authority figure who depicts himself as a peer. Its greatest value lies precisely in its character as Hersey's own, private commentary and witnessing made public; it rests on the sum of his work and reputation which he stakes on it. The trust which he preaches as the means to community and to individual responsibility and freedom is indispensable to the book; without it, Hersey could not say nor could a reader believe the things he urges. His description of the community based on trust, which he felt he had nearly attained at Pierson, is of "a place where the light-show of shifting clusters of identities could have full play; a setting where people could be themselves; an open place where communication would be free enough so that the many small circles would be aware—and respectful—of each other's existence." (87)

The repressive tendency of American society, with its alienated blacks and unenlightened Nixonian policies, and the trusting, yet skeptical search of the young and the visionary became the materials for two powerful works of fiction, *The Conspiracy* and *My*

Petition for More Space, which focus on the role of the writer as the creator of community and witness for both the rights and the responsibility of the individual. Having exercised his prerogative and ability, as a writer, to interpret a world whose character cannot be discerned without the support of a humanistic community and the exercise of affirmative choice, Hersey depicts the dilemma of the writer as the dilemma of twentieth century human life. His recent novel, *The Walnut Door* (1977), uses the dilemma of the young to compel the reader's active interpretation of a world in which the creative powers of an artist may be the only security—or an unknown danger.

CHAPTER VII

FROM DESIRE TO POTENCY:
THE WRITER'S REPUTATION

Two of Hersey's most recent novels, *The Conspiracy* (1972) and *My Petition for More Space* (1974), focus on writers whose concern with the quality of life constitutes the most sane and humanistic element of their times. The sensitive, yet corrupted, vision of Lucan and Seneca comes from the problem Hersey outlined in the writing of *The Algiers Motel Incident*. The Roman poet and the philosopher are caught in the web of being and seeming, dependent on Nero and their fellow citizens, and shaped by a community with defects as well as ideals; like Hersey's white liberal guilt, their Roman preoccupation with power is both the source of and the obstacle to creativity. Sam Poynter, in *My Petition for More Space,* is a clever dramatization of a creative human being reacting to and being shaped by a terrifyingly over-crowded world, yet managing a life of the imagination and a thirst for experience reminiscent of the questing Berson and the humbled Boman. The artisan of *The Walnut Door* possesses the power to stop time and call up love as he chooses. Like the war novels and racial books, these fictions deal with subjects of contemporary concern; they seem more pessimistic than previous works, yet in a sense they are less so. For citizens of the "Rome" and "New Haven" Hersey paints, the consciousness of art is an amazing, triumphant feat, made plausible by the structuring of each work.

Girgus comments that *The Conspiracy* displays "a new depth to Hersey's uncertainty over man's ability to survive with freedom and dignity," "a growing vision of man's unwillingness even to try."[1] Hersey, however, suggests in a letter to Girgus that his essential optimism—his ability to be a "skeptic" rather than a "scoffer"—has persisted in the two later novels.

> I work in small ways for what I believe in. Silone, Malroux, Dos Passos and Steinbeck—each in his young years—put their stamps on me when I was a youth; I saw each turn away from his own youth. I don't think I've turned away from mine, though perhaps I'm more abrasive now, not quite so gentle and—because the world has grown so crowded—not quite so hopeful as I once was. But I haven't quite given up on man. Crowding does make him wild, but it also makes him more canny, more ingenious.[2]

The pessimism Girgus notes in *The Conspiracy* is, as he states, evident in the deaths of Seneca and Lucan and in the existential failure of Lucan as a human being. The failure of the poet to transcend the decaying society seems less important, however, than the questioning, goading role he plays in it, a role which Sam Poynter in *My Petition for More Space* seems to inherit. Considering the constant emphasis Hersey has placed on the work of the artist as interpreter, recorder, preservor and dignifier of life, it is not surprising that he has used the theme as the central issue of three fictional works since his experience at Yale and in Detroit. Girgus discusses Lucan's question, "What is the responsibility of the writer?" somewhat as a side issue to the political and philosophical ideas in *The Conspiracy*, suggesting that Hersey may have been working through his own artistic problems in depicting Lucan's. He maintains that Hersey's artistry has been handicapped by his didactic concerns, as in the overly symbolic Epicharis whose words "sometimes sound like editorials in a liberal daily."[3] Hersey's tendency to moralize is not an unfortunate, unconscious failing on his part however, but a deliberate conviction and a highly developed skill traceable in every one of his works and most often tied to the role of the artist-communicator (Levinson, Daphne, Lynch, Lotus, Su-Ling, Hersey himself) as the catalyst of human survival in dignity and freedom. Thus, the role of the artist as discussed in *The Conspiracy* is central, not peripheral, and its relation to "message" in that book is not an occasion of fumbling by an overzealous fiction writer, but the conscious device of an effective craftsman.

The experience of Lillian Hellman and others during the McCarthy era (*The Conspiracy* is dedicated to Hellman) and of Hersey himself first as a young journalist whom Whittaker Chambers accused of being slanted in favor of Communist China, and then as an intellectual critic of the Johnson administration, make one suspect at once that Hersey is as much the "novelist of contemporary history" in this work as in others, despite its representing a clear departure in time and setting for this author. He has hinted at the nature of the book by commenting, in the letter cited above, that his new novel *"seems"* to be about a plot against the Emperor Nero. The appearance of the book in 1972, at the beginning of the Nixon scandals, was appropriate then and seems amazing now; it is a new testimony to Hersey's unfailing reportage and attempted guidance of his age.

Unlike Norman Mailer, whose message and intent are similar, Hersey chose once again in this work to employ a familiar literary form, depending for originality on his shaping of that form and the intensity of his message. In so doing he seems to catch his audience by surprise. The Book-of-the-Month Club stressed the suspenseful and historical aspects of the work in selecting it; it remained for readers to discover the sharply contemporary overtones of the book. In a true sense, the novel is a tantalizing product of Hersey's imagination, reinforcing Hersey's peculiar prophetic position in our literature.

Much as he did in writing *The Wall*, Hersey used his essentially journalistic techniques to design a fictional work. Rearranging historical materials in ways similar to his use of diaries and transcriptions from the Warsaw ghetto, he created a protagonist, Tigellinus, whose voice is the embodiment of suspicion and manipulation. Blind and paranoiac, Nero's adjunct is nonetheless spirited and clever as he sets out to discover and destroy "the conspiracy" of writers and poets. Ironically, the atmosphere of Nero's court receives the blame for causing the plot; artists respond to society rather than control it. This pronouncement by Lucan before his death expresses the paradox Hersey has depicted throughout his career. The power and position of the writer are not his by birth or divine right, but are passed to him by the community. A flawed community limits art, yet the mind open to beauty and truth can find it both at home and in neighboring cultures. Hersey's view of creativity, especially that of the writer, relies heavily on the notion that the gifted individual can and must both depend upon and lead the humanistic milieu which has shaped him. In figures like Levinson, the engineer, Boman, and Lotus, we see the qualified triumph of the cultured, creative artist who has communal support; in characters like Hester, Barry, Lucan, Seneca, and Sam Poynter we have similar creativity and aspiration, yet for varying reasons the supportive humanism has eroded. The insight and daring of these figures, like the courage of Medlar and John Fist, do more to define Hersey as an optimist than the overtly affirmative books. This persistent potential of art to mirror and yet grace the world is linked to Hersey's own life as a writer of didactic works. He preaches, ultimately, a lesson of self-trust to the reader; these minds, my mind, your mind, can discriminate, can act, can make human choices still. Although the worlds of the most recent novels are both terrifying and real, Lucan's and Poynter's insights are the true central concepts, entertaining and at the same time elevating, suggesting openness and possibility rather than the self-defeating vision of anguished characters in other contemporary works. *The Walnut Door* forces the reader to confront dual possibilities and to accept responsibility for the outcome.

The very fact of Hersey's persistent affirmation through his fiction and his nonfiction is the "real" behind the "ideal" his works envision. He and his characters seem to invite the reader to "go thou and do likewise." The plausibility of works such as *The Conspiracy* comes from Hersey's adroitness as a writer and also from his involvements with his community. The epistolary form of the novel is a good example of his journalistic, literary, and political interests giving appropriate shape to his material as an expression of his belief in individual and group power. Some reviewers found the constant letter-writing difficult to believe in; would high officials or conspirators commit such secret matters to a permanent form? The question is now enough to evoke painful smiles or jokes about tapes and tape recorders. For some years, Hersey has been concerned with the issue of secrecy in government and the infringing of basic civil rights by government agencies, matters which have recently been under serious public scrutiny. He has worked with Lillian Hellman, Jerome Wisener, Telford Taylor, Robert Silvers, and others, on the Executive Council of the Committee for Public

Justice. Its conference on the FBI, in cooperation with Princeton University's Woodrow Wilson School in 1971, is described in *Investigating the FBI*, edited by Pat Watters and Stephen Gillers, Doubleday, 1973. Currently he is a member of the Advisory Board of the Committee Against Government Secrecy, investigating Watergate and its sources over the last two decades. Although he characterizes his group involvements as "peripheral" to his life as a writer, they seem to be essential to his concept of art.

The choice of the epistolary form has literary advantages as well as political appropriateness. Seneca and Lucan employ the formal rhetoric appropriate to their characterization and role as writers, without seeming to force an occasion for it. Since Epicharis is clearly another Daphne, a free person who lives the ideal of individualism-in-community, her open advice-giving in the letters seems even more plausible than it might in a different narrative framework. Rather than disguising his ideas through dramatization—as he does rather effectively in *My Petition for More Space*—Hersey chooses in this work to keep them close to the surface. Discussion of ideas in writing is a logical exercise for Seneca and his contemporaries, and something Hersey himself has undertaken often. As Hersey uses the letter-writing device, it is a concise form of characterization appropriate to the atmosphere of a police state. Perhaps it is significant of Hersey's clever character development that reviewers cite Tigellinus and Paenus, rather than Lucan and Seneca, as interesting personalities revealed by their letters. It is true that Tigellinus' surveillance of others is the source of suspense and wonder at his determination, but his sharp, cool control is also the background for the naive thirst for freedom embodied in Lucan.

The work opens with the correspondence of Tigellinus and Paenus, head of the secret police of Nero's court. The atmosphere of suspicion and jealousy breeds the notion of a plot among poets and writers, whom Nero disdains as "men of thought, not of action."[4] The disdaining of writers, however, is accompanied by the ironic account of Nero's wish to commandeer a reputation as a poet and the implication that his breech with his youthful friend Lucan and his tutor Seneca comes from his usurping of the artistic and moral power proper to the writer. Characters in the novel are largely defined in terms of their respect for, fear of, or longing for such power. The first informant about the alleged plot, for example, is a would-be poet who ascribes to Nero the power to control his poetic reputation. Tigellinus, who seems in awe of nothing except Nero's powers as Emperor, willing to strip temples, prostitute women, and order the death of Seneca in order to enhance and protect that power, is unlike Nero and virtually everyone else in the book; he is characterized as a "barbarian" by Lucan because he is totally outside of the literary tradition and untouched by the power of art except as a tool in his courting of Nero. He is the ultimate Philistine. Although he seems to triumph, he is totally alone; he can bestow political favors, but no Roman shares his view of the world. Paenus, his cohort, bows to the system of rewards and punishment, yet he is not so isolated from other Romans. He can, for example, write of Lucan's and Seneca's deaths with sympathy, respect and authority. Like Lucan and Seneca, he shares in the heritage of which they write, power for the sake of the common good. Tigellinus is an alien in his own country. By skillfully isolating him as a ruthless, though clever, opportunist, Hersey exemplifies the degradation of a state in which the aesthetic and moral role of art is usurped, as in Nero's case, or ignored, as in Tigellinus' case.

The triumph of Tigellinus and the death of the poets, Hersey implies, presage the fall of Rome. Without the restraint of art, the social contract becomes brute force. Lacking the ideal supplied by art, the real collapses as a truly human entity. Nero, more civilized than Tigellinus, knows this. Seneca's disapproving absence from his court is a torture to him, as is the mockery of Lucan. In killing the poets, as in killing his mother, Nero kills the Roman tradition of which he is a part. *The Conspiracy* reverses the process depicted in *The Wall*. Noach, gathering true information, created community and prolonged as well as enhanced the life of his people. Tigellinus, gathering false information, is from the start in the process of separating himself and Nero from the community. Such separation of the government from the people is both murderous and suicidal.

Spurring Tigellinus in his deadly hunt for "conspirators" is Lucan's restless questioning of Seneca: "What are the responsibilities of a writer?. . . The idea of art sometimes nauseates me when I think of what is happening in Rome in broad daylight. . . ." (26) Lucan, who dies pronouncing the "conspiracy" a delusion of Tigellinus, is actually engaging in conspiracy, according to those who have usurped the powers of art, by posing such a question. Seneca's answer to the question, "A writer is a rebel," (254) emphasizes the inevitable conflict of art with even the best political system. "If anything can save mankind from its darker side, . . .it will be the example of those who search—those few men in every setting who try to find and live by the rules of wisdom; and who write down what little they learn." (254) Becoming a true rebel would mean exile, yet exile would not answer the aesthetic problem. A writer whose society cannot tolerate his criticism becomes an outsider; his representation of the society, his power to effect recognition, will suffer accordingly. Lucan's avoidance of Seneca is related to his unwillingness to undertake exile, to see the Rome of his day as an object foreign to himself. He seems to need the courage not only to break with Nero and with present Rome, but also to assume the role of moral authority within the culture before he can continue his poetry. At his death, Lucan realizes this and seems to be freed of the weakness of the past. Paenus describes Lucan's conversion to freedom and responsibility as simultaneous with the return of his poetic inspiration. At his death, when he is free of Nero, his poem comes to life.

Lucan could not be a writer when he avoided responsibility. His inability to support Seneca for the succession seemed to stem from his belief that the power would corrupt his uncle. The novelist depicts Seneca as fallible, yet noble in his willingness to assume responsiblity in spite of the threat of corruption. It is Lucan who is corrupt in his dependency, not Seneca in his self-trust. Although it is the business of the writer to depict life, he must not avoid responsibility for the kind of life he sees.

In the narrator of *My Petition for More Space*, Hersey creates a writer who is an ironic counterpart of the involved communicators in the previous works. Sam Poynter, waiting in line to present the petition for more space which actually constitutes rebellion in a nightmare of overpopulation, is convinced that he is special. Just as Lucan identified the chief problem of his culture, the abuse of power, the writer of government reports who insists he is an artist presses the inflammatory question of his own times. In a concise representation of Hersey's concept of the writer's relation to the culture, and the culture's to the writer, Poynter seeks for space to acknowledge his gifts and foster them, and thereby to create works of art to adorn and preserve the culture. Lack of space, however, is the determining factor in the culture of waitlines and sleeping halls. The writer yearns for the impossible, schemes for it, and in the process of hoping creates a kind of art work. His stream of consciousness as he waits to be denied his petition is an entertaining, humanistic, resourceful vision of the concrete world before him and of the world known only to his memory and imagination. Poynter's thoughts are evidence that he *is* special (mainly because he believes that he is special). The over-populated world must stifle the creative urge as carefully as it forbids the procreative urge, yet Poynter's mind seems capable of endless creative associations and interpretation. Unlike Orwell's Winston Smith, who must lose his individuality, the hero of Hersey's futuristic novel remains canny and essentially optimistic. As he leaves the petition area, his request made to seem ridiculous by the unseen bureaucrat at the window, and the relationship he had tried to build with a young woman on the line apparently ended, Poynter seizes on an unbelievable hope for more time, the subject of his next petition.

There seems no doubt that the unseen authorities of the crowded world will have to deny all petitions Poynter makes. The writer's resilence seems like insanity in the face of things. This may be Hersey's entire point in the novel. On the waitline, Sam's petition for more space had nearly incited a riot. By voicing the hidden desires and fears of his compatriots, the writer may become an agent of social change. By recognizing and creating beauty, he contributes both to the nearly unbearable present and to the ameliorated future which exists only in his dreams.

Sam's contribution to the present is outwardly a social phenomenon, not an aesthetic one. In the flawed society, his books remain unwritten, unshared, unformed. In the context of the novel, we must assume that Sam will not write until he has the time and space he needs, until society is reasonably equitable and humane. Because his artistry goads him, the writer must shape the present moment into the nearest possible approximation of the ideal. As he moves on the line, Sam strives for the paradoxical necessity of individuality-in-community. From the meager materials of his crowded life, drawing upon the personal and literary heritage his parents gave him, Sam strives to imitate his father, to "make his own space." His method to attain space, which he, as a child of his era, equates with peace of mind, is to practice a "discriminating intimacy" with the people who are pressed against him and around him. His writer's sensitivity and observation work toward his spiritual survival; he notes peculiarities in others and keeps mentally aloof from those he rejects. He cultivates his self-image, recognizing that his faults may be the result of the intolerable crowding and oppression of his adulthood. Taking strength from the past (in the style of Levinson and Lucan), Poynter directs his attention to his own survival in dignity. He then builds community; a relationship of whispering and touching with the young woman directly ahead of him in line.

Hersey's talent for storytelling and for obvious but entertaining allegory has probably never found a better expression than the tightly symbolic image of Poynter pressing his aroused body into Maisie's. The writer responds to his environment, to the physical closeness of the woman, yet he also creates something from the environment that may exist only in his perception. In the web of being and seeming which controls even the packed waitline, he chooses to imagine a possible love relationship with the woman whose face he never sees, but who *seems* to be what he hopes for. The sexual arousal of Poynter, accompanied by daydreams of sharing life as well as lust with Maisie, is an apt image of the affirmation the writer represents. Poynter combines the physical world with the imaginary; he effects a physical change as well as an inner change as he "points" urgently into the warm human being he sees and imagines ahead of him. The fact that sexual contacts on the waitlines constitute criminal actions intensifies Sam's arousal. The sexual encounter symbolizes the many ways in which Sam proves his identity as a writer—or, as Seneca described it, a rebel.

Sam also builds community, of sorts, with the taciturn man who insists that he is a painter of both houses and pictures. This artist saves Sam's life by distracting the attention of the mob when it realizes the threat implicit in the petition Sam wants to make for the space all desire but which does not exist anywhere other than in Sam's imagination. The painter begins a song, a strange lyric reminiscent of the myths of Kathy Blaw in *White Lotus.* The pidgin rock and roll lullaby quiets people, and also restores a sense of trust in the present. Significantly, the painter does not acknowledge any reason for friendship with the writer. Community may exist only within Sam's imagination; it seems alive because the writer's imagination works to give physical life to dreams, to express outwardly the shape of human experience. Sam's situation on the waitline is outwardly hopeless; inwardly it is rich, and the inner richness reshapes the outer hopelessness. He insists to Maisie that his reports "put a good face on things;"[5] his perception of life and his drive to record it invariably spring from optimism, despite the pessimism he also possesses. For Hersey, the desire to create art is at one with the desire to live, with the desire to create a life worthy to be represented in art. Sam despises the janitor at his elbow, who will be a survivor at any cost. Creativity, the expression of one's own perception of things, is both the source and goal of a truly human life.

Just as *My Petition for More Space* utilizes in a concise and dramatic way the constant themes of Hersey's work, the need for idiosyncratic vision within human society and the relationship of the writer with the community (of art with politics), the book also employs the direct and prophetic social criticism Hersey has continued to make since he defined his role in the early books. Again acting as the oracle of the obvious, he has seized upon a familiar truism, that population growth is out of control, and made a haunting tableau of an impending catastrophe most readers are aware of but would rather not face. This work, like many of his others, reveals Hersey as a social documentarian who can construct effective, yet artistic, modern morality plays. The repressive world of New Haven, constructed within the conventions of science fiction, is a convincing nightmare. Were it not for Poynter's ability to transcend this world in his thoughts, the work probably would deserve the label "derivative" of Huxley and Orwell which was given to *The Child Buyer* by some reviewers. In a sense, the familiar science fiction world is a precise instrument for conveying the documentary message; it functions as a symbol of the data on which it is based.

As an imaginary, rather than a statistical backdrop, it reinforces the notion of the writer's power to create possible worlds by questioning problems that seem impossible to solve and dangerous to consider. The reader can draw on *1984,* just as Sam draws on his knowledge of art, music and literature, to posit a way to endure—or perhaps prevent—the world of the waitline. The individual mind exercises control; Hersey's use of myth and convention seems to send the reader off on a quest like Sam's to deny the implications of the narrative setting. The world in which people wearily plod for hours to and from their jobs, in which fraternity is a literary convention because no one ever has a sibling, is enough like the world the reader knows, in which millions die of starvation each week, to alarm; it is also enough unlike the present to constitute warning rather than realism.

My Petition for More Space had a quiet reception. It has not been the subject of angry reviews, as were many of Hersey's previous books. Instead, newspaper and magazine critics have tended to summarize the book, then refrain from comment or else praise it warmly as another entertaining and meaningful Hersey work. Susan Heath's remarks in *Saturday Review/World* are somewhat typical:

> It is a novel in which, essentially, nothing happens. Yet its mounting tension sustains the action of the novel and compels you to keep turning the pages. . . . Hersey's is a vision that belongs, dreadfully to our time; its greatest power is, simply, that it is unbearably close to being true.[6]

In addition to using material which gravely concerns contemporary readers, and reiterating his own central themes, Hersey accomplishes in *My Petition for More Space* the careful creation of a modern narrative consciousness. His earlier attempts at this, the engineer, Boman, White Lotus, and perhaps Tigellinus, are partial and usually burdened by other concerns, such as Boman's technical descriptions of flying. Sam's perception of his world is a controlled, poetic whole; unlike White Lotus, this narrator need not compress an entire history in his account. More than he has ever done, Hersey depicts here the inner workings of a human mind. One can study this text closely, and derive an Aristotelian sense of pleasure in its unity and form despite the simple, predictable plot. Sam's monologue is pithy and exact, filled with images that relate to the subject of crowding and to the theme of imagination. An example of this is the hero's reverie about the maple trees on the walled-in village green. He imagines that the leaves whisper "Forest, forest, brother leaf" in memory of the lost natural conditions. Later, his mind returns to this instant, and contemplates the fact that "For two generations there has been no such thing as a brother—or a sister." He then constructs a necessarily imaginative bond of fraternity with the janitor, whom he envisions as Cain. The fear and rivalry of a brother, however, become acceptable, natural elements which his imagination is capable of restoring to the struggling world. Many of his thoughts revert to his parents, again stirring natural human aspiration, emotion, and action. Because he is a writer (or believes that he is one) and because Hersey is behind the characterization, Sam's report of what he sees and what is happening to him is concrete, filled with sensory description, and direct.

During the entire narrative, Sam the writer endangers his life by moving forward to present his petition for more space. He contradicts the motto of the society, "Survival Is Acceptance," by reshaping, reinterpreting the world he sees. Since any human being can do this, Sam represents the means of human survival Hersey insists is the only one worth pursuing. The impact of the work comes from the fact that Sam lives in a society which has lost the ability to hear the writer's words as anything but insanity. The questioner behind the window cannot acknowledge the prerogative of the artist to examine the assumptions of his society. In Nero's world, the power of the word was known and feared. In the anti-utopia the natural order is dying, and the impending death includes the naturally rebellious mode of the writer. Hersey, in the sixties, could ask where justice for blacks was hiding; there was room to conduct a search. Poynter, in asking for more space, bares the coming end of his society; there is no more space. Rather than debating the philosophical implications of his request, the bureaucrat breaks Sam down by dealing in outward facts and statistics. In the massively crowded world, there is no spiritual space for ideas to grow. It is not possible to turn around.

In choosing a familiar, possible topic for the book which seems at once so full and so simple, in using a not-too-distant future to warn of the death of civilization at the same time that he exemplifies it in the insanely hopeful Sam, Hersey has once again uttered prophetic warning. Perhaps, in view of his early concern about nuclear weapons, his rash stand on civil justice, his fear of government secrecy—all concerns which now seem like old truths—Hersey should be listened to sharply in this book.

Hersey's other public actions and his writings of the late seventies are interesting variations on and expansions of his youthful topics and beliefs. The list of accomplishments for these years seems to offer yet again a description of Hersey as a reporter with the world for a beat, tapping out deceivingly light fiction even as he makes careful pronouncements about prominent persons and events. In 1974, Hersey visited Jerusalem twice, producing a "Reporter at Large" piece for the *New Yorker* and a thematic essay about Israeli writers' obsession with time for *Saturday Review*. The *New Yorker* article draws on conversations with the children of Holocaust survivors, conveying the impression that the survivors' descendents are not proud of their forebears' clinging to life unless they distinguished themselves as heroic resisters.[7] The literary essay emphasizes the need to capture the present, fleeting moment in the context of a long past and an uncertain future—not unlike Hersey's own attempts to image and shape the present in relationship to the past and future, something central to his work since *The Wall*. Israeli writers, according to Hersey, sense the world as process. Intrinsic to this is the realization that, while a person seems to take on a completely new identity in sequential phases of life, there are connections to be made, usually by poets, between the apparently disparate selves of youth and age. " 'All culture is memory'," says one writer, an appropriate aphorism to be quoted by chronicler Hersey.[8]

Just as one might have predicted that Hersey would be both commissioned and compelled to write about Israel as a natural outcome of his early book about the Holocaust and the Warsaw survivors, so might one have expected him to report and comment on national politics. He offered a verbal portrait of Trumanesque Gerald Ford in a *New York Times* feature, "The President," in 1975,

since reprinted in hardcover.[9]   While the Ford piece does make clear
Hersey's liberal skepticism about him, the apparent honesty of Ford,
like that attributed to Truman, draws the writer's grudging praise.
In a retrospective introduction to the joint publication of Hersey's
profiles of Truman and Ford, *Aspects of the Presidency* (New Haven:
Ticknor and Fields, 1980), Hersey qualifies his admiration of Ford
still further, stating that Ford's decency was the decency of accommodation, and asserting that Ford's weakness was "a short communal memory."[10]   By contrast, Truman's rich sense of history con-
tributed to a moral fiber "as durable as brake lining." (6) Hersey's
discussion of his assignments to interview Truman and Ford—each
over a period of several days—makes clear this conviction that his
words have the power to make history, to "get down" for posterity
the truths of two contrasting presidencies. Robert H. Dahl, the Yale
political scientist who analyzes the historical importance of the two
profiles, asserts that the pieces reveal the scope of the office to be
far beyond that intended by the framers of the Constitution and suggests that they contribute to an effort to reconsider the American
system. The profiles, Dahl believes, suggest that a conservative and
enigmatic leader like Ford can seem more effective than a dynamic
and liberal thinker like Truman, because of the contradictory expectations and limitations we assign to the presidency. (xviii)

        Hersey's willingness to take public stands on politics and
politicians—his 1970 *Letter to the Alumni* expressed horror at what
he interpreted as Ronald Reagan's stifling of free expression by his
budget cuts in the University of California system—has demonstrated
repeatedly his notion that the individual must live out a commitment to a world community. Added to his active support of Stevenson and his rebuke of Johnson is a later challenge to Jimmy Carter
which overlaps with Hersey's insistence that freedom of expression
is the most vital factor in achieving full human life. A piece called
"An Inaugural Address," narrated by Jimmy Carter's persona, appeared in the *New Republic* on December 11, 1976 after its rejection
by *Saturday Review,* the magazine which commissioned the article.
Norman Cousins has explained that "The Hersey Episode" was a sad
failure of communication (especially ironic in view of Hersey's
career); according to Cousins, *Saturday Review* offered to publish
the article in an issue on business scheduled a few months after their

traditional inaugural edition.[11]   Hersey's piece seemed too narrow and polemical; the offer to publish it included the proviso that Jack Kilpatrick would write a contrasting analysis. Hersey, however, has not retracted the anger he demonstrated to reporters who told him *Saturday Review* was not going to publish his article; his comments at the time suggest he shared the view expressed in New York papers that *Saturday Review* had "suppressed" an "anti-business piece." He called the cancellation "disgusting," the worst incident of his journalistic career, and did not allude to an offer by Cousins' editor to print the essay in another context.

"An Inaugural Address: Attention Jimmy Carter" is an outstanding example of Hersey's belief in the writer's power and obligation to set up clear imperatives. His "Carter" pledges forthrightly to free government from Big Business, stating "The essence of Nixonism was the corporate mentality." The link between war and business is embodied in a powerful statistic: three times the amount of aerial munitions were manufactured for the war in Viet Nam as for World War II. A long catalogue of the control of government by business ranges from foreign policy issues—apartheid, world hunger, SALT—to domestic—pollution, health care, nuclear wastes and privacy. Promising to return business to a position of subservience rather than management in national affairs, the imaginary inaugural does not say *how* Carter will accomplish the contemporary feat of taming the military-industrial lion.[12]

Hersey's trust in the word and in his own unequivocal use of it have resulted in his being linked as critic-advocate to three significant writers, all of whom have much in common with his own way of living and writing. The author of *The Algiers Motel Incident* and *White Lotus* is the editor of *Twentieth Century Views of Ralph Ellison;* his introduction probes with Ellison the sources of the artist's inspiration, stressing the role of early memories and impressions.[13] When Lillian Hellman received the MacDowell Prize in 1976, an honor previously awarded to Eudora Welty, Norman Mailer, Edmund Wilson, Edward Hopper and Georgia O'Keeffe, Hersey depicted his friend, neighbor and confidante as not simply the conscience of her time, but as its life force.[14] As a rebel, Hellman has practiced creative dissent, insisting that life ought to be better than social conditions decree it for most people. Hellman's earthiness, her sensuality and concreteness, seems to be the key element, for Hersey, of her affirmation of existence. A third author, John Cheever, interviewed by Hersey in 1977, asserts that his most memorable experience has been the birth of his children, even though he and interviewer Hersey agree that there is a sharp distinction between fiction and autobiography.[15] Like Hersey, Cheever has been criticized for optimism, for his "fondness for light," as he describes it.

The psychological realism, earthiness and qualified optimism which Hersey obviously admires in his three famous contemporaries seem to be among his goals in the recently published novel, *The Walnut Door* (1977).[16] This is a puzzling book. In a letter to me in 1975, Hersey expressed the hope that, with my dissertation completed, I could read his future works simply for pleasure. It is certainly true that the "spellbinder" quality of this novel offers the kind of reading pleasure Hersey was clever at giving in *A Bell for Adano* and more subtle about in *Under the Eye of the Storm.* Like *My Petition for More Space*, the text is gnarled with puns and yet credible as social commentary and psychological realism. But the novel seems deliberately constructed to force the reader to choose between two equally possible outcomes. In *The Walnut Door*, the dual possibilities are more carefully balanced than in *Under the Eye of the Storm*, the novel in which Hersey first used this device. Using the beautifully constructed walnut door as a central image, Hersey seems to take real delight in the *craft* of his hero and his tale; reality and possibility lie within the reader's perception and choices as well as in the powerful hands of the artist-craftsman. On the one hand, the work is more polished than Hersey's previous being/seeming allegories; on the other, it has a roughness and cruelty about it which stem not from the sexual descriptions but rather from the cynical point of view. Carefully, even masterfully, the narrative makes clear that no outside agent will supply interpretation or resolution. The reader is alone, to take or to leave the clues for a "happy" ending— the "happiness" of which may be transitory but may also be permanent, like the solid door which promises and then both does and does not provide physical security to the female character.

The reader of *The Walnut Door* finds a sharp, vibrant tone

throughout which seems to convey both pleasure and pain simultaneously. "Contemporary history via sexual metaphor" might describe the book; but such a caption would not make clear that in this novel Hersey seems both to have more fun and to be more critical than in his other tales. An example which is particularly startling is the contraption worn by Mary Calovotto, a secondary character—a scarf with rollers attached, so that people will think she's fixing her hair. This image of a plastic culture seems especially effective. Through many such cynical images, the reader derives pleasure from the tale, pain from its truths—simultaneously. While this may be characteristic of all literature, it has not been the kind of statement Hersey's work has usually evoked from critics. (Reviewers were divided: one called it his best, others described it as pornographic, melodramatic.)[17]

The Walnut Door, like the object the title refers to, is the work of a skilled and playful, scornful and powerful craftsman. The writer of this book, like his carpenter protagonist Eddie Macaboy, creates a situation in which the reader, like the young woman Eddie first imprisons in her apartment and then frees, must make of the facts—polished and craftily manipulated as they are—a world as desirable as it is possible to envision it. Elaine Quinlan chooses affirmatively; her involvement with Macaboy follows an unhappy relationship she wants to avoid repeating, yet she invites the wily artisan to move into her apartment. Eddie has seemed to earn her trust, despite the signs of his trickery—his phone calls to other women inviting them to invest in the sound locks and doors of his one man "company," Safe-T Security-E Syste-M; his unlocking the walnut door without informing Elaine that she is free to leave her apartment after he had locked her in for days. The reader, who knows even more about Macaboy than Elaine does, seeing the scrupulous order of his workshop and the mess of his sleeping area, and witnessing his personal—erotic—involvement with his craft, will allow the possibility for Macaboy and Quinlan to live together constructively, but will have greater reservations about it than the young woman presently has. Despite the cynical tone, the pain of experience both young people have known, and their defiance of the norms of the love story (Elaine tries to seduce Macaboy, who holds out for a "meaningful" relationship—very much, however, on his own terms), the days of talk and meals during Elaine's captivity create a context in which their merged lives seem so mutually desirable that they can justifiably be gambled on by a reader who assumes that the long and clever "foreplay" represented by the erection and oiling of the door has bonded the lovers mentally. This conclusion can stand despite the fact that Macaboy is working on a new door and a new client at the end of the tale; evidence at the start of the novel indicates that Macaboy does not always become involved with clients.

The plot of the novel as I have described it thus far—hippie turned carpenter builds a door, sells it and a deadbolt lock to a young woman who has also taken part in a climate of sexual freedom related to the sixties, and then uses the locked door to overpower her by making her feel "safe" with him—seems at first bizarre and unrelated to Hersey's previous works. This is especially true because of the either/or plot resolution—the young people may/may not live together with a reasonable degree of mutual fulfillment. In several important ways, however, *The Walnut Door* exhibits the two strands of Hersey's long writing career, versatility and continuity. As a tongue-in-cheek moral fable, the tale is an interesting variation of a Hersey type; its humor surpasses that of its predecessors, *Under the Eye of the Storm* and *Too Far to Walk*. With its depiction of a crime-ridden New Haven peopled by the two young characters in search of stable values (Elaine's possessions, ranging from a dulcimer and a wok to a photo album, stand for her fragmented personality, as does Macaboy's compartmentalized living space) by numerous near-grotesques who are Elaine's "normal" neighbors; and by the couple's memories of their affluent upbringings, the book has some of the characteristics of a social melodrama. As defined by John Cawelti in *Adventure, Mystery and Romance,* this kind of tale offers rather serious social criticism within a narrative which moves from apparent moral and social disorder to an affirmation of the benevolence of the universe.[18] With this definition for comparison, one might say that Hersey's either/or resolution is a fairly skillful avoidance of the trap of melodrama. Its true kinship with such books, however, lies in its somewhat comical social realism reminiscent of Hersey's early employer, Sinclair Lewis. Cawelti points out that the combination of muckraking with social melodrama is a strong American tradition exemplified by works like *Uncle Tom's*

Cabin, Gone with the Wind, and *Main Street.* (202)

Where Hersey differs from such contemporary writers of social melodrama as Harold Robbins and Irving Wallace is clearly in popular appeal; *The Walnut Door,* with its equivocal ending, has not even appeared in paperback. Its intended audience seems narrow—an educated and affluent group. The suspenseful tale links sex with power and possible violence; as in *My Petition for More Space* these forces are centered in an artist. Sam Poynter can neither write nor engage in sex; Macaboy, though a carpenter rather than a would-be writer, constructs both of his "products"—doors and sexual interactions— with both skill and pleasure. As an artisan, Macaboy is unique among the communicator-heroes of the Hersey canon. His hand-crafted, strong and authentic doors are concrete signs of the values he cannot articulate in the spoken word. Like Levinson, Su-ling, Boman, Poynter and the other Hersey protagonists, Macaboy derives both pleasure and meaning from culture and art; his bedtime reading is Conrad, his carpenter's accompaniment is Beethoven. His way to initiating communication with Elaine is to tell her that Bennington girls (she is one) have always reminded him of Mondrians. With typical undercutting, Macaboy qualifies this to "imitation Mondrians." This exchange is an example of Macaboy's power to tell the truth in a harmful, unpolished way, exemplifying the interest he feels for the spoken word. In linking Macaboy's doormaking to his relishing of literature, music and sex Hersey seems to be concentrating on the artist's delight in craft itself and power over others resulting from it. The ex-hippie college dropout is a two-faced hero whom we, like Elaine, would like to believe in and hope for. We link him to the power of creation, to making things "fit together," suggestive not only of sex but also of coherence and stability in a world where walnut doors are unavailable objects and "oyster-shell plastic toilet seats" abound. Despite the "reversible" qualities of this book— which would allow one to construct an interpretation of it as a nihilistic statement about contemporary inability to love—two factors prevent me from doing so. One, linked to my own sense of wanting to be right about my interpretation of Hersey's view of art, suggests that this book too, is about the "honorable survival" Hersey set out to describe as a young man, and the way that art "makes people want to live." This external evidence and personal bias can be supplemented convincingly by contemplating—as Elaine does for many days—the walnut door itself. This second basis for my interpretation of the work gathers, I believe, the values of the novel and of Hersey as a writer, into both a useful and pleasurable unifying symbol.

Hersey assumes that all readers will appreciate the walnut door as an object. The Aida-whistling Macaboy can produce that which few of us can easily buy, even if we can afford it: "a pure door, an essence." (53) This flush door, "as safe as Hoover Dam," will have beauty in "the dance of grains." It will be a solid walnut door, naked and heavy. In the description of the door, Hersey seems to have a great deal of fun making the door represent an ideal American masterpiece, a technologically authentic, aesthetic and practical *thing*. The naked Macaboy has skin which "glistens like a space suit." His priestly intent is to produce a perfect surface as representative of nature as a seascape. The Yankee Macaboy—his family has lived in New England for generations—will produce a door as tough, authentic and mysterious as Bogey's face, without the "sucking Nixonism" of veneer, without the bevels and whorls a Puritan would despise. His precision and skills are equivalent to those needed for the most exotic technology. The crafting of a door, safe as a bank vault, nearly becomes a sexual experience. In fact, Macaboy may be aroused by his work when he hears Elaine's telephone voice and determines to pursue her.

Though the door thus carries a weight of American themes, it is able—like a beautifully constructed tale—to exist as a whole more valuable than its parts or materials. The very inaccessibility of handcrafted doors gives this object its affirmation. With this comes, I believe, an alternately fond and despairing respect for the creator of the door. Someone who can do this can also build a life; even if this proves untrue (as the novel permits one to speculate), at least Macaboy can make these admirable objects whose existence the reader must value. (Is Hersey having fun with names again? "Make-a-buoy?" Or, since the hero does not necessarily come of age, does he simply "make a boy" of himself again? Too many other punnish possibilities occur to continue.)

The doors Macaboy constructs are beautiful. Their existence, and the joy of creating them—especially in the pop-culture ambience of New Haven as Hersey presents it—makes life, despite all of the squalor, the sufferings of growing up in an inauthentic culture, seem valuable. Yet this affirmation is teased by the fact that Macaboy controls the function of the door. By reversing the lock, he imprisons Elaine: it is Macaboy, not the door, that will determine her safety or lack of it. Two recurrent Hersey themes, the moral power of the poet/storyteller and the power of the individual mind to shape reality seem at work in Macaboy's deceit. Furthermore, just as Hersey's tales seem to be actions-in-the-world as much or more than they are aesthetic objects, so the door—with its enduring and intrinsic value—is manipulated by its maker so that it plays an active role in the shaping of a sexual encounter and, perhaps, a relationship of enduring value.

For Elaine, who initially resents Macaboy's manipulation (he sells doors by warning lone women about the danger of break-ins), the door cannot be known separately from its maker. Its solid presence, because Macaboy has locked her in, causes long reveries and dreamlike memory sequences during which she attempts to define and accept her own character. Ultimately, through the dialogue she and Macaboy engage in when he opens the walnut door to bring her food over the five days of her vigil, the wary and unpredictable Elaine "feels safe." She is in love with Macaboy. At the end of the tale, we see him intent upon his art and the deception that goes with it; but he has packed a suitcase to stay at Elaine's.

While the door (art) is solid enough, relationships (real life) have a shifting and perplexing quality. Both characters seem to define themselves in terms of their fathers (perhaps this accounts for my impression that Elaine is a less convincing character than Macaboy). Each defines the father's flaw they fear reliving. For Macaboy, it is his father's failure to "be himself" (not especially well defined in the story); for Elaine, it is her father's unpredictability. This part of the narrative seems to serve two purposes: it carries much of the historical-social commentary by presenting the values, spiritual and material, to which the two have been exposed; and it is the focus for each character's sexual identity. Macaboy seems to doubt his sexual prowess; Elaine seems to regret hers.

Since the outcome of the sexual encounter (that is, whether the relationship will endure beyond it) is virtually left to the reader's preference, the door dominates the tale. Its beauty and power, and the craft which designed and constructed it, have permanence and value. It is difficult to conclude that the communication and sexual encounter the door drew forth from the man and woman have not also a similar authenticity and value. None the less, it is much clearer that the craft is more powerful than that the craftsman can love. The power of the artist, as in *My Petition for More Space,* seems to be the one reality that can capture the ideal. Such an interpretation of Hersey's most recent novel suggests more strongly than ever, because the parable is given a cynical universe, his conviction over a long career that art, storytelling and mythmaking demand extraordinary commitment but are essential to human life. Though Macaboy's other efforts may fail, his artistry will enhance the lives it touches.

Hersey's personal work to improve the position of writers in American society has included practical, effective labor toward protective copyright laws and contrast agreements as a member of P.E.N. and the Authors Guild. Testifying before the House Judiciary Committee on May 26, 1965, Hersey uttered publicly the belief he has dramatized in the books:

> I think the special thing is that writers speak to the human spirit. They are the conscience and the recorders of our society. Their works should be seen by the children. We want them to be and feel that they should be. But if you encroach on the aleady precarious livelihood of our poets, our most gifted writers, their wood notes may turn sour. Or, worse, they may be forced into kinds of employment which would in act deprive them of their own free voices.[19]

Hersey's didactic approach to the role of the writer has indeed qualified the contribution he has made to contemporary art. His subversion of form to idea places him in a category of writers who do not fully meet traditional critical standards of originality and formal design. In a sense, however, Hersey's public work for his beliefs and the rhetoric of his novels and journalism identify him with the group of people Frye sees as fulfilling now the poet's ancient social role. "Those who express the ideas and symbols that hold society together are no longer the poets; they are rather men of action with a power over the sententious utterance operating mainly outside literature. . . ."[20] Hersey's journalistic style and form would be classified as functional prose in Frye's system, far removed from the creativity of the poet.

Although Frye's is not the only voice in modern literary criticism, the practice of this singularly important critic of categorizing socially concerned prose as unimaginative is powerfully indicative of the mainstream of literary criticism. Hersey benefits more fully from appraisals which endorse journalism and the documentary or which compare him with noted writers who also have less than exalted critical reputations. Truman Capote, for example, has referred to Hersey as one of several "styleless stylists" who write in a way that is difficult, admirable, and popular.[21] In addition to Hersey, Capote mentions Graham Greene, Somerset Maugham, Thornton Wilder, Willa Cather, J. P. Marquand, and Jean Paul Sartre as writers whose style does not block communion between the writer and reader.

Samuel Beckoff, a former C.U.N.Y. professor who is an admirer of Hersey's early work, points to current interest in journalistic writers, including Arnold Bennett and George Gissing, as a means of assessing Hersey's contribution. Discussing Leslie Fiedler's rejection of Hersey as a sentimental do-gooder, Beckoff elaborates this position:

> I like Fiedler—the critic, that is, not the novelist—and I do respect most of his literary judgments; however, I think he misses the point of Hersey's reputation as an authetnic, contemporary, *American* novelist. As such, I would expect that novelist to be issue-oriented, streamlined in style and technique, journalistically trained, and somewhat removed from the closet of academically oriented writers. Yes, Hersey is in the tradition of the issue-oriented and journalistically trained writers such as Warren and Steinbeck, but also Dana, Sinclair Lewis, Hemingway, Breslin, Wicker, Drury,—and why not Daniel Defoe, too?[22]

Beckoff adds that, while he admires experimental novelists, Hersey has made a more valuable contribution to contemporary society and literature than has, for example Thomas Pynchon. He cites a review by Frank Kermode of biographies of Gissing and Bennett as applicable to the accomplishment of Hersey. Speaking of Bennett, Kermode comments that Bennett "knew what he could and could not do," and thus was not one of the "obsessed technologists" from James to the New Novel. His was a public which appreciated skill and craftsmanship though not extreme experiment.[23] Elsewhere in the article, Kermode compares the period of Bennett and Gissing to our own, arguing that the same kinds of social forces which affected Gissing, Wells and Bennett continue to affect our own times.

With increasing recognition of the role of journalistic writers in shaping the culture, it is possible that Hersey will not continue in the "limbo" which he calls his sphere between the mass market and the endorsement of literary criticism. As the kind of writer always present in literate societies, pencil and opinions ready, Hersey seems part of a needed reportorial tradition. His varied, complex and socially relevant works express in form and theme the freeing role of the imagination, and the ideas by which he has lived, and by which he has helped to free his fellow artists and his readers from inertia and despair. Although he does work in another realm than that of our most cherished writers, his contribution in his chosen mode is superior.

Dwight MacDonald's placing of Hersey as Midcult, while in MacDonald's views a pejorative description, gives further testimony to Hersey's accomplishment. He assigns such works as Wilder's *Our Town*, Hemingway's *The Old Man and the Sea* and MacLeish's *J.B.* to Midcult because while they have been popular with the educated classes, received some praise from critics, and Pulitzer Prizes as well, they are full of "constant editorializing" and probably can be summed up by the atrociously vague line of Wilder's Stage Manager, " 'There's something way deep down that's eternal about every human being from Our Town'."[24]

MacDonald's additional reason for holding Midcult in disdain is its resemblance to the Popular Culture which, by way of ideas and stylistic borrowing from High Culture, has brought it forth as a bastard offspring. Guilty of formula writing, the built-in-reaction, and lack of standards, Midcult writers such as H. G. Wells, John Steinbeck, J. P. Marquand, Pearl S. Buck, Irwin Shaw, Herman Wouk and John Hersey oppose faith to cleverness, offer liberal moralizing instead of talent, submerge their work to the spectator's expectations, and worst of all, corrupt the High Culture by using ideas and forms which it has generated.[25]

MacDonald, in some ways, has offered cogent truth about Hersey. Grouping him with Steinbeck, Wells, and Buck, MacDonald unwittingly identifies not only Hersey's shortcomings but also his chosen area of work. No doubt Hersey would be pleased to stand with such writers in American letters. Steinbeck and Buck, in fact, seconded Hersey's nomination by Mark Van Doren to the American Academy of Arts and Letters, as did Van Wyck Brooks and Douglas Moore. Stripped of the critic's derogatory description, the names Steinbeck, Wells, Buck and Hersey convey to the educated reader not questions about their ultimate reputations as authors so much as images of comfortable but critical commentators and engaging storytellers. Like the contemporary writers Hersey most admires—Robert Penn Warren, Arthur Miller and Lillian Hellman—they have concerned themselves seriously with their contemporaries' options, choices, mistakes and accomplishments.

There is not much in Hersey's work that reflects the mass culture's use of formula writing or lack of standards, moral or literary. (MacDonald has not specified the kind of "standards" Midcult lacks.) Indeed, Hersey's evident attempt both to avoid the trap of the formula writer and the label of "journalist" have led him to produce such varied works as *The Marmot Drive, The War Lover, Under the Eye of the Storm,* and *My Petition for More Space.* It is, in fact, Hersey's avoidance of any settled form which has helped to keep his reputation undefined and made him difficult to analyze.[26] Although Hersey does moralize openly in such works as *A Single Pebble* and *The Algiers Motel Incident,* as well as by implication in *Hiroshima, The Child Buyer* and *White Lotus,* his idea of the writer's role decides his preacher's stance. Unlike even writers of such fame as Steinbeck and Buck, Hersey's moral vision is unique and the rhetoric which accompanies it is a deliberate part of his authorial intention. Although at times—in company with Sartre, Dos Passos, and Dreiser—the moral commitment of this artist leads him to choose forms that become flat, to write passages that openly plead or persuade, one cannot imagine Hersey in a brilliant moment of literary inspiration such as he displays from time to time, editing out anything that conveys the sense of his role as artist to the reader.

In this respect, Hersey is like MacDonald's beloved *New Yorker,* "Midcult with a difference." MacDonald disparages all of Midcult until he faces the existence of the magazine he works for. Its formula, he says, reflects the taste of the editors, not their fear of the readers; such personal editing leads to "extra-formula happy accidents."[27] (Certainly, one can ask, wasn't the editors' decision to print *Hiroshima* in one issue one of those "happy accidents" the *New Yorker* has offered the public?)

Hersey's vision, derived as it is from the High Culture, is nevertheless idiosyncratic, a quality MacDonald has described as proper to great writing. The existential vision Hersey offers is his own capturing of the dominant social thought of his times. Elaborating and making plausible the dilemma of Sispyhus-man, Hersey performs a service to numbers of people who might not otherwise understand the philosophical mood of the times, or who like to relax with a story which does not insult their intelligence nor demean their lives. Beyond this rather homely accomplishment (homely to critics alone) the works are interesting reflections and chronicles of the time by a respected and well-informed observer.

The categories of high, middle and low culture are not yet defined in any wholly satisfactory way. Edward Shils has observed that the practitioner of "mediocre culture" often reaches heights in certain new or relatively new genres of his own field "to the point where, if the genre is admissible, his work can take on the lineaments of superior cultural achievement."[28] In an age noted for nonfiction, the author of such journalism as *Hiroshima, The Wall,* and *The Algiers Motel Incident* must be reckoned with as more than "mediocre." If Hersey is middlebrow, he is middlebrow with a difference, a writer who works from personal standards and convictions rather than from mores dictated by his publisher's interpretation of public wishes. A writer who is consistently grouped not only with Steinbeck and Buck by critics who dislike him, but with Faulkner and Wilder by those who admire him[29] is unique enough in this respect to be an "original." Hersey's brow, raised in concern, compels attention. It is a dignified, silver-haired brow that has towered over its peers.

NOTES

INTRODUCTION

[1] David Sanders, *John Hersey* (New York: Twayne Publishers, Inc., 1967), p. 139.

[2] Samuel B. Girgus, "Against the Grain: The Achievement of John Hersey" (unpublished Ph.D. dissertation, University of New Mexico, 1972), p. 10.

[3] Albert Camus, *The Myth of Sisyphus and Other Essays*, trans. by Justin O'Brien (New York: Random House, 1955), p. 90.

[4] Maxwell Geismar, "John Hersey: The Revival of Conscience," in *American Moderns* (New York: Hill and Wang, 1958), p. 186.

[5] R. W. B. Lewis, *The Picaresque Saint: Representative Figures in Contemporary Fiction* (Philadelphia: J. B. Lippincott, 1956), p. 76, quoted by permission of Harper & Row, Publishers, Inc.

[6] John Hersey, ed., *The Writer's Craft* (New York: Alfred A. Knopf, 1974), p. 4. All subsequent references to this book are cited parenthetically in the text.

[7] Germaine Bree, *Camus and Sartre: Crisis and Commitment* (New York: Delacorte Press, 1972), p. 70.

[8] —, "The Novel of Contemporary History," *The Atlantic Monthly*, November, 1949, p. 1.

[9] Interview with Hersey.

[10] Hersey, "The One Without Whom. . .," *Yale Daily News*, January 18, 1967.

CHAPTER I

[1] Wayne C. Booth, *The Rhetoric of Fiction* (Chicago: The University of Chicago Press, 1961), pp. 397-398. Reprinted from *The Rhetoric of Fiction* by Wayne Booth by permission of the University of Chicago Press. © 1961 by The University of Chicago.

[2] John Hersey, *Men on Bataan* (New York: Alfred A. Knopf, 1942), p. 32. All subsequent references to this book will be included parenthetically in the text.

[3] Sanders, *John Hersey* (New York: Twayne Publishers, Inc., 1967), p. 23. Copyright 1967 by Twayne Publishers, a division of G. K. Hall and Co., Boston.

[4] J. Donald Adams, "New Books in Review," *Yale Review*, xxxii (Summer, 1943), p. 191.

[5] John Hersey, *Into the Valley* (New York: Alfred A. Knopf, 1943), p. 50. All subsequent references to this book will be included parenthetically in the text.

[6] Samuel B. Girgus, "Against the Grain: The Achievement of John Hersey" (unpublished Ph.D. dissertation, University of New Mexico, 1972), pp. 23-23.

[7] *Ibid.*

[8] John Hersey, "The Novel of Contemporary History," *The Atlantic Monthly* (November, 1959), p. 82.

[9] Girgus, p. 24. See Diana Trilling, "Fiction in Review," *The Nation*, February 12, 1944, pp. 194-195.

[10] *Ibid.*, p. 26.

[11] Randall H. Waldron, "The Naked, the Dead, and the Machine: A New Look at Norman Mailer's First Novel." Reprinted by permission of the Modern Language Association from Randall H. Waldron, "The Naked, the Dead, and the Machine: A New Look at Norman Mailer's First Novel," *PMLA* 87 (March, 1972), p. 272.

[12] Letter from Hersey to Girgus, quoted by Hersey in a letter to me.

[13] Warren French, "Fiction: A Handful of Survivors," in *The Forties: Fiction, Poetry Drama,* ed. Warren French (Deland, Florida: Everett/Edwards, Inc., 1969), p. 16.

[14] Albert Van Nostrand, *The Denatured Novel* (New York: Bobbs-Merrill, 1960), p. 81.

[15] John Hersey, *A Bell for Adano* (1944, rpt. New York: Knopf, 1945), vi. All subsequent references to this book will be included parenthetically in the text.

[16] —, "Alternatives to Apathy," *United Nations World*, May, 1947, p. 20.

[17] Northrop Frye, *The Critical Path: An Essay on the Social Context of Literary Criticism* (Bloomington: Indiana University Press, 1971), p. 64.

[18] John Hersey, "Engineers of the Soul," *Time*, October 9, 1944. Reprinted by permission from *Time*, The Weekly Newsmagazine; Copyright Time Inc. 1944. Subsequent references are noted parenthetically in the text.

[19] —, "Letter from Chungking," *The New Yorker*, March 16, 1946, p. 87.

[20] —, "A Reporter in China," *The New Yorker*, May 25, 1946, p. 58.

[21] —, "Two Weeks Water Away: A Reporter in China," *The New Yorker*, May 18, 1946, p. 68.

[22] Sanders, p. 39.

[23]Maxwell Geismer, "John Hersey: The Revival of Conscience," in *American Moderns* (New York: Hill and Wang, 1958), p. 186.

[24]Mas'ud Zavarzadeh, *The Mythopoeic Reality: The Postwar American Nonfiction Novel* (Urbana, Illinois: University Press, 1976), pp. 93-102.

[25]Sanders, p. 49.

[26]Kingsley Widmer, "American Apocalypse: Notes on the Bomb and the Failure of the Imagination," in *The Forties: Fiction, Poetry and Drama* (Florida: Everett/Edwards, Inc., 1969), p. 142.

[27]Alfred Kazin, *Bright Book of Life: American Novelists and Storytellers from Hemingway to Mailer* (Boston: Little, Brown and Co., 1971), p. 218.

[28]Giggus, pp. 58 ff.

[29]Frye, p. 81.

[30]John Hersey, *Hiroshima* (New York: Alfred A. Knopf, 1946), p. 106. All subsequent references to this book will be included parenthetically in the text.

[31]Booth, p. 198. Reprinted from *The Rhetoric of Fiction* by Wayne Booth by permission of the University of Chicago Press. © 1961 by the University of Chicago.

CHAPTER II

[1]John Hersey, "A Fable South of Cancer," *'47, Magazine of the Year*, April, 1947, pp. 113-141.

[2]—, "Profile: The Old Man," *The New Yorker*, January 3, 1948, pp. 28-37; January 10, 1948, pp. 30-40; January 17, 1948, pp. 30-41; on Bernard Baruch. "Mr. Secretary Marshall," *Collier's*, March 29, 1947, pp. 11-13, 48-51; April 4, 1947, pp. 18-19, 71-73; April 12, 1947, pp. 24, 78-81; on General

George C. Marshall. "Mr. President," *The New Yorker,* April 7, 1951, pp. 42-56; April 14, 1951, pp. 38-53; April 21, 1951, pp. 36-57; April 28, 1951, pp. 36-52; May 5, 1951, pp. 36-53, on Harry S. Truman.

[3] David Sanders, *John Hersey* (New York: Twayne Publishers, Inc., 1967), p. 138.

[4] David Daiches, "Record and Testament," *Commentary,* April, 1950, p. 385.

[5] Alfred Kazin, "John Hersey and Noach Levinson," *The New Yorker,* March 4, 1950, p. 26.

[6] Maxwell Geismar, "Experiment in Genocide," *Saturday Review,* March 4, 1950, p. 14.

[7] —, "John Hersey: The Revival of Conscience," *American Moderns* (New York: Hill and Wang, 1958), p. 182.

[8] Edward Weeks, review in *The Atlantic,* March, 1950, p. 72.

[9] William Stott, *Documentary Expression and Thirties America* (New York: Oxford University Press, 1973), p. 314.

[10] Hersey, "The Mechanics of a Novel," *The Yale University Library Gazette,* xxvii (July, 1952), p. 8.

[11] Alvin Rosenfeld and Irving Greenberg, Editors, *Confronting the Holocaust: The Impact of Elie Wiesel* (Bloomington: Indiana University Press, 1978), p. 11.

[12] Hersey, "The Mechanics of a Novel," p. 4.

[13] *Ibid.,* p. 11.

[14] Emmanuel Ringelblum, *Notes from the Warsaw Ghetto,* edited and translated by Jacob Sloan (New York: McGraw Hill, 1958), xxiii.

[15] Chaim Kaplan, *Scroll of Agony,* translated and edited by Abraham I.

Katsch (New York: MacMillan, 1965).

[16]Hersey, *The Wall* (New York: Alfred A. Knopf, Inc., 1950), p. 3. All subsequent references to this book will be included parenthetically in the text.

[17]Stott, p. 17.

CHAPTER III

[1]Samuel B. Girgus, "Against the Grain: The Achievement of John Hersey" (unpublished Ph.D. dissertation, University of New Mexico, 1972), p. 134.

[2]John Hersey, ed., *The Writer's Craft* (New York: Alfred A. Knopf, 1974), p. 12.

[3]—, "The Novel of Contemporary History," *The Atlantic Monthly*, November, 1949, p. 82.

[4]Irving Howe, "Symbolic Suburbia," *New Republic*, November 16, 1953, p. 17.

[5]Howard Mumford Jones, "New England Parable," *The Saturday Review*, November 7, 1953, p. 22.

[6]Maxwell Geismar, "The Crazy Mask of Literature," *The Nation*, November 14, 1953, p. 404.

[7]David Sanders, *John Hersey* (New York: Twayne Publishers, Inc., 1967), p. 79.

[8]Girgus, p. 132.

[9]John Hersey, *The Marmot Drive* (New York: Alfred A. Knopf, Inc., 1953), pp. 12-13. All subsequent references will be to this edition and will be cited parenthetically in the text.

[10]Northrop Frye, *The Critical Path* (Bloomington: Indiana University

Press, 1971), p. 81.

[11] Leslie Fiedler, "The Novel in the Post-Political World," *Partisan Review* (Summer, 1956), pp. 358-365.

[12] Samuel Beckoff, ed., *Four Complete American Novels* (New York: Globe, 1960), p. 8.

[13] John Hersey, *A Single Pebble* (New York: Alfred A. Knopf, 1956), pp. 304. All subsequent references to this book are to this edition, and are cited parenthetically in the text.

[14] Beckoff, p. 628.

[15] Ian Watt, *The Rise of the Novel* (Berkeley: University of California Press, 1967), p. 117.

[16] Hersey, in a letter to Girgus quoted in a letter to me, cites Silone, Malroux, Dos Passos and Steinbeck as influences in his youth.

CHAPTER IV

[1] David Sanders, *John Hersey* (New York: Twayne, 1967), p. 75.

[2] *Ibid.*

[3] Letter from Hersey to me.

[4] Robert N. Hudspeth, "A Definition of Modern Nihilism: Hersey's *The War Lover*," *The University Review*, 35 (Summer, 1969), p. 243.

[5] Randall H. Waldron, "The Naked, the Dead, and the Machine: A New Look at Norman Mailer's First Novel," *PMLA* 87, No. 2 (March, 1972), p. 272.

[6] Samuel B. Girgus, "Against the Grain: The Achievement of John Hersey" (unpublished Ph.D. dissertation, University of New Mexico, 1972), p. 242.

[7] Hudspeth, p. 246.

[8] John Hersey, *The War Lover* (New York: Alfred A. Knopf, 1959), p. 1. Subsequent references to this novel will be to this edition and will be included parenthetically in the text.

[9] —, *The Child Buyer* (New York: Alfred A. Knopf, 1960), p. 167. All subsequent references to this book are to this text and will be included parenthetically in the text.

[10] Editorial note preceding "What Shall We Do With the Gifted Child," *The New Republic,* October 10, 1960, pp. 21-26. The article is a collection of critical comments about *The Child Buyer* by such writers as B. F. Skinner, Margaret Halsey, Carl F. Hansen, William Jay Smith, and Robert Gorham Davis. Further references will be documented by page numbers in the text. Quoted material is reprinted by permission of *The New Republic* © 1960. *The New Republic,* Inc.

[11] Girgus, p. 281.

[12] Wayne Booth, *The Rhetoric of Irony* (Chicago: The University of Chicago Press, 1974), p. 268. Subsequent references to this text are noted by page numbers in parentheses.

[13] Arthur Burton, "Existential Conceptions in John Hersey's Novel: *The Child Buyer,*" *Journal of Existential Psychology,* 2 (Fall, 1961), pp. 243-258.

[14] Sanders, p. 144.

[15] Girgus, p. 256.

[16] Norman A. Brittin, *A Writing Apprenticeship,* 3rd, ed. (New York: Holt, Rinehart and Winston, Inc., 1963), p. 55.

CHAPTER V

[1] Eric F. Goldman, *The Tragedy of Lyndon Johnson* (New York: Alfred

A Knopf, 1969), p. 419. Subsequent references are noted parenthetically within the text.

[2] John Hersey, *Here to Stay* (New York: Alfred A. Knopf, 1963), p. 244. All subsequent references to this book are to this edition and are cited parenthetically in the text.

[3] David Sanders, *John Hersey* (New York: Twayne Publishers, Inc., 1967), p. 125. Copyright 1967 by Twayne Publishers, Inc., and reprinted with the permission of Twayne Publishers, a division of G. K. Hall and Company, Boston.

[4] *Ibid.,* p. 127.

[5] Samuel B. Girgus, "Against the Grain: The Achievement of John Hersey" (unpublished Ph.D. dissertation, University of New Mexico, 1972), p. 161.

[6] *Ibid.,* p. 169.

[7] Edwin Morgan, "Sleeping Bird," *New Statesman and Nation,* June 25, 1965, p. 1018.

[8] William Stott, *Documentary Expression and Thirties America* (New York: Oxford University Press, 1973), p. 157.

[9] John Hersey, *White Lotus* (New York: Alfred A. Knopf, 1965), unpaginated author's note. All subsequent references to this book are to this edition, and are included parenthetically within the text.

[10] Michael Haltresht, "Dreams, Visions and Myths in John Hersey's *White Lotus,*" *Western Georgia College Review,* May, 1973, pp. 24-28.

CHAPTER VI

[1] Granville Hicks, "The Undergraduate Faust," *Saturday Review,* March 19, 1966, p. 29.

²John Hersey, *Too Far To Walk* (New York: Alfred A. Knopf, 1966), p. 3. All subsequent references to this book are to this edition, and will be cited parenthetically in the text.

³Leslie Fiedler, "The Novel in the Post-Political World," *Partisan Review* (Summer, 1956), p. 361.

⁴John Hersey, unpublished graduation address at Browning School, June 5, 1963 (Mimeographed).

⁵John Hersey, *Under the Eye of the Storm* (New York: Alfred A. Knopf, 1967), pp. 1-2. All subsequent references to this book are to this edition and are included parenthetically within the text.

⁶Edward Weeks, review of *Under the Eye of the Storm, The Atlantic,* April, 1967, p. 141.

⁷J. F. Fixx, review of *Under the Eye of the Storm, Saturday Review,* March 18, 1967, p. 33.

⁸Richard Sullivan, review of *Under the Eye of the Storm, The Critic,* June, 1967, p. 78.

⁹J. C. Pine, review of *Under the Eye of the Storm, Library Journal,* February 15, 1967, p. 793.

¹⁰Albert Camus, *The Myth of Sisyphus and Other Essays,* trans. by Justin O'Brien (New York: Alfred A. Knopf, Inc., 1955), p. 91.

¹¹Hersey, during an interview with me, November, 1973.

¹²John Hersey, *The Algiers Motel Incident* (New York: Alfred A. Knopf, 1968), p. 32. All subsequent references to this book are to this edition and are cited parenthetically in the text.

¹³Yale Kamisar, "Was Justice Done in the Algiers Motel Incident?" *New York Times,* March 1, 1970, IV, 10:1.

¹⁴John Hersey, "The Mechanics of a Novel," *The Yale University*

Library Gazette, July 1952, p. 10.

[15]—, "The One Without Whom," *Yale Daily News,* January 18, 1967. My note is taken from pp. 3-4 of a typed copy supplied by Hersey. Emphasis added.

[16]—, Dedication Speech for John Hersey High School, November 10, 1968. My note is taken from p. 2 of a typed copy supplied by Hersey.

[17]—, *Letter to the Alumni* (New York: Alfred A. Knopf, 1970), p. 137. All subsequent references to this book will be to this edition and will be cited parenthetically in the text.

CHAPTER VII

[1] Samuel B. Girgus, "Against the Grain: The Achievement of John Hersey" (unpublished Ph.D. dissertation, University of New Mexico, 1972), p. 302.

[2] Hersey, in a letter to Girgus, quoted in Girgus, p. 306.

[3] Girgus, p. 298.

[4] John Hersey, *The Conspiracy* (New York: Alfred A. Knopf, 1972), p. 3. All subsequent references will be cited parenthetically in the text.

[5] —, *My Petition for More Space* (New York: Alfred A. Knopf, 1974), p. 38. All subsequent references will be cited parenthetically in the text.

[6] Susan Heath, review of *My Petition for More Space, Saturday Review/World,* September 21, 1974, p. 26.

[7] John Hersey, "Israel: successors," *New Yorker,* December 16, 1974, pp. 46-82.

[8] —, "Israeli Writing: an Obsession with Time," *Saturday Review,* April 5, 1975, p. 19.

[9] —, *The President* (New York: Alfred A. Knopf, 1975).

[10] —, *Aspects of the Presidencey: Truman and Ford in Office*, intro. Robert A. Dahl (New Haven: Ticknor and Fields, 1980), p. 145. Further references to this book are noted parenthetically in the text.

[11] Norman Cousins, "The Hersey Episode," *Saturday Review*, January 8, 1977, pp. 6-8.

[12] John Hersey, "An Inaugural Address: Attention Jimmy Carter," *New Republic*, December 11, 1976, p. 17.

[13] —, ed., *Twentieth Century Views of Ralph Ellison* (New York: Prentice-Hall, Inc., 1973).

[14] —, "Lillian Hellman," *New Republic*, September 18, 1976, p. 25.

[15] —, "John Cheever, Boy and Man," *New York Times Book Review*, March 26, 1978.

[16] —, *The Walnut Door* (New York: Alfred A. Knopf, 1977). Further references will be cited parenthetically in the text.

[17] See Peter Gardner, Review of *The Walnut Door*, *Saturday Review*, September 17, 1977, pp. 38-39; also Sylvia Martin, "John Hersey's Literary Porn," *Chicago Tribune*, September 11, 1977, p. 8.

[18] John G. Cawelti, *Adventure, Mystery and Romance: Formula Stories as Art and Popular Culture* (Chicago: University of Chicago Press, 1976), p. 202. Further references will be cited parenthetically in the text.

[19] John Hersey, quoted in *Authors Guild Bulletin*. Reprinted by permission from the *Authors Guild Bulletin*, June-July 1965, p. 7. Copyright © 1965 The Authors Guild, Inc.

[20] Northrop Frye, *The Critical Path* (Bloomington: Indiana University Press, 1971), p. 82.

[21] Truman Capote, quoted in *Writers at Work, The Paris Review Inter-*

views (New York: The Viking Press, 1959), p. 295.

[22] Letter from Beckoff to me, October 28, 1974. Beckoff, in a letter dated October 13, 1977 expressed reservations about Hersey's novels after *A Single Pebble*, though he repeated his belief that journalistic writers constitute an important group in American literary history.

[23] Frank Kermode, "Buyers' Market," *The New York Review,* October 31, 1974, p. 4. Kermode states that a journalist's sense of technique is "inescapably and honorably related to the idea of craft." Reprinted with permission from the *New York Review of Books.* Copyright © 1974 Nyrev, Inc.

[24] Dwight MacDonald, "Masscult and Midcult," *Against the American Grain* (New York: Random House, 1962), p. 40.

[25] *Ibid.,* pp. 37 ff.

[26] David Sanders, *John Hersey* (New York: Twayne Publishers, Inc., 1967), p. 137.

[27] MacDonald, p. 68.

[28] Edward Shils, "Mass Society and Its Culture," *Daedalus* (Spring, 1960), p. 301.

[29] Frank Stanton, "Parallel Paths," in *Ibid.,* p. 349.

BIBLIOGRAPHY

Primary Sources

A. Books by John Hersey

Men on Bataan. New York: Alfred A. Knopf, 1942.

Into the Valley. New York: Alfred A. Knopf, 1942. New York: Bantam, 1966.

A Bell for Adano. New York: Alfred A. Knopf, 1944. New York: Avon Books, 1956.

Hiroshima. New York: Alfred A. Knopf, 1946. New York: Bantam, 1966.

The Wall. New York: Alfred A. Knopf, 1950.

The Marmot Drive. New York: Alfred A. Knopf, 1953. New York: The Popular Library, 1960.

A Single Pebble. New York: Alfred A. Knopf, 1956. New York: Bantam, 1968.

The War Lover. New York: Alfred A. Knopf, 1959. New York: Bantam, 1960.

The Child Buyer. New York: Alfred A. Knopf, 1960.

Here to Stay. New York: Alfred A. Knopf, 1963.

White Lotus. New York: Alfred A. Knopf, 1965. New York: Bantam, 1967.

Too Far to Walk. New York: Alfred A. Knopf, 1966. New York: Bantam,

1967.

Under the Eye of the Storm. New York: Alfred A. Knopf, 1967. New York: Bantam, 1968.

The Algiers Motel Incident. New York: Alfred A. Knopf, 1968.

Letter to the Alumni. New York: Alfred A. Knopf, 1970. New York: Bantam, 1971.

The Conspiracy. New York: Alfred A. Knopf, 1972.

Twentieth Century Views of Ralph Ellison, ed. New York: Prentice-Hall, 1973.

My Petition for More Space. New York: Alfred A. Knopf, 1974.

The Writer's Craft. New York: Alfred A. Knopf, 1974.

The President. New York: Alfred A. Knopf, 1975.

The Walnut Door. New York: Alfred A. Knopf, 1977.

Aspects of the Presidency. New Haven: Ticknor and Fields, 1980, ed. Robert H. Dahl.

B. Selected Articles and Short Stories

"Alternatives to Apathy." *United Nations World,* May, 1947, pp. 20, 21, 75, 76.

"The Death of Buchan Walsh." *The Atlantic Monthly,* April, 1946, pp. 80-86.

Dedication Speech for John Hersey High School, November 10, 1968. (Type-written).

"Dialogue on Gorki Street." *Fortune,* January, 1945, pp. 149-151.

"Engineers of the Soul." *Time,* October 9, 1944, pp. 99-102.

"A Fable South of Cancer." '47, *Magazine of the Year*, April, 1947, pp. 113-141.

"An Inaugural Address: Attention Jimmy Carter." *New Republic*, December 11, 1976, p. 17.

Interview at John Hersey's home, November, 1973.

"Israeli Writing: an Obsession with time." *Saturday Review*, April 5, 1975, p. 19.

"John Cheever, Boy and Man." *New York Times Book Review*, March 26. 1978.

"Kamikaze." *Life*, July 3, 1944, pp. 68-75.

"Letter from Chungking." *The New Yorker*, March 16, 1946, pp. 80-87.

"Letter from Shanghai." *The New Yorker*, February 9, 1946, pp. 74-82.

"The Life of the Word." *Images*, Arlington Heights, Illinois: John Hersey High School, 1969, p. 1.

"Lillian Hellman." *New Republic*, September 18, 1976, pp. 25-27.

"The Mechanics of a Novel." *The Yale University Library Gazette*, xxvii (July, 1952), pp. 1-11.

"The Novel of Contemporary History." *The Atlantic Monthly*, November, 1949, pp. 80-84.

"The One Without Whom. . ." *Yale Daily News*, January 18, 1967.

"The Pen." *The Atlantic Monthly*, June, 1946, pp. 84-87.

"Reporter at Large: Israel: Successors." *The New Yorker*, December 16, 1974, pp. 46-82.

"A Reporter in China." *The New Yorker*, May 18, 1946, pp. 59-69; May 25,

1946, pp. 54-69.

"A Short Wait." *The New Yorker,* June 14, 1947, pp. 27-29.

Speech at Browning School Graduation, New York, June 5, 1963. (Mimeographed).

"Why Were You Sent Out Here?" *The Atlantic Monthly,* February, 1946, pp.
88-91.

Secondary Sources

Adams, J. Donald. Review of *Into the Valley. Yale Review,* xxxii (Summer,
1943), p. 191.

Alexander, Edward. *The Resonance of Dust.* Columbus: Ohio State University
Press, 1979.

Authors Guild Bulletin. June-July, 1965.

Balliett, Whitney. Review of *The War Lover. The New Yorker,* December 19,
1959, p. 141.

Beckoff, Samuel D., ed. *Four Complete American Novels.* New York: Globe,
1960.

Booth, Wayne C. *The Rhetoric of Fiction.* Chicago: The University of Chicago
Press, 1961.

—. *The Rhetoric of Irony.* Chicago: The University of Chicago Press, 1974.

Bree, Germaine. *Camus and Sartre: Crisis and Commitment.* New York: Delacorte Press 1972.

Burton, Arthur. "Existential Conceptions in John Hersey's Novel: *The Child
Buyer." Journal of Existential Psychology,* 2 (Fall, 1961), pp. 243-258.

Camus, Albert. *The Myth of Sisyphus and Other Essays.* Translated by Justin O'Brien. New York: Random House, 1955.

Cawelti, John G. *Adventure, Mystery and Romance.* Chicago: University of Chicago Press, 1976.

Daiches, David. "Record and Testament." Review of *The Wall. Commentary,* April, 1950, pp. 385-388.

Fadiman, Clifton. Review of *Men on Bataan. The New Yorker,* June 6, 1942, p. 62.

Fiedler, Leslie. "The Novel in the Post-Political World." Review of *A Single Pebble. Partisan Review,* 23 (Summer, 1956), pp. 358-365.

Fixx, J. F. Review of *Under the Eye of the Storm. Saturday Review,* March 18, 1967, pp. 33-34.

French, Warren B. "Fiction: A Handful of Survivors." *The Forties: Fiction, Poetry, Drama.* Edited by Warren B. French. Deland, Florida: Everett/ Edwards, Inc., 1969, pp. 7-32.

Frye, Northrop. *The Critical Path: An Essay on the Social Context of Literary Criticism.* Bloomington: Indiana University Press, 1971.

Geismar, Maxwell. "The Crazy Mask of Literature." Review of *The Marmot Drive. The Nation,* November 14, 1953, p. 404.

—. "Experiment in Genocide." Review of *The Wall. Saturday Review,* March 4, 1950, pp. 14-16.

—. "John Hersey: The Revival of Conscience." *American Moderns: From Rebellion to Conformity.* New York: Hill and Wang, 1958, pp. 180-186.

Girgus, Samuel B. "Against the Grain: The Achievement of John Hersey." Unpublished Ph.D. dissertation, University of New Mexico, 1972.

Goldman, Eric F. *The Tragedy of Lyndon Johnson.* New York: Alfred A. Knopf, 1969.

Heath, Susan. Review of *My Petition for More Space*. *Saturday Review/World*, September 21, 1974, p. 26.

Hicks, Granville. "The Undergraduate Faust." *Saturday Review*, March 19, 1966, p. 29.

Hollowell, John. *Fact and Fiction*. Chapel Hill: University of North Carolina Press, 1977.

Howe, Irving. "Symbolic Suburbia." Review of *The Marmot Drive*. *New Republic*, November 16, 1953, p. 17.

Hudspeth, Robert N. "A Definition of Modern Nihilism: Hersey's *The War Lover*." *The University Review*, 35 (Summer, 1969), pp. 243-249.

Huse, Nancy Lyman. *John Hersey and James Agee: A Reference Guide*. Boston: G. K. Hall, 1978.

Jennings, Frank G. "Black Market in Brains." Review of *The Child Buyer*. *Saturday Review*, September 14, 1960, p. 21.

Jones, Howard Mumford. "New England Parable." Review of *The Marmot Drive*. *Saturday Review*, November 7, 1953, p. 22.

Kamisar, Yale. "Was Justice Done in the Algiers Motel Incident?" *New York Times*, March 1, 1970, IV, 10, p. 1.

Kaplan, Chaim A. *The Warsaw Diary of Chaim A. Kaplan*. New York: Collier Books, 1973.

Katz, Alfred. *Poland's Ghettos*. New York: Twayne, 1970.

Kazin, Alfred. *Bright Book of Life: American Novelists and Storytellers from Hemingway to Mailer*. Boston: Little, Brown and Co., 1971.

—. "John Hersey and Noach Levinson." Review of *The Wall*. *The New Yorker*, March 4, 1950, pp. 96-100.

Kermode, Frank. "Buyers' Market." *The New York Review*, October 31,

1974, pp. 3-4.

Lampell, Millard. *The Wall*. New York: Alfred A. Knopf, 1961.

Langer, Lawrence L. *The Holocaust and the Literary Imagination*. New Haven: Yale University Press, 1975.

Lewis, R. W. B. *The Picaresque Saint: Representative Figures in Contemporary Fiction*. Philadelphia: J. B. Lippincott, 1956.

MacDonald, Dwight. *Against the American Grain*. New York: Random House, 1962.

McDonnell, Thomas P. "Hersey's Allegorical Novels." *The Catholic World*, July, 1962, pp. 240-245.

Morgan, Edwin. "Sleeping Bird." Review of *White Lotus*. *New Statesman and Nation*, June 25, 1965, p. 1018.

Pine, J. C. Review of *Under the Eye of the Storm*. *Library Journal*, February 15, 1967, p. 773.

Review of *Too Far to Walk*. *Newsweek*, March 14, 1966, p. 104.

Review of *The War Lover*. *Time*, October 5, 1959, p. 102.

Ringelblum, Emmanuel. *Notes from the Warsaw Ghetto*. New York: McGraw-Hill, 1958.

Rosenfeld, Alvin and Irving Greenberg, ed. *Confronting the Holocaust*. Bloomington: Indiana University Press, 1978.

Sanders, David. *John Hersey*. New York: Twayne Publishers, 1967.

— "John Hersey: War Correspondent Into Novelist." *New Voices in American Studies*. Edited by Ray B. Browne. Lafayette, Indiana: Purdue University Press, 1966, pp. 49-58.

Schnedler, Jack. "*Catch-22*'s Joe Heller: He's Back After Thirteen Years. . . ."

Review of *Something Happened*. *Chicago Daily News*, October 3, 1974, The Arts, pp. 4-5.

Shils, Edward. "Mass Society and Its Culture." *Daedalus* (Spring, 1960), pp. 288-314.

Stanton, Frank. "Parallel Paths." *Daedalus* (Spring, 1960), pp. 347-353.

Stern, Daniel. "Notes on Reputation." Review of *Too Far to Walk*. *Harper's Magazine*, April, 1966, p. 120.

Stott, William. *Documentary Expression and Thirties America*. New York: Oxford University Press, 1973.

Sullivan, Richard. Review of *Under the Eye of the Storm*. *The Critic*, June, 1967, p. 78.

Van Nostrand, Albert. *The Denatured Novel*. New York: Bobbs-Merrill, 1960.

Waldron, Randall H. "The Naked, the Dead, and the Machine: A New Look at Norman Mailer's First Novel." *PMLA*, 86 (March, 1972), pp. 271-277.

Watt, Ian. *The Rise of the Novel*. Berkeley: University of California Press, 1967.

Weeks, Edward. Review of *The Wall*. *The Atlantic Monthly*, March, 1950, p. 72.

—. Review of *Under the Eye of the Storm*. *The Atlantic*, April, 1967, p. 141.

"What Shall We Do with the Gifted Child?" Review of *The Child Buyer* by B. F. Skinner, Margaret Halsey, Carl F. Hansen, William Jay Smith and Robert Gorham Davis. *The New Republic*, October 10, 1970, pp. 21-26.

Widmer, Kingsley. "American Apocalypse: Notes on the Bomb and the Failure of the Imagination." *The Forties: Fiction, Poetry and Drama*. Edited by Warren B. French. Deland, Florida: Everett/Edwards, Inc., 1969, pp. 141-164.

Writers at Work: The Paris Review Interviews. Edited by Malcolm Cowley. New York: The Viking Press, 1959.

Zavarzadeh, Mas'ud. *The Mythopoeic Reality: The Postwar American Non-fiction Novel.* Champaign-Urbana: University of Illinois Press, 1976.

Zielinski, Siegfried. "History as Entertainment and Provocation: The TV Series 'Holocaust' in West Germany." *New German Critique,* Winter, 1980, pp. 81-96.

Zoll, Donald Atwater. *The Twentieth Century Mind: Essays on Contemporary Thought.* Louisiana: Louisiana State University Press, 1967.

INDEX